NON RENEWABLE

Creating Highly Motivating
Classrooms for All Students

Creating Highly Motivating Classrooms for All Students

A Schoolwide Approach to Powerful Teaching with Diverse Learners

Margery B. Ginsberg, Raymond J. Wlodkowski

JOSSEY-BASS
A Wiley Company
www.josseybass.com

Published by

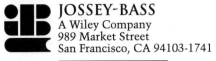

JOSSEY-BASS
A Wiley Company
989 Market Street
San Francisco, CA 94103-1741

www.josseybass.com

Library of Congress Cataloging-in-Publication Data
Ginsberg, Margery B., 1954–
        Creating highly motivating classrooms for all students : a schoolwide approach to powerful teaching with diverse learners / Margery Ginsberg, Raymond Wlodkowski.
        p. cm. — (The Jossey-Bass education series)
        Includes bibliographical references (p. 295) and index.
        ISBN 0-7879-4330-4 (alk. paper)
        1. Effective teaching—United States. 2. Motivation in education—United States.
        3. Multicultural education—United States. 4. School improvement programs—United States.
        I. Wlodkowski, Raymond J. II. Title. III. Series.
LB1027 .G546 2000
371.102—dc21   00-008481

FIRST EDITION
HB Printing   10 9 8 7 6 5 4

The Jossey-Bass Education Series

Contents

We dedicate this book to Matthew Aaron Ginsberg-Jaeckle and Daniel Mark Ginsberg-Jaeckle. They anchor our understanding of what it means to love a child.

Preface

This book is about teaching students with a diversity of backgrounds, cultures, and interests in ways that support their intrinsic motivation to learn. We provide a pedagogical framework and concrete strategies that school staff and educators can employ in three contexts: professional development related to school renewal, professional development related to K–12 teaching, and teaching strategies for K–12 classrooms. Because the same framework can guide staff development and K–12 teaching, we address these contexts as integrated streams throughout the book. We also adapt staff development exercises for school renewal, using them as classroom teaching strategies across content areas and grade levels.

This book also describes how school-based teams can be prepared to serve as staff developers, school renewal facilitators, and instructional leaders. Although we realize that our focus is ambitious, our work in some of this nation's schools with the highest poverty levels among students has convinced us of this: highly motivating classroom instruction for *all* students rarely occurs in isolation from certain schoolwide strengths. One of these strengths, seen in this country's most successful schools, consists of educators who regularly support one another in order to create optimal learning conditions for their students and themselves.

Supporting and nurturing motivation among all students is a universal challenge, seen in all classrooms. Even when circumstances for learning seem optimal—for example, classes are a reasonable size, students and teachers respect one another and share a sense of purpose, and schools and families work together well—motivation is a moving target. This has always been so. There never was, nor is there now, any place in the United States where all children are exactly alike and all the conditions that influence them at school and at home uniformly contribute to academic success.

School renewal strategies and pedagogical frameworks informed by sound research can serve as a compass to guide possibilities. But every person is shaped by multiple social contexts, and every person is influenced in some way by the realities of racism, poverty, and other forms of social injustice. Easy answers are insufficient.

Understanding and encouraging motivation is an ongoing process. It requires educators to examine and reconsider their own histories, experiences, and interpretations. It requires an investment in understanding the perspectives and struggles of students and the communities in which they live. And it requires educators to apply such understandings to ways in which they can struggle, with students, against societal inequalities.

Within the scope of this book, we cannot undertake all the investigations necessary to the endeavor of motivation. What we have undertaken to do is to demonstrate how to align teaching strategies so that they are supportive of students' intrinsic motivation within and across cultural groups. Synthesizing the research and literature concerning learning theories, cultural studies, and other disciplines that inform teaching practice, we offer a macrocultural approach to motivation. We present an overarching conceptual design that supports racial, ethnic, cultural, and language diversity among students. It offers an understanding of how to design motivating learning experiences and support schoolwide change without stereotyping, being overly prescriptive, or operating on the assumption that *diversity* means disadvantage or anything other than white and middle class.

Our framework is based on the notion that *all* individuals are motivated to learn and that the role of both teachers and staff developers is to encourage, elicit, and support this intrinsic motivation. Intrinsic motivation (learning because one wants to), as opposed to extrinsic motivation (learning because one wants only to gain external rewards), is encouraged and supported through attitudes of respect, learning experiences that are relevant and engaging, and opportunities to identify success in ways that matter to oneself and others. We believe that educational success is not only significant in helping students to experience their full humanity but also a necessary condition for shaping a pluralistic democracy. In schools that have implemented the principles and ideas in this book with breadth and depth, we have seen multiple indications of success, including increases in standardized test scores. We would, however, like to express our belief—as indicated in the case study in Chapter Two—that increases in test scores are a *by-product*. The ultimate goal is for adults and students, from *all* backgrounds, to experience a deep sense of purpose and meaning in intellectual study, civic responsibility, and daily life.

Audience

Although our immediate reader is the staff developer, this book will prove useful to a much broader audience: teacher educators, teachers, administrators, and other facilitators of school change will find assistance in developing and elaborating upon their own approaches to instructionally focused school renewal. Teachers can also independently distill from these chapters principles of intrinsic motivation and new teaching strategies for use in their classrooms. With the motivational framework as a guide, the strategies in the book have been developed and refined in some of the most socially, economically, racially, and culturally diverse classrooms in the nation. This book draws from this school-based research to help teachers everywhere encourage intrinsic motivation and create supportive schools in which motivation to learn is a central theme.

We have also written this book for school administrators. It is interdisciplinary, combining the best strategies we know about change, professional development, and instruction. This broad focus offers leadership support for administrators who are implementing significant instructional changes. It can also serve as a guide to continuous school improvement.

This book will provide support to district leaders as they work on school improvement. All our school renewal initiatives have been designed to develop the vital role of central office staff, including coordinators of federal programs, and garner support for their work in meaningful districtwide change. Ultimately, the charge of many district staff is to support student success. Frequently, however, other administrative responsibilities make it difficult to envision ways to support continuous learning and school-based action across a vast number of schools short of importing a blueprint model. In contrast, our ideas are intended to inspire creativity and enhance skills that respect the uniqueness of each school and each school district.

Overview of the Contents

This book is divided into three sections, or parts. From time to time you will notice some repetition that we allowed in order to produce stand-alone chapters for readers' easy reference when employing the information and strategies. In addition, it has been challenging to present ideas about classroom teaching, adult learning, and school renewal in a single volume. As you will see in Chapters Five through Eight, we typically present strategies related to K–12 teaching toward the beginnings of these chapters and strategies for working with adults in the area of school renewal toward the ends. However, some strategies apply to *both* K–12 teaching *and* school renewal. We have learned that teachers, administrators, and staff developers appreciate efficiency as well as an opportunity to experience and critique a strategy before implementing it. Therefore we present many of the strategies with two purposes: to model an instructional approach that can be applied to K–12 classrooms and to present, in the form of the instructional content, a discussion related to school renewal.

Part One (Chapters One through Three) is designed to heighten awareness about motivation and culture, the features of a culturally responsive school, and culturally responsive curriculum. Although Part One contains some practical suggestions on various topics, Part Two (Chapters Four through Eight) is the section that comprehensively defines, examines, and *applies* the motivational framework. Part Three contains guidelines for organizing school renewal initiatives, designing professional development agendas, and conceptualizing an approach to evaluation. To avoid making the book too dense and possibly overwhelming, we present particular kinds of information where we believe readers will find these points of interest to be most relevant.

Chapter One, "Culture and the Motivation to Learn," discusses some of the theoretical underpinnings of the motivational framework. It examines why motivation is important, the relationship between motivation and culture, and ways to understand the concept of culture. Chapter Two, "Critical Features of a Culturally Responsive School," provides an overview of what culturally responsive schools often think about and grapple with. We discuss motivational plans for lesson design, schoolwide adult learning and planning, and awareness about the change process. A case study illustrates how a culturally responsive school might look.

Chapter Three, "Culturally Responsive Curriculum," briefly explores some important curriculum considerations. By curriculum, we mean the *content* of instruction, but of course our focus remains *how* to teach rather than *what* to teach. We believe that the day-to-day relationships and interactions between teachers and students, which play out primarily through how teachers teach, profoundly influence students' intrinsic motivation. The stories that children most frequently bring home about school are about the ways that their teachers have demonstrated, or failed to demonstrate, respect, humor, and flexibility as they teach. In this chapter we examine such essentials as encouraging multiple perspectives, integrating subject matter so that it resembles the way learning occurs in "real life" (that is, so that it is authentic), and helping students make connections between new learning and their existing experiences and frames of reference. This chapter also provides recommendations for one group frequently excluded from the dialogue on multicultural curriculum, teachers of young children.

Part Two is the heart of the book. The first chapter in this section, Chapter Four, gives definition to the Motivational Framework for Culturally Responsive Teaching, providing a sample lesson to demonstrate the framework in practice. The subsequent chapters in Part Two are devoted to discussing and applying each of the four motivational conditions that the framework comprises: establishing inclusion, developing a positive attitude, enhancing meaning, and engendering competence. Each condition embodies two related criteria: *respect* and *connectedness* for inclusion, *relevance* and *choice* for attitude, *engagement* and *challenge* for meaning, and *authenticity* and *effectiveness* for competence. Chapters Five through Eight present a broad range of K–12 classroom and staff development activities to demonstrate how to create each motivational condition. These activities generally apply to classroom teaching and school renewal. That is, our professional development activities exemplify what we encourage teachers to do in their classrooms.

Chapter Five addresses establishing inclusion based on principles of respect and connectedness. One of the exercises, for example, shows how to create a communication agreement among participants that contributes both to an inclusive sense of community in a classroom and to a sense of community *schoolwide.* This chapter also contains a section on dealing with conflict and negotiating resistance.

Chapter Six focuses on developing a positive attitude toward learning based on the principles of personal relevance and choice. This chapter provides the greatest number of school renewal activities because the attitudes of teachers are *fundamental* to schoolwide change. Many of the activities demonstrate how to present ideas to adults in ways that are relevant to their needs and interests and respectful of the notion of self-determination. Although most of the exercises encourage interactive dialogue and respect the varied profiles of intelligence, we also offer suggestions for using the minilecture to present the principles of relevance and choice. We outline key points that can guide staff developers when making presentations about the motivational framework. Simultaneously, we show how to use *human highlighters* and *response cards* to ensure that, even during lectures, different perspectives are heard. These two approaches to teaching encourage a positive attitude toward the content being presented, and they are strategies that teachers can apply immediately in their classrooms. Along with several other school renewal and teaching strategies, Chapter Six also presents ways teachers can find more time for collaborative planning, teaching, and reflection.

Chapter Seven examines enhancing meaning and deepening learning through activities that challenge and engage students (including adult learners). These activities include using metaphors and stories, case studies, simulations, action research, and framed summaries.

Chapter Eight focuses on engendering competence, addressing the criteria of authenticity and effectiveness. It offers assessment strategies that encourage success in ways that matter to learners of all ages. This chapter also addresses one of the most politically charged issues in education—grading practices. In our experience, educators consistently express appreciation for opportunities to safely explore and discuss this topic. Chapter Eight also pulls together everything that has been learned about the motivational framework. We introduce assessment strategies as a means by which adults can demonstrate their competence in designing highly motivating instruction or approaches to school renewal.

As earlier stated, Part Three, containing the final two chapters, describes how to organize school renewal initiatives, design professional development agendas, and conceptualize an approach to their evaluation. Chapter Nine, "Organizing a Districtwide Initiative," delineates components for success. These components are necessarily idealized; in reality district and school resources are limited, commitments are often tentative (especially at first), and change processes are unpredictable. Although there is no substitute for insight and imagination in such situations, we have learned quite a lot about the virtues of *informed* improvisation. To a significant extent, this knowledge was gained in concert with Peggy Bullion.

Chapter Ten, "Designing Training Institutes and Work Sessions," outlines some key professional development topics and their related goals and activities. Staff developers and educators can use this information to select strategies that match their training purposes. The chapter also offers some sample training agendas for professional development institutes.

The Resource offers some guides for evaluating school renewal with respect for the imperfections of one's recommendations. The design, collection, and analysis of data, and conclusions are invariably influenced by the interpretive lenses through which all involved have been socialized and educated.

Terminology

It is always a challenge to find language that is accessible and meaningful to others. We would therefore like to briefly explain some of our choices in terminology. Most frequently, when referring to what has been variously called *continuous school improvement, school change, school restructuring, schoolwide reform,* or *school reculturing,* we use the term *school renewal.* We mean it to refer to an ongoing process, rooted in deep values about educational equity, that enhances the vitality and effectiveness of the school as a whole.

When referring to issues related to race, ethnicity, or culture, we frequently use the term *cultural diversity.* We realize that this term has been criticized at times for subsuming and homogenizing, for example, racial, ethnic, economic, sexual, physical, or age-related identities. Further, since the 1960s, when many social scientists used terms like *culturally deprived* and *culturally disadvantaged,* terms that speak of cultural difference have often run the risk of connoting disadvantage, inferiority, or any condition other than white and middle class. Our work has primarily been in schools that serve diverse student populations, such as Spring Woods High School in Houston, where there are many ethnicities, recent immigrants, and several languages and multiple dialects. A common feature in most of the schools with which we have worked is that the students live in or near urban communities and many families are low income. With our focus on practical, macrocultural applications of theory, a term that accommodates a broad range of students seems pragmatic, hence our choice of cultural diversity. We know, however, that vocabulary choice not only *represents* how individuals think, it *influences* how they think, and we therefore struggle with the imperfections of our choice.

We use the term *culturally responsive teaching* to mean the understanding and constructing of culturally respectful and motivationally aligned pedagogies. We use the terms *instruction* and *pedagogy* interchangeably. To some, instruction implies an approach to teaching that undermines self-direction or encourages passivity. We tend to prefer this term, however, because it is widely used in schools and is accessible to the audiences we hope to engage. Overall, our greatest challenge has been rethinking, with *all* kids in mind, ways to collectively test the limits of our imagination and our commitment to social justice.

The Scope of the Challenge

The enterprise of school renewal is optimistic and the support offered by local, state, national, and global politics is, at best, unreliable. Further, although we are fundamentally respectful of human potential, we know firsthand the rigor required to build a dream. The ideal of schools in which adults love teaching, students enjoy learning, and communities rally round is rife with challenge. We have to admit that we have yet to find theories, structures, and activities that eradicate periods of stagnation and defeat. We spend a significant amount of time trying to help people convince themselves not to give up.

Moreover, the theme of culturally responsive teaching is a loaded issue, still subject to much debate and with many objectives still unrealized in most of today's classrooms. In this book we try to make a significant contribution toward helping educators establish culturally responsive schools and classrooms, but we are fully aware of the complexities that schools and their staff must address in the pursuit of this objective. Obvious in this regard are the historical and contemporary inequities that students confront and that all of us must continually attempt to understand and struggle to resolve.

Acknowledgments

This book is the consequence of invaluable conversations and many different forms of encouragement from family, friends, colleagues, teachers, and students. We are especially grateful to those people who have worked closely with us to put ideas into action. Peggy Bullion, former staff developer for the Okinawa District of Department of Dependents Schools (DoDDS), worked with us during our early stages of developing districtwide initiatives rooted in principles of culturally responsive teaching. She made the line between dreams and action permeable in ways that continue to inspire. Sonny Zinn is a great teacher and friend. In addition to what she has told us, we have learned from the example of her life.

Other people who have nurtured our work along include Suzanne Benally, Eloise Hambright-Brown, Lorenzo Garcia, Winona Emerson, Joan Davies, Pat Schaffarczyk, Norma Martinez, Wilma Sagara, Anne Muse, Challice Rickard, Elizabeth Thornton, Anita Villarreal, and Amy Anderson.

We would also like to express our gratitude to Gale Erlandson, senior editor of Higher and Adult Education at Jossey-Bass, who believes in this work and supported the creation of this book with insight and patience. Finally, for listening and supporting us wholeheartedly, even when they have other perspectives, we would like to extend our warm appreciation to Margery's parents, Kathryn and Aubrey Ettenheimer.

January 2000   MARGERY B. GINSBERG
                                                RAYMOND J. WLODKOWSKI

The Authors

Margery B. Ginsberg is an independent researcher and consultant in Boulder, Colorado, with a background as a teacher on two Indian reservations, university professor, and Texas Title I technical assistance contact for the U.S. Department of Education. She works nationally and internationally to provide support for instructionally focused, comprehensive school renewal. Her most recent books are *Diversity and Motivation: Culturally Responsive Teaching* (with Raymond Wlodkowski, 1995) and *Educators Supporting Educators: A Guide to Organizing School Support Teams* (with Joseph F. Johnson Jr. and Cerylle A. Moffett, 1997). In addition, her work provided the foundational material for the video *Encouraging Motivation Among All Students* (1996). Ginsberg holds a Ph.D. degree in bilingual/multicultural/social foundations of education from the University of Colorado-Boulder.

Raymond J. Wlodkowski is research professor in the School for Professional Studies at Regis University, Denver. A licensed psychologist who has been a teacher for four decades, he specializes in motivation, learning, cultural diversity, and professional development. He received his B.S. degree (1965) in social science and his Ph.D. degree (1970) in educational psychology, both from Wayne State University in Detroit. His books have been translated into Spanish, Japanese, Chinese, and Korean. His awards for teaching, writing, and research include the Phillip E. Frandson Award for Literature and the University of Wisconsin-Milwaukee Award for Teaching Excellence.

Chapter One

Culture and the Motivation to Learn

No pessimist ever discovered the secrets of the stars, or sailed to an uncharted land, or opened a new heaven to the human spirit.
HELEN KELLER

Motivation is a concept that is intended to explain one of the most elusive questions, Why do we do what we do? Implicit in seeking to answer this question is educators' hope that they might better understand motivation in order to encourage student learning. Scholars, however, differ in their assumptions about motivation because it is something that can be neither directly observed nor precisely measured. Thus motivation researchers examine people's signs, behavior, words, and stories for indications of their interest, effort, perseverance, and completion. Although much of the information gained in this way can yield valuable clues about teaching and learning, it is still extremely challenging for educators to identify the intentions and understand the behaviors of students. Becoming sensitive to the motivation of students who have been socialized in similar ways and who share common histories is no easy task. When students have different patterns of socialization, histories, and worldviews, interpreting their will and purpose is even more difficult and misconceptions are common. The behaviors we associate with different attributes, including intention, imagination, and even cognitive genius, are likely to depend on

1

our own ethnic and cultural backgrounds and thus to vary significantly. As Vivien Gussin Paley (1990) reminds us, "None of us are to be found in sets of tasks or lists of attributes; we can be known only in the unfolding of our unique stories within the context of everyday events" (p. xii).

Because both conceptions of wisdom and research indicate that motivated students will surpass unmotivated students in learning and performance, educators typically want to gain more knowledge of motivation in order to give all students the best chance possible to have an excellent education. When we teach we may see that the same student who responded apathetically to a lecture energetically interacts with peers on any number of topics in the hallway after class. Realities of this sort help us to know that individuals *are motivated* even when they are not motivated to do what we would like them to do. In addition, this example is initial evidence that if we would like people to be motivated to learn, then students and teachers alike need to find learning activities intrinsically satisfying. To consistently learn well, we all have to feel respected, believe that what we are learning and doing is relevant, and accept challenges that we can imagine effectively accomplishing (Wlodkowski and Ginsberg, 1995; Csikszentmihalyi, 1997; Lambert and McCombs, 1998).

Another formidable truth is that enthusiastic teaching begets motivated learning. Often this kind of teaching reflects a unity with something that is greater than ourselves, a congruence with our dreams. When Charles Garfield (1986) studied older *peak performers*—adults who were sixty or older, who loved their work, and who in the eyes of their peers were excellent at what they did—whatever their occupation, they had one thing in common. They saw their work as being about something greater than themselves. For some, work was connected to a spiritual belief, and for others work's importance was the social contribution it made or the beauty of the work itself. As educators, one of our greatest challenges is to help ourselves, the adults with whom we interact, and *all* of our students to experience a sense of deep purpose in learning that can prevail against cynicism, anxiety, and feelings of being overwhelmed. Communities of learners with this sense of commitment are more likely to have the motivation to steadily improve their conditions for learning, contributing to a cycle of hope that is presently absent in the lives of many students and, too often, the lives of their teachers as well.

Intrinsic Motivation and the Influence of Culture on Learning

Theories of intrinsic motivation respect the influence of culture on learning. According to this set of motivational theories, it is part of human nature to be curious, to be active, to initiate thought and behavior, to make meaning from experience, and to be effective at what one values (Lambert and McCombs, 1998). These primary sources of motivation reside in all of us, across all ethnic and cultural groups. When people can see that what they are learning makes sense and is important according to their values and perspectives, their motivation to learn emerges. Like a cork rising through water, intrinsic motivation surfaces because the environment elicits it. What is culturally and emotionally significant to a person evokes intrinsic motivation (Wlodkowski and Ginsberg, 1995).

Our emotions are socialized through culture. For example, one person working at a task feels joy and continues. Another person working at the same task feels frustrated and does not persevere. And yet another person feels frustrated but continues with increased determination. Each person has been socialized with a different set of cultural norms, and therefore the circumstance that elicits joy, frustration, or determination may differ across ethnic and cultural groups because of people's differences in definitions of novelty, hazard, opportunity, and gratification and in accepted, appropriate responses to these perceptions (Kitayama and Markus, 1994). To a large extent the response that a person has to a learning activity reflects his or her ethnic or cultural background.

From this viewpoint, effectively teaching *all* students requires culturally responsive teaching. Even though each student's internal logic for doing something may not coincide with the teacher's logic, it is nonetheless a reality. To be consistently effective, the teacher has to accommodate that logic. This can be particularly challenging when students or their families have had experiences that suggest their ethnic or cultural views are not considered valid and the teachers lack similar experiences or have not examined such experiences. It can be particularly detrimental to students when such teachers rely on unquestioned assumptions about effort and reward as driving forces in student learning.

Anthropologists Signithia Fordham and John Ogbu (1986) have examined the connection between academic performance and students' perception of the relationship between effort and reward. Their research addresses the disinvestment in education that has occurred for many students of color whose families have lived for generations in the United States and have been denied employment and education commensurate with their efforts. As a consequence of this experience, especially in urban schools with large numbers of African American students, it is not uncommon for these students to conceal or diminish their ability to achieve. Doing well in school may seem futile to them and as "acting white." Stated differently, being smart is seen as the opposite of being cool (Tatum, 1997).

Among the other scholars who have examined the disconnect between effort and reward for many of this nation's students, Claude Steele and Joshua Aronson (1995) of Stanford University have addressed *stereotype threat*. Their research indicates that when students are placed in a situation in which poor performance, for example on a standardized test, would support the stereotype of inferior ability because of ethnicity or gender, their performance suffers when compared to the performance of those who do not labor under such preconceptions. When black students and white students were given a test that they were told measured their academic abilities, black students did less well than whites. But when a control group of black students and white students were told that the test did not have any significance but was merely a laboratory tool, the difference in performance disappeared (Singham, 1998).

The task of understanding, talking about, and working against racism and its consequences may seem formidable. Nonetheless, the pernicious effects of racism are still at work in the United States, and the connection between social status and academic performance cannot be ignored.

With such deep-rooted historical and contemporary inequalities at work and amidst a host of ideologically based notions about student-teacher relations, teaching based on theories of intrinsic motivation is not easily put into action. The extrinsic orientation to motivation continues to dominate school culture, with the carrot and stick as a fundamental metaphor. In the extrinsic perspective on motivation the focus of learning is on prizes, grades, eligibility for select courses, vocations, colleges, and so forth. When students do not respond to these incentives, a sociopathological view of underachievement tends to prevail, that is, the view that something is wrong with the student. Even though for many students the connection between effort and extrinsic reward is neither obvious nor desirable as a main reason for learning, those who do not respond to carrots and sticks are likely to be described as lacking ambition, initiative, or self-direction.

This is evident even in the language educators often choose. It is not uncommon, for example, to hear an educator ask, "How do I motivate them?" Although the question may be well intended, it implies that students are inert, that they do not own their motivation but require motivation from someone more powerful. When educators lack awareness that students are motivated by shared definitions of respect, meaning, and success, they find it easy to view students from a deficit perspective. For many students, this is an invitation to disconnect from learning altogether.

Sadly, most dropouts offer, among many other reasons for leaving school, one clear statement about their relationship to school, "Nobody really cared" (Steinberg, 1992). According to the Children's Defense Fund (1996), every day 2,833 children drop out of school. Every thirty-four seconds a baby is born to a mother who did not graduate from high school. Every twenty-five seconds a baby is born into poverty. Schools and universities graduate a disproportionately low number of low-income and ethnic minority students (Wlodkowski and Ginsberg, 1995). The economic implications of this distribution include an income differential between young male college graduates and high school dropouts of 200 percent (Springfield, 1998). Because the importance of extrinsic rewards such as grades and grade point averages increases as students advance in school, it is legitimate to question whether extrinsic motivation systems are effective for significant numbers of students across racial, ethnic, and cultural groups. It is reasonable to propose that as long as educational systems continue to connect motivation to learn to extrinsic rewards and punishments, students whose cultural norms, beliefs, and values differ from the dominant school norms will in large part be excluded from academic engagement and success.

Since we know that students whose socialization accommodates the extrinsic system tend to move ahead in school, whereas students whose socialization does not tend to fall behind, we propose a culturally responsive pedagogy based on intrinsic motivation to correct this imbalance. This approach to teaching, based on the Motivational Framework for Culturally Responsive Teaching, is respectful of different cultures and is capable of creating a common culture that all students and their teachers can accept.

The framework is composed of four motivational conditions that the teacher and students continuously create or enhance. They are as follows:

1. *Establishing inclusion* refers to employing principles and practices that contribute to a learning environment in which students and teachers feel respected by and connected to one another.
2. *Developing a positive attitude* refers to employing principles and practices that contribute to, through personal and cultural relevance and through choice, a favorable disposition toward learning.
3. *Enhancing meaning* refers to bringing about challenging and engaging learning. It expands and strengthens learning in ways that matter to students and have social merit.
4. *Engendering competence* refers to employing principles and practices that help students authentically identify that they are effectively learning something they value.

These conditions work in concert and are essential for developing among all students an intrinsic motivation for learning. The chapters ahead will further explain each motivational condition, document their importance, and describe strategies to create them in classrooms and schools.

Personal Appreciation for the Concept of Culture

Our achievement of educational equity will rest on an understanding that the most favorable conditions for learning vary from person to person. This variation occurs even though all people share the characteristics of being naturally curious and wanting to make meaning of their experiences. Teachers who engage students in learning have always been aware of the differences in the ways students make sense of the world and interpret the learning environment. Resisting the narrow lists of attributes or behaviors that have been associated with specific groups of people, these teachers seek to understand these differences through direct relationships with students, their families, and various communities.

Another kind of understanding that is a foundation for educational equity springs from examining how myths and stereotypes are shaped and used to maintain power and privilege. Even in teacher education programs that introduce multicultural curriculum, prospective teachers can distance themselves from historical and social realities (Ladson-Billings, 1991). However, an awareness of how people are socialized to accept inequalities makes it possible for teachers to expose and disrupt the cultural narratives that maintain unequal rules, practices, and power in classrooms and communities. Learning about cultural diversity needs to address more than simply understanding different beliefs, customs, and orientations that operate in the classroom. It should include an understanding of the ways one's own values and biases have been shaped and the ways one can provide meaningful opportunities for learning that are not simply the repackaging or disguising of dominant perspectives. These ideas are illuminated in the work of such scholars as Lawrence-Lightfoot (1998), Irvine (1997), Cochran-Smith (1995), and King (1997).

Several approaches can help educators personalize the concept of culture. First, it is useful to examine why the term *culture* seems elusive for many people and to examine what we know about culture as a concept and as an educational opportunity. Although culture is something we are all taught, that teaching is generally implicit and culture is conveyed to us unsystematically (Schein, 1992). This is one of the reasons why it is difficult for anyone to describe in explicit terms who he or she is culturally. Our beliefs, values, and usual patterns of interaction most often work subconsciously. It is no surprise then that we are most likely to experience uniqueness as cultural beings when we are in the presence of those who appear different from ourselves. For example, a person from a family or community that values and models emotionally demonstrative behavior as a sign of open and honest communication may confuse, offend, or embarrass a person whose family or community controls emotion as a demonstration of reverence for that which is greater than oneself. When a person meets others whose family or community orientations differ from the person's own, it is seeing someone similar to and yet different from oneself, provoking questions one might not otherwise think to ask. Contrast and dissonance awaken us to important assumptions we have made and make it possible for us to deepen and expand the discovery of rich variation within and between cultural groups.

The most obvious cultural characteristics that people observe are physical. Ethnicity, race, gender, and physical ability are often the antecedents to recognizing possible differences in experiences, beliefs, values, and expectations. Physical characteristics, however, provide only a cursory sense of who a person is. Families, jobs, organizational ties, and lifestyles develop a repertoire of behaviors in each person; we cannot obtain a clear view of who a person might be culturally because the view is always complex. Similarly, unique personal histories, politics with which people have struggled, and psychological traits interact dramatically to distinguish individuals from other members of their primary cultural groups. The subtle complexity of who we are makes it difficult to define any human being according to a static list of expected characteristics. It is a mistake to tell ourselves we know another person's cultural identity when the sole criteria are observable characteristics and behaviors. The influences of ethnicity, race, gender, language, sexual orientation, physical ability, age, and social class do not in and of themselves fully define our cultural being.

This is one of the primary reasons why there are no fixed scripts for teaching in a culturally diverse classroom. In most urban classrooms it is easy for a teacher to misconstrue the motivation as well as the capability of students who vary in the ways they speak or remain silent (Delpit, 1988), ask for or boldly display knowledge, (Health, 1983), prefer to work as individuals or as members of groups (Ladson-Billings, 1994), and connect information.

Therefore, when we do not acknowledge the variation and distinction among cultural groups, we may be thinking in terms of a single set of cultural norms. In the United States, this set of norms typically consists of the values, beliefs, and behaviors of the historically dominant Northern European–American middle class. When we accept these norms as universal, we are likely to see differences as deficits. For example, some students have learned the cultural norm that respect for one's teachers is demonstrated by deferring to the information the teacher presents. If a teacher expects students to actively question a lecture or interact eagerly in a seminar, students who reserve judgment out of respect could conceivably be misjudged as linguistically or cognitively limited, underprepared, lacking in initiative, easily intimidated, or arrogant.

The presumption of deficit in individuals who fail to conform to the expectations and standards that are commonly associated with the dominant culture, of which schools have been a microcosm, is one of students' primary reasons for dropping out of secondary and postsecondary education. Throughout the literature on retention and attrition, the dropout phenomenon is attributed to a broad range of institutional barriers that fail to take into account the expectations and experiences of students from various cultural backgrounds (Smith, 1989; Butler and Walter, 1991; Adams, 1992).

Although there is still much ambiguity associated with finding ways to understand and respect cultural pluralism, most theorists agree that culture is a deeply learned confluence of language, values, beliefs, and behaviors that pervades every aspect of a person's life, and that each person's culture is continually undergoing minor changes. What culture *is not* is an isolated, mechanical aspect of life that can be used to explain phenomena in the classroom or that can be learned as a series of facts, physical elements, or exotic characteristics (Ovando and Collier, 1985). In the words of Geertz (1973), "The human being is an animal suspended in webs of significance she or he has spun. I take culture to be those webs, and the analysis of it to be, therefore, not an experimental science in search of a law, but an interpretive one in search of meaning" (pp. 5, 29).

Geertz's perspective is fundamental to the strategies presented in this book, as are the perspectives of other scholars who refuse to reduce human beings to fragmented pieces of information. In addition to perpetuating stereotypes, such reductionism perpetuates a tendency to view *difference* in ways that keep white people in the center, or place of normality (Cochran-Smith, 1995; King, 1997).

When we engage in stereotyping, we make assumptions about the "average" characteristics of a group and impose those assumptions upon all individuals within a group. For example, some people believe that all European Americans are individualistic because as a group they are commonly considered more individualistic than other groups (Sue, 1991). Yet all cultural groups exhibit a great deal of heterogeneity among their members. "Seek first to understand" is a bit of wisdom that has been generated by many ethnic and cultural communities. This advice attempts to guide people to respect and relate to others as complex beings. It also suggests that as educators we need to examine narratives about privilege and power that presume that student success or failure can be understood as simply a personal, familial, or cultural attribute.

Both educators and learners have beliefs and values about teaching. These are culturally transmitted through narratives shaped by economics, history, religion, mythology, politics, and family and media communication. As mentioned earlier, the ways in which we experience a learning situation are mediated by such narratives. No learning situation is culturally neutral. If we teach as we were taught, it is likely that we will sanction individual performance, advocate personal "objectivity," and condone sportslike competition in testing and grading procedures. Such teaching represents a distinct set of cultural values that for many of today's students is at best culturally unfamiliar and at worst a contradiction of the norms and values of their gender or ethnic backgrounds. As just one of several possible examples, many students find themselves in a dilemma if they have been socialized to value modesty and cooperation in their families and communities but are expected to be self-promoting and competitive in educational settings.

Few educators would care to admit that the way they teach compromises the learning of members of various cultural groups. Yet to avoid the cultural issues in and influences on our teaching situations under the guise, for example, of maintaining academic standards, treating everyone alike, or waiting for society to change undermines the success of *all* children and, ultimately, everyone's shared future.

One way to gain insight into the elusive concept of culture is to consider the research of sociologist Robin M. Williams Jr.

(1970, pp. 454–500), who has identified cultural themes and orientations that generally reflect the Anglo-Saxon influence in the United States and that may or may not be operative in the classroom as a consequence of educators' belief systems. Selected themes have been condensed (Locke, 1992), and in the following list, they are accompanied by alternative perspectives that may reflect the values and beliefs of some or many students in our classrooms.

1. *Theme: achievement and success.* People emphasize rags-to-riches stories.
   Alternatives. People believe personal generosity is the highest human value. Rags-to-riches stories are rooted in a cultural mythology that overlooks the social, political, and economic forces that favor certain groups above others and that make achievement as much a matter of privilege as of personal desire and effort.

2. *Theme: activity and work.* People see this country as a land of busy people who stress disciplined, productive activity as a worthy end in itself.
   Alternatives. People believe caring about and taking time for others is more important than being busy; discipline can take many forms and should be equated with respect, moral action, and social conscience; sustenance is a higher value than productivity.

3. *Theme: humanitarian mores.* People value spontaneously coming to the aid of others and having sympathy for the underdog.
   Alternatives. People value being selective about whom they will help; for some, personal gain takes precedence over kindness and generosity; for others, human emotion is to be avoided because it makes them feel vulnerable and inept.

4. *Theme: moral orientation.* People judge life events and situations in terms of right and wrong.
   Alternatives. People feel that there is no objective right or wrong and that such perspectives tend to favor and protect the most privileged members of society; finding meaning in life events and situations is more important than judging.

5. *Theme: efficiency and practicality.* People emphasize the practical value of getting things done.

Alternatives. People believe that process is just as important as product and that it makes the strongest statement about what individuals value; living and working in a manner that values equity and fairness is both practical and just.

6. *Theme: progress.* People hold the optimistic view that things will get better.

   Alternatives. People believe that the idea of progress assumes human beings can and should control nature and everything that happens to them and that instead we ought to acknowledge, respect, and care for that which we have been given, that which is greater than ourselves, and that which is—like life— cyclical. (Interestingly, many languages in North America and around the world do not have a word for progress.)

7. *Theme: material comfort.* People emphasize the good life; conspicuous consumption is sanctioned.

   Alternatives. People believe a good life is defined by sharing and giving things away. The idea that life will be good if one owns many possessions leads to insatiable behaviors.

8. *Theme: freedom.* People believe in freedom with an intensity others might reserve for religion.

   Alternatives. People believe that freedom without justice is dangerous; limiting freedom is necessary for equality; accepting the limitations of freedom is a sign of respect for others.

9. *Theme: science and secular rationality.* People have esteem for the sciences as a means of asserting mastery over the environment.

   Alternatives. People believe the earth is a sacred gift to be revered and protected. The notion of scientific objectivity is based on the mistaken presumption that human beings are capable of value-neutral beliefs and behaviors.

10. *Theme: individual personality.* People believe every individual should be independent, responsible, and self-respecting; the group should not take precedent over the individual.

    Alternatives. People believe sharing and humility are higher values than ownership and self-promotion; self-respect is inseparable from respect for others, for community, and for that which is greater than oneself. Individualism can promote aggression and competition in ways that undermine the confidence and self-respect of others; independence denies the social, cultural, racial, and economic realities that favor members of certain groups over others.

As with all information, the research on culture can seem daunting. Yet to be mindful of how we may appear to others and to be respectful of how difficult it is to know another person's views and beliefs—that is, to be much more thoughtful about how we teach—does not mean that any of us has to be someone he or she is not. But it does mean we ought to be able to question assumptions that are often embedded in the preparation, professional development, and ongoing socialization of educators. After all, most teachers are genuinely eager to positively influence the learning of others.

When we clarify our own cultural values and biases, we are better able to consider how they might subtly but profoundly influence the degree to which learners in our classrooms feel included, respected, at ease, and generally motivated to learn. The range of considerations found in Williams's cultural themes can be helpful as we think of questions to ask ourselves about our own assumptions and as we construct reflective questions that can enhance the learning experience we are creating with our students. Here are examples of such questions; each question is followed by ideas for action.

1. Are ways of doing things in my classroom clear so that students who are accustomed to different ways of doing things at home or in their communities of origin can understand and negotiate alternative approaches?

Ideas. It may be important to model behavior, provide visible examples of expectations, and elicit information about clarity of communication through student polls or written responses. A common norm among U.S. teachers is that students will raise their hands when they have questions. Some students, however, are embarrassed about publicly identifying what they do not understand. The anonymity of writing or of conferencing with peers and then sharing the group's information with a teacher can facilitate communication. In addition, some teachers use the *fist-to-five* approach to check for clarity. Students might, for example, raise all five fingers on a hand when they understand what they have learned so well that they could teach it to someone else. Four fingers mean they understand it but would be cautious about teaching it. Three fingers mean they have a good start but are confused about some things. Two fingers mean they don't get it. One finger means they are struggling not to give up.

2. Have I examined the values embedded in my discipline that may confuse or disturb some students?

Ideas. Ask questions that encourage students to present alternative perspectives; construct student panels so students can discuss issues from diverse perspectives with their peers.

3. Are the examples I use to illustrate key points meaningful to my students and sensitive to their perspectives?

Ideas. Give one example from your own experience and then ask students to create their own examples to illustrate different points, providing an opportunity for group discussion; acknowledge the experiences of people with different backgrounds; be aware of nonverbal language such as physical stance and gestures.

4. Do I have creative and accurate ways to learn about students' lives and interests?

Ideas. Use three-by-five-inch cards as *door passes,* requesting students to write a response on the card to a question you have asked and then to use card as their ticket to leave when class is over. Position yourself at the door to collect the cards. This has the added benefit of allowing you to make contact with each and every student. (Questions for older students might ask: What is one connection that I was able to make between what we learned today and an interest or goal I have? What is one question I wish I had asked today but I was too confused or distracted at the time to think of it? or, If I were teaching this topic, I would want to be sure to include . . . ?) Create a display for which students submit photos or original reminders about themes that vary from month to month (for example, an experience I had that I will always remember; one of the most beautiful places I've been; something that still surprises me); work with students to generate the themes and ask for volunteers to design and manage the display). Instead of buying posters, ask students to make them on different topics, including "words of wisdom," to post on the wall for inspiration. Invite two students to lunch one day a week and do more listening than talking, acknowledge birthdays and cultural occasions, share information about yourself, keep a hot-water urn with hot chocolate packets and tea bags at the back of the class and make it a site for informal dialogue, and if you can, visit the homes of students. The section on inclusion in Chapter Five presents additional ideas, although most teachers already have a host of ways to become more familiar with the lives and interests of students. The goal is to make a regular point of including all students in one's efforts.

Over 75 percent of public school teachers are white, and thus many will recognize the experience that Peggy McIntosh (1989) has poignantly described: "As a white person I had been taught about racism as something which puts others at a disadvantage, but had been taught not to see one of its corollary aspects, white privilege, which puts me at an advantage. I was taught to see racism only in individual acts of meanness, not in invisible systems conferring dominance on my group" (p. 10).

Moreover, many of us have been socialized, regardless of our racial, ethnic, or cultural membership, to think of the United States as a just society. It is hard to imagine that each of us is responsible for everyday actions that can be viewed as dismissive of or discriminatory toward others. The learning environment provides a meaningful context for addressing and redressing the ways in which bias occurs. Learning about who we are culturally, as individuals and as educators, can create a consciousness that is personally, professionally, and socially empowering in ways we may have never dreamed.

Chapter Two

Critical Features of a Culturally Responsive School

*Although the connections are not always obvious, personal
change is inseparable from social and political change.*
HARRIET LERNER

Both school success and school failure are often rooted in the
larger societal and institutional structures that are outside the
scope of this book. Nonetheless, we would be remiss not to mention that school success or failure is often a political as well as an
educational challenge. Schools are parts of larger systems that
inevitably share responsibility for policies and practices that influence the extent to which educators participate in continuous
school renewal. Educators' enthusiasm and commitment are easily eroded by politicians who attend to the appearance of success
within rules-driven bureaucratic systems. Their strident rhetoric
too often ignores the necessary positive influence of imaginative
leadership, clean lines of responsibility, adequate financial
resources, and—at all levels—environments that foster collaboration, trust, and continuous learning. There is an obvious link
between such things as positive management of overarching structures and school quality.

Just the same, we have enough examples of successful schools
to know that formidable obstacles are being overcome, even in
some of the most troubled locations. A characteristic of these successful schools is their teachers have a bedrock belief that all of

their students are capable of learning at high intellectual levels. This belief is fortified with a clear focus on the relationship between professional practice and student learning. Student motivation is a central concern of instruction. It is also a central concern of the total school environment and of continuous adult learning. These schools not only enjoy cultural diversity but understand its relationship (as examined in Chapter One) to student success. They are culturally responsive schools, respecting cultural, ethnic, and racial diversity; seeking to engage the intrinsic motivation of students from diverse backgrounds; creating a safe, inclusive, and respectful learning environment; deriving teaching practices from principles that apply across disciplines and cultures; and agreeing that academic success and civic virtue are inseparable ideals (Wlodkowski and Ginsberg, 1995).

This chapter summarizes some of the school-based factors beyond instruction that influence student motivation in culturally responsive schools: using motivational plans to guide instruction, employing schoolwide planning, and establishing a vision of educational equity. It also illustrates schoolwide planning through the story of King Middle School, a fictitious school that is a composite of some of the most promising conditions for student success we have experienced in our work.

Motivational Plans to Guide Instruction

As we pointed out in Chapter One, an understanding that the most favorable conditions for learning vary from person to person is crucial to achieving educational equity. Because learning is the act of making meaning from experience, involving all students in learning requires respect for students' different ways of seeing the world and interacting in a learning environment. The keen ability of an Inupiat hunter to discern sea, stars, and ice from a small boat in the Arctic Ocean is a motivational and intellectual challenge as profound in its own way as that facing a systems analyst deciphering a federal budget at a computer terminal (Wlodkowski, 1999). The crucial question for educators is not, How motivated or intelligent is this person? but, How is this person motivated or intelligent?

Every instructional plan ought to be a motivational plan. Finding an instructional design for most subject matter is not an enormous challenge (Rothwell and Kazanas, 1992). However, most instructional designs do not adequately deal with ethnic and cultural diversity. Frequently, teachers try to deal with diversity independently, relying on their own intuition and spontaneous decision making, which are necessarily limited by their own experiences and beliefs. The difficulties with this approach are most apparent when student motivation seems low or diminishing. Without an adequate guide for planning and for finding ways to revise, refine, or build upon a planned learning experience, teachers often feel helpless, hopeless, and prone to blame the learners for the difficulties. When teachers turn to books on motivation, the vast range of competing theories can simply confuse them further. When they turn to books about ethnic and cultural diversity, they find many are group specific. Although such books can yield valuable clues to motivating instruction, the challenge is to think broadly while simultaneously respecting the unique bonds of specific groups and the unique attributes of individuals. As discussed in Chapter One, if teachers fail to acknowledge variations among individuals in ethnic and cultural groups—variations influenced by such factors as social class, gender, family narratives about historical and contemporary political conditions, and personal interpretations of those same conditions—they risk stereotyping or narrowly bracketing students according to prescribed lists of characteristics (Hilliard, 1989; Irvine and York, 1995).

Teachers need plans for fostering motivation that are flexible and that help them respond coherently to the complexities of human diversity. Without a plan, motivation too often becomes a process of trial and error, lacking cohesion and continuity. With a plan, there is greater opportunity for all students to experience academic success. A comprehensive instructional framework and concrete strategies for motivational planning are discussed in detail in Chapter Three. A sample plan is presented in Chapter Eight.

A Schoolwide Approach Supporting Learning and Renewal

A school that seeks to be highly motivating for all students aligns its goals and practices for professional development; scheduling; governance; parent, family, and community involvement; counseling; and discipline with its goals and practices for curriculum, instruction, and assessment. This coordination is what is meant by comprehensive schoolwide planning. It makes it possible for all a school's component parts to work in complementary ways toward common ends. It is difficult, for example, to imagine a successful school that advocates rigorous intellectual habits for students but provides limited time for teachers to engage in critical and creative thinking. The same disjunction is apparent in a school that encourages the voices of many different groups of people to be heard in curriculum planning but that maintains a strict hierarchy in school governance.

Certain conditions are fundamental to comprehensive, schoolwide planning. As introduced in Chapter One and as elaborated on in Chapter Seven, the same four conditions that underlie intrinsic motivation to learn are necessary for effective schoolwide planning. Both the adults and students throughout a school need to

- Feel respected and connected as members of a learning community
- Have educational experiences that are personally relevant and that support meaningful decision making, giving them a favorable disposition toward new learning through such experiences
- Engage in challenging learning that has genuine social merit
- Co-create authentic ways to know that their effective learning is increasing their personal competence in ways that they value and can communicate to others

It is to achieve these conditions that (as you will see in Chapter Six) we apply the motivational framework to school development as well as to student motivation and learning. Seymour Sarason (1982) has remarked that "one of the unverbalized assumptions undergirding the organization and thrust of our schools is that the conditions that make schools interesting places for children can be created and sustained by teachers for whom these conditions exist only minimally, at best." This book addresses applying such conditions to both teachers and students. To illustrate one of the many ways a culturally responsive school might look, a description of a culturally responsive middle school follows. Although King Middle School is fictional, its story reflects successful practices at schools such as Horizons Alternative School in Boulder, Colorado, Spring Woods High School in Houston, Texas, and Cabrillo Elementary School in Fremont, California.

King Middle School is located in a rural agricultural community fifty miles from a large city. Its students have diverse backgrounds. Approximately 50 percent speak English as a second language, and 45 percent are members of migratory families. Approximately 85 percent qualify for free or reduced-price lunch.

For some time, King Middle School educators, parents, and community members have been working together as an adult learning community to study, develop, and apply highly motivating, culturally responsive pedagogy to support the academic accomplishment of all students. As a result, the school has eliminated pullout programs that require teachers to label students and limit their regular classroom instruction. Teachers throughout the building have agreed to share responsibility for all students through pedagogy that allows students to be motivated learners and valued community members. In fact, motivation to learn and serve is now the signature of the King Middle School community.

To contribute to this effort, King Middle School maintains a large literacy center, which is staffed by faculty, parents, and members of local organizations and which remains open in the evenings. The center is a haven in many ways for students, families, community members, and staff. Students and families who are in the process of acquiring English visit the center to develop reading, writing, and oral language skills. A broad range of students frequently stop by for one-on-one assistance with assignments or to work together in the teahouse area. In the teahouse, where there is always hot water for tea and hot chocolate, it is not uncommon to see students meeting with their *advocates*. An advocate is an adult friend who gets to know a few students well and provides personal support for their success throughout their stay at King. Students also drop by the literacy center to join in ongoing book discussions, plan community-based projects with local artists and other service learning volunteers, observe demonstrations, contribute to technology-based projects that are routinely facilitated by visiting scientists or engineers, engage in independent research, or read silently on the comfortable pillows in the fiction loft. The center is particularly proud of its ability to stimulate student interest and awareness by offering a broad range of literature by ethnically and culturally diverse authors. In fact, the book lists that inform library acquisitions are often designed by students.

The literacy center not only responds to student and community interests but also provides a context in which teachers can learn new ways to support literacy across the curriculum. At least once a month teachers volunteer as coaches in the writing center. This helps them fine-tune their ability to teach literacy skills and encourages strong, consistent expectations for high-quality writing across the curriculum. In fact, in concert with students, teachers at King Middle School have created a literacy rubric that guides skill development in the center and defines expectations for high-quality reading and writing in all courses.

Adult members of the school community are especially committed to learning that builds confidence and motivation through teamwork, creativity, problem solving, and community action. The school's vision statement reflects this commitment. A banner hanging over the front door reads, "King Middle School, a place where youth and adults successfully work together to learn and strengthen our community."

King Middle School has developed a model for supporting adult learning that helps the school achieve this vision. King funds permanent substitutes who can be assigned to free up teams of teachers called *interdisciplinary learning teams*. One of the functions of each of these professional learning teams is to follow the work of a historically low-performing student throughout a quarter. Team members present pieces of the student's work, and the team tries to understand student characteristics as well as such influences on the student as the environment, instruction, and support. Together, team members brainstorm ideas that could strengthen the student's motivation, knowledge, and skill. The emphasis is on strengthening the motivational conditions that influence success rather than on "fixing" the student. Using the Motivational Framework for Culturally Responsive Teaching, which informs the instructional design of lessons, team members consider: (1) What might be done to create a stronger sense of respect for and connectedness with the student; what might increase his or her sense of emotional safety? (2) How might the choices offered and the personal relevance of the learning experience be strengthened? (3) How might the learning experience more effectively challenge and engage this student (even to the extent that the student might lose track of time)? (4) How might the assessment process create authentic evidence of emerging skills to encourage a sense of hope in the student and help him or her see the ways in which strong learning really matters?

King Middle School also has a *schoolwide instructional leadership cadre*, comprising two people from each interdisciplinary learning team, the principal, some parents, and representatives of the site-based decision-making team. The members of this cadre are building their capacity in highly motivating and culturally responsive pedagogical practice in concert with a district-level team comprising parents, community members, the assistant superintendent, and district-level curriculum representatives. Their primary goals, as reflected in the school's vision statement and school improvement plan, are to support teacher performance throughout the entire school so that pedagogy consistently encourages student motivation, to enhance student performance so that all students experience high-quality academic success, and to help students experience their value to their community and the world.

As described earlier, teacher performance is developed by regularly examining the work of low-performing students. It is also developed through two-hour bimonthly meetings of the interdisciplinary professional learning teams, led on a rotating basis by team members. Each team, as mentioned, has two members who are part of the instructional leadership cadre, to ensure that all staff are aware of and have access to new books, materials, and demonstration sites that may be of interest. However, the school makes a concerted effort to safeguard against promoting the power of a few. Everyone is encouraged to share resources and practices that can influence student learning. These learning teams, sometimes referred to as *study groups,* regularly apply their learning in the collaborative design of interdisciplinary lessons. In addition, every other week teachers visit each other's classrooms to observe classroom practice, identify interactions that contribute to success among all students, and share ideas for strengthening student success. Several times a year, a team of teachers visits another school to engage in dialogue about school improvement efforts and to learn from the host school's classrooms and community programs. All teachers are encouraged to present what they are learning and doing at local universities, at professional conferences, and at school-sponsored community forums with parents, service learning partners, business partners, and other members of the community.

Teachers refer to classroom visits that occur within their school as *partnership observation and dialogue.* The goals that teachers set for partnership observation and dialogue are consistent with the goals they have identified at professional performance meetings with colleagues and school administrators. For example, one goal might be to find ways to help the lowest-performing students heighten their intellectual stature in the classroom and community. A second goal might be to share ideas on how to make the "real-life" experiences and values of all students a more regular and highly visible part of curriculum. Insights from partnership observation and dialogue influence the lessons plans that the professional learning teams develop.

The two-hour block of time for professional learning team activities is provided by students' participation in community service. Twice a month on Tuesday afternoons students work in pairs or small groups to maintain a community garden and prepare meals for the community food share program, develop a school-based day-care center with parents and community representatives, work with local visual artists on public displays and maintain exhibits of student art throughout the building, create films with a local video artist about important social and community issues, share computer skills through English as a second language (ESL) teaching at the learning center of a nearby migrant housing complex, assist in the school-based community health clinic, adopt a grandparent at the local nursing home, or read to and play with children at the community homeless shelter. Students are always encouraged to develop their own projects.

Community service is an important part of the family and community involvement in the school. Parent, community, and student volunteers coordinate the program. For this reason, the community service coordination center is located in the school's community room. The community room, a colorful room that invites people in with comfortable furniture, a soft-drink machine, and the work of students, staff, and parents on the wall, also has a washing machine and dryer for the community's use.

Parent and community volunteers work with students to create a community service newsletter that keeps the public informed of important outcomes and opportunities. At the end of every quarter, students display something they have created as a consequence of their community work. It might be a piece of literature, original art, or a photographic journey. Each display offers a well-written one-page summary of the student's experience. Displays and summaries may chronicle significant learning derived from the twelve hours of family service or the twelve hours of service to the school that are also required in addition to the community work. The summaries become part of a folio titled the "King Middle School Community Service Process," which parent volunteers maintain.

Parents serve many other roles at the school as well. For example, they work with older students to coordinate an initiative that helps students new to the school feel respected and connected right away. Approximately one hundred older students serve as friends and advisers to small groups of new students, who meet regularly throughout their first year. To further contribute to a family atmosphere at King, all homeroom classes include sixth, seventh, and eighth graders. This heightens students' concern for one another throughout the school. Because parent participation is essential to creating and sustaining these kinds of school-based innovations, several parents have become interested in full-time work at the school. Funded by a grant submitted by parents and teachers, five parents are assistants in training, participating in a paraprofessional training program that benefits parents and the school.

As its vision statement reflects, King Middle School requires that students work respectfully together; engage in motivating learning experiences that have personal, cultural, and community relevance; and experience success. In all classrooms, teachers use four questions to guide lesson development and to refine learning experiences. Just as they use similar questions to examine student work, teachers regularly ask themselves: (1) How does this learning experience contribute to developing a community of learners who feel respected and connected to one another? (2) How does this learning experience offer meaningful choices and focus on personal and cultural relevance? (3) How does this learning experience engage all students in challenging learning that has social merit? (4) How does this learning experience support each student in knowing that he or she is becoming more effective in learning he or she values and can use in authentic ways? Once a week, each teacher adds to his or her professional portfolio the lesson that he or she believes best supported the motivation of all students. Teachers also include their written responses to the four previous questions in relation to this lesson. These portfolios are an important part of the ongoing peer review and support process.

The students also use four similar questions to self-assess, in writing, their overall performance and set personal goals at the beginning, middle, and end of every learning experience. A focus group of students helped to write the four questions so that they could be clear from a student's perspective. Answers to these questions also provide feedback to teachers on the effectiveness of classroom pedagogy. The questions that guide self-assessment are: (1) What have I done to demonstrate respect and support for other people in our classroom and in the community, and how can I build on that? (2) What kinds of decisions have I made that have helped me academically and what kinds of decisions make sense now? (3a) When was I so involved in learning that time seemed to fly? (3b) What are at least two things I can do to have this feeling more often? (4a) What are some of the things I have been doing in school that allow me to feel successful? (4b) How are they important to other people as well as to me? (4c) What might I do more of? These questions help students to think deeply about their learning. They also inspire teachers to organize student learning around complex problems and issues that students care about and to support students as decision makers who are becoming increasingly self-directed.

Computer usage that supports learning is integrated into all subjects. For example, a science teacher and math teacher collaborated to help student teams design original research on student-generated environmental questions. One student research team investigated the influence of pesticides on the health of people who live in rural communities. They designed Internet surveys to be filled out by county health officials, medical clinics, migrant labor centers across the country, and professors at colleges and universities. (They developed a separate questionnaire with which they could personally interview people in their neighborhoods). The students also used technology to compute and report their findings and to write and send an article to the local newspaper. They also developed charts and graphs for presentations to the local health board and to an environmental health class at a nearby college. (As part of preparation for all public presentations, students practice listening and responding to the kinds of strong, divergent opinions that often arise in public discourse.) The students are currently exploring ways to solve the problems they identified as a part of their research. As people who are becoming expert in some aspect of solving an environmental problem, they will eventually host an exhibition of their recommendations for their families and other community members.

The King Middle School governance council, cofacilitated by the principal and an elected parent, comprises teachers, parents, the assistant principal, a counselor, a district office liaison, students, and community members from several organizations. It meets once a month at night, with students providing child care. The council assesses the progress of the school toward its vision, proposes solutions to complex issues that will eventually be considered by the broader school community, guides the implementation of a policy to attract and retain staff members from ethnically and culturally diverse backgrounds, and garners community resources to provide support for improving the curriculum for ethnic and cultural plurality. The school principal is a co-learner who helps maintain a school culture that respects multiple perspectives.

King Middle School is proud that its students score above the national norms and that it has been recognized for the numbers of students from all backgrounds who score well above the required competency levels on state tests. However, the school is understated about this because it believes that test scores are a consequence of that which it most values—being a stimulating place of learning in which all students feel respected and supported as individual people, students, and world citizens.

Establishing the motivational conditions that undergird student learning requires complex decisions about pedagogy, curriculum, and the overall school environment. But, as King Middle School illustrates, what happens throughout an entire school is a powerful influence on the effectiveness of any educator. In addition, students, parents, and community members generally intuit the insincerity of a school that declares it is responsive to the needs of all of its students but that lacks a comprehensive focus. They become frustrated, for example, by such contradictions as personally and culturally relevant curriculum accompanied by grading policies that penalize students for taking risks and making mistakes. Good schools always see themselves as works in progress and maintain a comprehensive focus on all the processes that contribute to student success.

Although not exhaustive, the following questions have been useful to the schoolwide planning process and to ongoing renewal in some of the nation's most successful ethnically diverse schools. They are predicated on research about multicultural schools and classrooms (Nieto, 1992; Ladson-Billings, 1994; Grant and Gomez, 1996; Wlodkowski and Ginsberg, 1995), successful high-poverty schools (Johnson and Ginsberg, 1996; Knapp and Turnbull, 1990; McLaughlin, 1990), school restructuring (Newman and Associates, 1996; Boyer, 1995; Hopfenberg, Levin, and Associates, 1993), and change processes (Fullan, 1993; Darling-Hammond, 1993).

- Are we maintaining a focus on highly motivating teaching and the academic success of every student, and ensuring that this focus permeates all decision making? (This focus includes providing structural support for social membership and a sense of belonging, positive attention to students' attitude toward learning, attention to the experiences and interests that students bring to the classroom, personalized and challenging academic opportunities, and clear criteria for success that responds to students' values.)
- Are we thoughtfully experimenting with promising schoolwide policies and innovations, including organization and management structures, that support an ambitious vision of student success, especially when old practices are not working?
- Are we, as educators, frequently, passionately, and substantively learning together, sharing our challenges, and collaborating to strengthen instructional practice?
- Are we, as a school community, experiencing the enhanced communication structures, rich diversity of relationships, and shared leadership that will allow us to create the most inclusive and democratic environment for adults as well as children and youth?
- Are we being loyal to a "no excuses" policy that precludes us from blaming parents and labeling children and that encourages us to model and promote responsibility ourselves?
- Are we becoming increasingly aware of our own cultural experiences, assumptions, inner feelings, and patterns of behavior so that we can be authentically supportive of all students' cultural experiences, assumptions, inner feelings, and patterns of behavior?
- Is individual and cultural inclusiveness a core value and accountable practice so that each member of the school community feels a genuine sense of belonging?

- Is our school a place where families and community members enjoy mutual respect as well as opportunities for important decision making and contributions?
- Does our school look like it belongs to all of us?
- Are we coordinating our resources for everyone's success?
- Do we have well-identified ways to examine school and student growth? Are we sharing the results with our community?

These questions contribute to an examination of currently accepted ways of thinking, helping schools to recognize their strengths and challenges. The ability to recognize accomplishments and contradictions may seem straightforward, but, as each of us knows, we live in a society in which political cliché readily blurs what is actually happening. Perhaps commercial advertising provides the most perverse example of this. If we say that all of our students are talented, but we have evidence that whole groups of children are not succeeding, we have a rather significant contradiction. Culturally responsive schools predicate continuous school improvement planning upon consistent reflection, a challenging vision of student performance, and ambitious goals that cannot be separated from a heartfelt commitment to caring about students as people.

Awareness of the Complexity of Innovation

Catalyzing and supporting such an ambitious continuous improvement focus is not a straightforward, lockstep process. On this topic, scholarship abounds (Fullan, 1991; Darling-Hammond, 1993; Senge, 1990). Perhaps one of the greatest challenges for educators is maintaining their belief in the efficacy of ongoing collective examination and courage in a quick-fix political climate.

Strong schools never stop looking for substantive ways to enhance their vitality. The spirit of invention is foundational to their development. However, this perspective can render a school vulnerable amid shifting political climates and ideologies. Inventive schools suffer as well from the unfortunate jealousies directed toward maverick people and organizations. Recall Proverbs, "Wrath is cruel, and anger is outrageous, but who is able to stand before envy?" To these contests add the personal fatigue that accompanies a profession dedicated to human beings and their lives, the surprises of everyday life in complex communities, and limited resources. Resisting the temptation to field quick fixes to complex questions, even if such resistance seems to come at the expense of self-empowerment and inspired dreams, is something with which even the most successful schools struggle.

Clearly, getting everyone in a school to hold on to the rope and pull in the same direction for the sustained periods of time that it takes for a school to learn to do something well is no small task. Loss of control, doubt, concerns about competence, more work, and past resentments reside among the personal concerns. According to researchers such as Carl Glickman (Glickman, Hayes, and Hensley, 1992) and Michael Fullan (Fullan and Miles, 1992), we also know these complications exist.

- As schools become empowered conflict increases because participants in the decision-making process take their responsibilities seriously. In fact, conflict is not only inevitable but fundamental to successful innovation.
- Assessment information tends to cultivate dissatisfaction and possibly blame when we have the *cardiac approach* to student learning: "in our hearts we're doing fine."
- When they lack new information, people make decisions that reinforce the status quo.
- People need strong encouragement to change, even in directions they desire, but such encouragement is effective only under conditions that allow people to react, to form their own positions, to interact with other implementers, and to obtain technical assistance.
- Schools commonly underestimate the amount of professional development needed to support educational innovation. Lasting learning is most likely to occur when teachers have significant and regular opportunities to study together, plan together, observe each other's classrooms, examine student work in ways that catalyze new insights, and visit other schools.
- Change is a process, not an event. Significant change takes a minimum of three years to five years to fully implement, and

comprehensive and systemic change initiatives only begin to take hold in that period.

- Once there is some immediate success, schools may press for more short-term success at the potential cost of long-term student gains because they question whether they will see similar results in subsequent years. They can adopt an attitude of "more goals, faster success" at the expense of a focus on "fewer goals, greater significance."
- Criticism develops on the outside, especially as a school gains success and recognition.

Culturally responsive schools use information on change and innovation to normalize their experiences with the complex, nonlinear process of continuous improvement and to create processes that sustain educators' sense of shared purpose and responsibility. This is one of the reasons why they often have a no-blame policy and shared covenants or agreements about communication and professional norms to which a staff can periodically refer. One norm, for example, might be, "We commit to assisting adults who are threatened or challenged by changes occurring in the school. In return, all adults in the school agree to be supportive or constructively critical" (Conley, 1993). A process for creating professional agreements is outlined in Activity 16 in Chapter Five.

Educators in successful culturally responsive schools engage in ongoing dialogue about many of the aforementioned challenges associated with innovation. Some schools, for example, regularly distribute articles that discuss change, innovation, cultural diversity, and instructional practice so that teachers in study groups and at faculty meetings can consider ideas from these articles in relation to their own experiences, to schoolwide norms, and to the goals embedded in their school improvement plans. In such schools, as educators and community members heighten their awareness of the complexity of innovation, there tends to be agreement that there are no panaceas, only opportunities and commitments. Amid the frustration that is an inevitable part of moving ideas forward, the school community benefits when adults work hard to take responsibility for themselves.

A Powerful Vision of Educational Equity with Supportive Leadership

In successful schools, acceptance of challenge as opportunity is strengthened by a shared, heartfelt vision. It varies in wording and evolves over time, but it consistently acknowledges a shared belief among educators, students, parents, and community members in two inseparable ideals: making education work for kids and caring for the communities from which the kids come.

As a profession we educators have learned quite a lot about the technical, emotional, and cultural attributes of exceptional schools, even though we also recognize that there is no blueprint for change. For example, and as illustrated in the King Middle School case study, a culturally responsive school manifests a powerful schoolwide vision of educational equity. This vision is informed by a continuous cycle of well-coordinated, motivationally focused innovation, feedback, and redesign. And it is supported by strong leadership in the form of a skillful administrator or a flatter hierarchical structure such as a school leadership team of culturally diverse educators, parents, community members, and when appropriate, students. Several theorists believe that forceful leadership is the factor that contributes most directly to major effective changes in classroom practice that become incorporated into everyday routines (Crandall, 1983; Loucks, 1983).

King Middle School was described as having three forms of leadership—the principal, the governance team, and the instructional leadership cadre. In some schools, however, every staff member is on one of many different kinds of leadership teams, all with a distinct school renewal focus. Such schools often also have a steering committee that consists of team representatives and other members of the school community that the school feels ought to be represented.

In the culturally responsive school, concerted effort is devoted to making certain that multiple voices from the community are heard. In a community that is largely African American, for example, a school would seek representation from organizations such as the National Association for the Advancement of Colored People (NAACP), the Urban League, and churches and community centers that serve African American families. But it would also welcome the participation of other groups that could inform its comprehensive focus on ethnic and cultural pluralism.

People from the community play a particularly vital role in culturally responsive schoolwide innovation. They not only represent critical perspectives but can act as the conscience of the community and the conscience of serious school improvement initiatives. Often when resources become scarce and other forms of support begin to fade, it is parents and community members who maintain an unrelenting vision of what is necessary and possible. It is ironic that parents are at times maligned for one of their greatest contributions to education—activism in the face of adversity.

Clearly, a school's vision of educational equity is also a vision of social justice. Schools that are culturally responsive aspire to the principles of a just society. That is, they aspire to create themselves as pluralistic democracies. In spite of the obvious social injustices that exist in the broader world, they know that if they wait for massive social change before trying to create a great school, the students who have the most to lose are the ones who already suffer. Typically, then, these schools see themselves as agents of change and agents of their own empowerment, finding it easier, for example, to ask for forgiveness for mistakes than to seek permission for each innovative idea. In other words, they see themselves as having the authority to act. This sense of agency helps such schools rise above any despair born of the momentary or episodic confusion that comes with taking risks. It also diminishes their tendency to assign blame.

The blending of technical, emotional, and cultural attributes in exceptional schools is like creating improvisational jazz. Rather than working with music as a set of isolated variables, the jazz artist hears many different sounds at the same time and works with them so that many sounds become one—symmetry through diversity. Educators who inspire student success have this facility in common with the jazz artist, a personal ability to blend and weave differences into a unified whole. Overall, culturally responsive educators and schools manifest the meaning of courage because, even though realizing at times that they are afraid, they still dare to question themselves, to be powerful, and to use their strength in the service of their vision.

Chapter Three

Culturally Responsive Curriculum

To have one's individuality completely ignored is like being pushed quite out of life. Like being blown out as one blows out a light.
EVELYN SCOTT

In a culturally responsive school the classroom is a place where teachers and students engage in serious work and where *all* students are genuinely expected to succeed. This perspective is communicated through curriculum and instruction that reciprocally interact so that *what* students learn is motivationally and educationally aligned with *how* students learn. Inadequate, misleading, or irrelevant content combined with motivating instructional practice is at best noneducative and at worst miseducative. This chapter discusses the key aspects of a culturally responsive curriculum that make it a transformational curriculum.

Transformational Curriculum

Curriculum can be defined as a formal course of study. In a culturally responsive school, curriculum is transformational. This means that students examine subject matter from many different cultural, political, and academic perspectives and apply those perspectives in ways that have social merit (Banks, 1997; Nieto, 1992; Butler, 1993). In addition, students see themselves and others equally and realistically represented in all resources for learning.

Transformational curriculum extends beyond cultural content. It includes real-life ways of integrating and organizing cultural, social, scientific and environmental, and civic learning across subject areas. In doing so, it enhances transfer of knowledge from one academic task to another, from subject to subject, and from school to outside life. Further, it deepens the meaning of learning and cognitive value of learning because students are able to make authentic connections to their experiences, frames of reference, and interests (Caine and Caine, 1991).

Compartmentalized learning, in contrast, interferes with some of our highest educational goals and in particular with students' ability to construct meaning, because it does not correspond to the way human beings experience life. It defines a world once removed from the way we actually interact with the world. Individuals do not generally encounter in everyday life isolated and vicarious experiences similar to their academic math experiences, social studies experiences, and so forth.

When we compartmentalize learning and isolate it from reality, it is like giving a person a paint-by-number book rather than the tools and guidance he or she needs to create an inspired piece of art. It deprives people of the opportunity to give shape and meaning to their own experiences and abstractions. This has motivational and cognitive implications. But it also has political implications. If we are to interrupt the anger and apathy that can result when people experience social, political, and economic alienation, we must help students find meaning in going to school. As professionals, we burn out when we are treated like appliances (Meier, 1995); students do the same. Students require involvement in issues that really matter to them and interaction with others about these issues. If we are to create conditions in which all students can see themselves as social, political, and intellectual leaders, then we need to shape curriculum with students' experiences, perspectives, and interests in mind.

Beyond Heroes and Holidays

Implicit in a curriculum that allows students to examine subject matter from many different cultural, political, and academic perspectives and apply those perspectives in ways that have social merit are regular opportunities for students to understand how ethnic and cultural experience is integrated into an individual's total experience. Through these opportunities we transform learning so that students are able to apply their emerging understanding of different ethnic and cultural perspectives to issues and events, and to integrate that understanding into the way they interact with others and take action in the world. In other words, we help students to experience culture not only as a point of affirmation and celebration but as a source and mediator of influence and empowerment.

This approach can be clearly distinguished from what has come to be known as the *heroes and holidays*, or *contributions*, approach to curriculum. A classroom focus on heroes and holidays results in an emphasis on discrete cultural elements, people, or celebrations. It introduces a few individuals who have achieved exceptional acclaim or a few exotic rituals and ceremonies, often without any meaningful context (Banks, 1997). Not infrequently this approach supplants a thoughtful examination of the historical experiences and contemporary issues that integrate the perspectives of many different ethnic and cultural groups. Just as important, it trivializes complex events and, at times, sacred belief systems. One of the many consequences is that students, parents, and community members become frustrated with the insincerity of this superficial activity and react accordingly.

These results are also true of the *additive approach,* in which content is added to the curriculum without changing the curricular structure. For example, an educator might teach literature from the perspectives and points of view of the dominant group but add a novel by a person of color (such as *The Color Purple,* by Alice Walker) to the reading list (Banks, 1997). Although the additive approach can be a first step toward integrating ethnic content and different points of view, it does not substantively alter the way curriculum is developed.

Where to Begin

Initiating and building transformational curriculum can seem overwhelming. It is not easy to create wholeness in the ways we help students understand and use information, given the limitations on our own opportunities to learn and the structure of the typical school day. In culturally responsive schools, educators, working either as individuals or in study groups, see curriculum transformation as part of a process that will take longer than a single lifetime. Nonetheless the starting points they have found are informative, as the following examples show.

1. *Add a culturally significant issue to every lesson.* Some educators begin by adding some aspect of culture or issue of equity to every lesson or unit. Often they "share the ownership of knowing" (Oldfather, 1992) by becoming co-learners, engaged in inquiry with their students. In the study of the American Revolution, for example, a social studies and a language arts teacher might work with students to learn about the various groups in addition to male European Americans who were in the colonies during that time. A simple KWL chart (What do we know? What do we want to know? How will we create and share evidence of our learning?) can guide the process. Educators may replace the question, What do we know? with, What have you heard? (creating an HWL chart). This alteration is respectful of students who are modest about their sources of knowledge.

Perhaps students will want to identify not only the colonists' grievances against King George III but also the grievances of women, American Indians, and African Americans of that time. Alternately, students may want to apply the wording and intent of the Preamble of the Constitution of the United States to diverse groups of people living in the United States at that time. Having done so, they might then suggest amendments. Finally, students might use this process to create a document that informs student rights in the classroom (Eldridge, 1998). There are many ways to merge new content with old, learning with students as you go.

2. *Be conscientious about sharing information about women of color.* Like all curriculum, multicultural curriculum can unwittingly perpetuate the overrepresentation of men that exists in society as a whole. Such overrepresentation is often present in the illustrations as well as the content of reference materials. This is why many educators are becoming increasingly conscientious about regularly including perspectives on and information about women of color in course content. An extensive bibliography of books about women of color can be found in *Teaching Strategies for Ethnic Stud-*

ies (Banks, 1997) as well as in *Multicultural Teaching: A Handbook of Activities, Information, and Resources* (Tiedt and Tiedt, 1995). Using local individuals as resources may also be helpful.

3. *Access local human resources.* Most educators who are working toward transformative curriculum rely on the human resources in their own communities. They seek assistance from district-level curriculum specialists and resource centers; reference librarians; parents, families, students, and community members representing local cultures; multicultural bookstores; and representatives of political and professional organizations. Parents are typically particularly underrepresented when educators are garnering resources. Not only is a multicultural curriculum advisory board with parents, teachers, and community members of benefit to the school, but individual parents are often more than willing to locate culturally relevant music, art, literature, and a host of community resources for their children's teachers.

In a culturally responsive school such assistance helps educators to identify content and perspectives that not only complement the existing curriculum but may conflict with it. Often, when we try to help students resolve conflicting perspectives, we are able to work through our own conflicting views too (Butler, 1993).

4. *Locate transformational curriculum resources that include extensive bibliographies.* There are many excellent books on K–12 multicultural transformational curriculum, many of which contain extensive bibliographies and references for videotapes and films: see, for example, Banks (1997); Grant and Gomez (1996); Grant and Sleeter (1998); Ladson-Billings (1994); Tiedt and Tiedt (1995).

In Grant and Gomez's book, for example, Geneva Gay (1996) discusses a multicultural school curriculum, and one of her suggestions is to include a group that frequently feels excluded from the dialogue on multicultural curriculum, teachers of young children. She suggests that educators

- Institute a cross-ethnic Adopt-a-Grandparent Program, in which students from one ethnic group choose grandparents from another ethnic group.
- Use ethnic games and folk dance as ways for students to practice gross motor coordination for recreation and to develop skills for physical education.

- Ask culturally diverse individuals regularly to facilitate class-room story time through personal or mediated appearances.
- Change the focus of routine seasonal activities (for example, discussing pilgrims and drawing turkeys at Thanksgiving) to reflect ethnically diverse experiences and practices. For example, use Thanksgiving as an opportunity to explore different locations in which students have lived and what it feels like to be in a new home, or to explore a theme like friendship by thinking about how American Indian children and European American children during the colonial era might have felt about each other around the time we associate with Thanksgiving.

One of the primary purposes of a multicultural transformational curriculum, especially during students' early years, is to influence habits of the mind. If we wish students to respect themselves and others, to enjoy learning, to question established practices and assumptions through thoughtful inquiry, and to see themselves as effective civic participants, then they need to experience such expectations from childhood as an explicit part of their learning.

Examine Existing Materials for Fairness

In addition to the previously mentioned suggestions, it is important to work with students so that they become conscientious about seeing themselves and others more accurately and equitably reflected in course content. There are several excellent guides for evaluating curriculum content for realistic portrayals of members of diverse ethnic and cultural groups, for fair representation of people, and for honest attempts to break down stereotypes and prejudices. One such guide is *Ten Quick Ways to Analyze Children's Book for Racism and Sexism* (Council on Interracial Books for Children, 1980). It is easy enough, however, to design your own customized checklist.

In upper elementary grades and beyond, one approach is to ask students to consider what they might look for in a text or other print materials if they were evaluating ethnic and cultural fairness. Although they would probably express these criteria differently, a typical list might include

- Visibility (implying that members of diverse groups are of equal importance and significance)
- Realistic portrayals (implying that there is diversity within and across groups)
- Realistic interpretations (implying that there is more than one way to understand an issue, situation, or group of people)
- Authentic acknowledgment of historical and contemporary challenges (implying that it is important to acknowledge prejudice and discrimination as ongoing challenges each person must address for the benefit of all)
- Linguistic respect for groups and genders (implying that it is important for language to reflect the involvement of both genders and to refer to groups in ways that acknowledge their own ways of seeing themselves).

These criteria can be used to examine text materials and supplementary resources. With a partner, students might agree to examine ten or more randomly selected pages of a book, using the criteria to which they have agreed and looking at content and illustrations to determine whether or not the text appears to represent the experiences and perspectives of people from diverse backgrounds. The goal is not to discard print materials that manifest bias but rather to make informed decisions about how to use them and when to provide additional resources to ensure equitable and realistic learning materials. To encourage students' conscientious use of published materials, some teachers put examples of bias on display in their classrooms as students find them. This activity also informs students' own writing.

Find the Time to Form Collegial Study Groups

Educators work within the normal constraints of a twenty-four-hour day. This is one of the reasons why a culturally responsive school functions as a learning community rather than a collection of isolated teachers and classrooms. As isolated professionals, teachers would find it nearly impossible to develop expertise in every aspect of education, that is, instructional practice, curriculum, and school-wide issues such as governance; parent, family, and community involvement; and so forth. However, ideas and commitment are the currency of professional exchange.

Of course, one of the constraints that overwhelms professionals working in isolation is also a challenge for those working together. Consistently, educators ask, "How will we find the time?" There are several resources to assist schools that seek to find time for staff collaboration. Mary Ann Raywid (1993), Carlene Murphy (1997), and Sue Francis, Stephanie Hirsh, and Elizabeth Rowland (1994) provide excellent examples of the ways that schools across the United States are successfully creating ongoing, collaborative schoolwide learning among adults. The suggestions in Activity 12 in Chapter Six may also be helpful for schools seeking to find practical ways for teachers to find the time to learn together.

Multicultural curriculum study groups are one example of how educators use time well in collaboration. Such study groups work together to locate resources and curriculum expressive of and committed to multiple and divergent perspectives. In addition, study group members examine new and existing curriculum to see how well it connects with the social context of students' interests and experiences and with the types of information that intrigue a range of students. Like all curriculum content, multicultural content has little meaning to students if it fails to connect with their experiences, frames of reference, and interests.

In addition to examining course content, multicultural curriculum study groups provide an opportunity for teachers to co-create lessons that integrate diverse ethnic and cultural perspectives. As mentioned earlier, when integration of perspectives and academic concepts occurs across disciplines there are many benefits in addition to multicultural understanding. This is illuminated in the following example of a middle school unit on the solar system.

Middle School Unit: The Solar System

Four subject areas, social studies, language arts, science, and math, converge to provide students with a multifaceted understanding of the stars. In social studies students learn various cultural beliefs about the heavenly bodies while in language arts they read legends and stories and make connections between the perspectives of culturally diverse authors. Students then write their own stories. They share these stories with younger students, who provide illustrations and book jackets for the authors.

In science, the students construct sundials, study the life of a star, and construct models that depict this life cycle and its interactions with other forces. They also discuss how this life cycle might be represented in the legends they are reading and writing. In addition, science and social studies teachers help students examine the social, political, and environmental implications of space exploration, and students develop interview questions to learn about different perspectives on space exploration from astronomers, astronauts, environmentalists, government officials, and community members of different ethnic origins. Students who are studying another language, translate interview questions into that language and agree to interview two people who are native speakers of that language. Students also work together in teams to design experiments that will provide direct experience with the environmental implications of space technology and exploration.

In math, students learn the mathematics of rudimentary astronomy. They also analyze data and develop charts and graphs based on the space exploration questionnaires they developed in science and social studies classes.

For a culminating project, the art, woodshop, and technology support teachers help students create original displays and videos that will teach family and community members about the ways the stars have influenced the stories human beings tell; the systems of belief related to the stars, within and across cultures; some ways contemporary astronomers know what they know about the sun and the stars; and the social, political, and environmental implications of space exploration.

Teachers who are new to or experienced with interdisciplinary, thematic multicultural planning will find *Teaching Strategies for Ethnic Studies* (Banks, 1997) particularly helpful. The first few chapters, in particular, clarify the meanings of terms like *race, ethnicity,* and *culture* and provide examples of concepts that are significant to a pluralistic democracy and thematic learning. In addition, *Educating Everybody's Children: Diverse Teaching Strategies for Diverse Learners* (Association for Supervision and Curriculum Development, 1995) provides many valuable examples of ways that educators can use students' prior knowledge to develop thematic approaches to learning. The development of a semantic web is one particularly useful pedagogical device. The theme of the Harlem Renaissance (p. 55), for example, helped teachers and students identify and categorize topics for exploration. Teams of teachers worked together to choose a topic, research it, and develop a lesson plan upon which others might elaborate. Lesson plans were then combined to produce a curriculum unit. This is just one example of how teacher and student interests can shape curriculum.

A transformational curriculum offers educators ways of integrating and organizing cultural, social, and civic learning across subject areas. It can transform the ordinary to the extraordinary, creating new patterns that can call forth one of the motivational foundations for intellectual rigor—wonder.

Chapter Four

A Motivational Framework for Culturally Responsive Teaching

Out of clutter, find simplicity.
ALBERT EINSTEIN

Learning theory has been dominated by the field of psychology. However, a predominantly psychological interpretation of learning has significant limitations, as explained by Jarvis (1987), Cunningham (1989), and Wlodkowski and Ginsberg (1995). In particular, psychology has used mostly Eurocentric assumptions and values in explaining why students are academically successful and in labeling those who are not. But human responses to situations and consequent human behaviors may differ across cultures. It is quite possible, for example, for two people who have been socialized differently to feel two completely different responses to the same experience. And even when their initial responses are similar, say, for example, that both of them feel frustrated, their subsequent actions might differ. One might continue with enhanced determination, whereas the other might decide that participation is futile. Because the socialization of emotions is influenced by cultural experiences, the motivational response a student has to a learning activity reflects this influence and its associated complexity. Psychology offers at best an incomplete understanding of this remarkable intricacy (Hall, 1997).

Motivation, that is, why people do what they do, or the natural human capacity to direct energy in pursuit of a goal, is a vital construct within the realm of many disciplines—philosophy, sociology, the study of spiritual ideology, economics, linguistics, anthropology, political science, and a host of other disciplines, including the field of education. In education alone, the expansive knowledge base that informs the way educators think about student motivation and learning contains theories that address multiple intelligences, language acquisition, brain-based learning, constructivism, cooperative learning, foundations of literacy, multicultural education, performance assessment, student-centered learning, and experiential learning. What has been missing is a larger theory, or *ecology*, through which educators can synthesize motivational concepts from various disciplines in order to begin to develop a comprehensive and cohesive understanding of motivation. The theory of intrinsic motivation provides that synthesis, and it is the foundational theory for the Motivational Framework for Culturally Responsive Teaching.

In this chapter, we discuss the importance and function of the Motivational Framework for Culturally Responsive Teaching, henceforth referred to simply as the motivational framework. This motivational framework provides educators with a *macrocultural* pedagogical model. In other words, it is built on principles and structures that are meaningful within and across cultures and that are especially applicable to the learning of students from families that have historically not experienced success in school systems. It does not compare and contrast groups of people as a microcultural perspective would; it does not, for example, identify specific ethnic groups and prescribe approaches to teaching according to each group's presumed characteristics and orientations.

The purpose of the motivational framework is to unify teaching practices that elicit the intrinsic motivation of *all* learners, so that educators can consistently design learning experiences that matter to and support the success of *all* students. Therefore we have sought to make the framework broad enough that it accommodates the range of ethnic and cultural diversity found in most schools. It also integrates the variety of assumptions addressed on many fronts—educational, social, cultural, and psychological (Singham, 1998). Most of all, it seeks to explain how to create compelling and democratic learning experiences that honor the diverse perspectives, values, and talents that students bring to the classroom.

The Four Conditions of the Motivational Framework

As outlined earlier, the Motivational Framework for Culturally Responsive Teaching offers a holistic and systematic representation of four motivational conditions:

1. Establishing inclusion
2. Developing a positive attitude
3. Enhancing meaning
4. Engendering competence

Establishing inclusion refers to employing principles and practices that contribute to a learning environment in which students and teachers feel respected by and connected to one another.

Developing a positive attitude refers to employing principles and practices that contribute to, through personal and cultural relevance and through choice, a favorable disposition toward learning.

Enhancing meaning refers to bringing about challenging and engaging learning. It expands and strengthens learning in ways that matter to students and have social merit.

Engendering competence refers to employing principles and practices that help students authentically identify that they are effectively learning something they value.

The four motivational conditions work in concert with each other. When educators plan carefully, the conditions form a set of intersecting dimensions that simultaneously and reciprocally interact to influence motivation and learning within and across cultural groups. The following is an example of a plan for employing the four conditions so they work together in a two-hour high school U.S. history class. The goal or, in contemporary language, the *content standard,* is for students to understand the causes of the Revolutionary War.

Understanding Conflict:
An Examination of the Causes of the Revolutionary War

1. Motivational Condition: Establishing Inclusion

The learning experience contributes to the development of participants as a community of learners who feel respected by and connected to one another and to the teacher.

Teaching Strategies

A. Students work in collaborative groups to think of things that might make them "fighting mad." Each group selects a volunteer to report on its findings.

B. Each group has a small pile of beans in the center of its table. Every time a student speaks, she or he takes a bean. Students work together to ensure that everyone comfortably and equitably contributes. The number of beans each student accumulates contributes to this awareness.

2. Motivational Condition: Developing a Positive Attitude

The learning experience offers meaningful choices and promotes personal relevance to contribute to participants' positive attitude.

Teaching Strategy

Students select one of three different topics to explore in a small group.

A. One group makes a list of the colonists' grievances against King George III. They then compare and contrast the kinds of things about which the colonists were "fighting mad" with the kinds of "fighting mad" feelings they previously identified among themselves, identifying themes and patterns.

B. Another group makes a list of what might make East Coast American Indian tribes "fighting mad" at King George and at the colonists. They then compare and contrast that list with the kinds of "fighting mad" feelings they previously identified among themselves, identifying themes and patterns.

C. Another group makes a list of reasons that African American people had to be "fighting mad." They then compare and contrast that list with the kinds of "fighting mad" feelings they previously identified among themselves, identifying themes and patterns.

3. Motivational Condition: Enhancing Meaning

The learning experience engages participants in challenging learning that has social merit.

TEACHING STRATEGIES

A. Students select three different sources to investigate in order to refine their lists of the potential sources of the anger or rebellion of colonists, American Indians, or African Americans during the revolutionary period and to respond to questions such as the following:

1. Were all the members of the colonial group you are researching equally opposed to the authority of the British government?

2. What were other conflicts the group was dealing with during this period of time?

3. How was this group's role either directly or indirectly significant in the Revolutionary War?

Sources of information might include the Internet, literature, and interviews with knowledgeable community members or with historians at a local university.

B. Students select three different ways to represent their findings. One of these representations must be written in paragraph form. The other two representations might take the form of a visualization exercise for the entire class, a short play, a poem, a piece of art, a photographic display, a collage, a time line, a PowerPoint presentation, a song, a mock interview, or some other format that students determine.

4. MOTIVATIONAL CONDITION: ENGENDERING COMPETENCE

The learning experience creates participants' understanding that they are becoming more effective in authentic learning that they value.

TEACHING STRATEGIES

A. Students examine samples of excellent student work from previous classes and note common attributes of different products. Students use these observations to develop a rubric for high-quality work. Next, they examine how to determine the difference between works receiving grades of A, of B, and of C and agree that any work receiving a grade lower than a C will be considered incomplete.

B. Each student identifies one person in the school and one person in the community to whom she or he will present the group's work and then elicit feedback.

C. In addition to receiving a grade, each student will complete a self-assessment that identifies (1) personal contributions to group work, (2) things that were difficult or frustrating and what can be learned as a consequence, (3) something surprising that was learned, and (4) a goal based on this experience.

The following outline delineates the four questions the conditions address and the two criteria for each motivational goal or condition. These questions and criteria can act as a compass, helping teachers to be reasonably sure both when planning and when teaching that they are continuously supporting motivation to learn among all students. A diagram of the motivational framework is shown in Figure 4.1.

Establishing Inclusion

Question. How does the learning experience contribute to the development of participants as a community of learners who feel respected by and connected to one another and to the teacher?

Criteria. Respect and connectedness.

Developing a Positive Attitude

Question. How does the learning experience offer meaningful choices and promote personal relevance to contribute to participants' positive attitude?

Criteria. Choice and relevance.

Enhancing Meaning

Question. How does the learning experience engage participants in challenging learning that has social merit?

Criteria. Challenge and engagement.

Engendering Competence

Question. How does the learning experience create participants' understanding that they are becoming more effective in authentic learning that they value?

Criteria. Authenticity and effectiveness.

Conclusion

In the chapters ahead, each of the four motivational conditions will be explained and exemplified in detail as they apply to student learning, staff development, and school renewal. By using criteria

**Figure 4.1. Motivational Framework for
Culturally Responsive Teaching.**

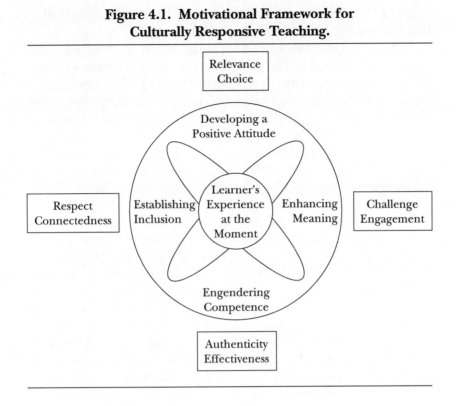

instead of rules we are able to provide a more multidisciplinary and interpretive approach. As we remarked earlier, criteria are more like a compass than a map. Try as theorists may to find hard and fast rules, the challenge and beauty of teaching is that human beings can never be reduced to a simple set of variables.

Each of the motivational conditions contains an initial verb as a way of emphasizing its dynamic and continuous state of existence. And once again we emphasize that these conditions are interrelated. They are simultaneously reciprocal. Each affects all the others. The conventional psychological model of perceiving, thinking, and acting is a linear process that may occur far less often than previous theorists have thought. There is evidence that in matters as profound as perspective transformation and cultural identity, most people change through immediate action in response to intercultural challenges, with little deep rational reflection and planned action (Taylor, 1994).

Thus the simultaneously and reciprocally interacting motivational conditions in Figure 4.1 are an evolving family of intersecting dimensions that join with and act as part of learning to influence individuals' motivation at any given moment. For example, without the establishment of inclusion (a sense of respect and connectedness that contributes to emotional safety) and the development of a positive attitude, the enhancement of meaning (the actual learning of something challenging) may not occur with equal ease and energy. Then it may be nearly impossible to engender competence, that is, for students to experience success that has academic or social merit. Moreover, even when some conditions are met, others may not be. We have all been in classrooms where there was an exhilarating feeling of inclusion, where students felt safe to face risky academic challenges, and yet where there were few challenges to be found. Similarly, there are teachers who work with students to establish inclusion, who contribute to a positive attitude, and who offer stimulating challenges, but who also use competitive grading that builds distrust and ultimately undermines motivation. Therefore, all four conditions must be present and work together to evoke and sustain participants' intrinsic motivation. This interaction may occur over time, but ultimately, there must be harmony among the conditions. We call this harmony *pedagogical alignment*—the coordination of procedures in teaching that ensures maximum consistent effect and motivation (Wlodkowski and Ginsberg, 1995). The Motivational Framework for Culturally Responsive Teaching is a harmonious means for creating compelling learning experiences in which *all* students can attain success that matters—to themselves and to their communities.

Chapter Five

Establishing Inclusion

Remember the sky you were born under, know each of the stars' stories.
JOY HARJO

Establishing inclusion means that all students become part of an environment in which they and their teacher are respected by and connected to one another. In other words, the classroom or school possesses agreed-upon norms that create safety, acceptance, and harmony so that students and teachers are able to manifest and learn from diverse values, perspectives, and ways of interacting. Establishing inclusion not only diminishes the feelings of cultural isolation that can deteriorate the motivation to learn but also fosters an environment that encourages students to be their authentic selves and, consequently, to take the risks that are fundamental to personal development and academic performance. When students do not feel included, they are far more likely to guard their resources, strengths, and perceived weaknesses. Inclusion, therefore, is at the core of genuine empowerment, agency, and academic success. One might simply say that it allows students to tell and hear their stories and to make sense of things without fear.

From a scientific perspective, when students are encouraged by the learning atmosphere to use their own social and cultural strengths, they can construct cognitive connections that make knowledge relevant and bring it within their personal control (Vygotsky, 1978). In doing so, students become knowledge builders rather than knowledge resisters. There is a spate of research on

51

this topic, but it is also simply common sense that students who feel alienated will achieve less than those who do not. This is the very real threat of being in the minority of any classroom, school, or society. Most of us can easily recall what became of our motivation in a class or during a time in which we felt excluded. We are social beings, and our feelings of inclusion or exclusion are enduring and irrepressible.

The strategies presented in this chapter can contribute to creating a *climate of respect* and can enable students to *feel connected to one another.* Like all strategies in this book, they accommodate intracultural and intercultural differences.

Please note that throughout Chapters Five, Six, Seven, and Eight, in the activity sections titled "Process," terms such as *teacher, professor,* and *staff-developer* may be substituted for the term *facilitator,* as appropriate. Similarly, terms such as *seminar, workshop,* or *institute* may be substituted for the word *class.* We use *participants* as an all-inclusive term to describe anyone from elementary school student to staff developer who is a learner in a class. Also, in describing the materials for each activity we do not list ordinary notepaper and pens or pencils, and obviously, any appropriate materials can be substituted for the specific ones we mention.

Each of these chapters concludes with a list of the activities presented, organized by audience, students or educators. Many of the activities are effective both for students and for educators engaged in professional development and school reform. When an activity is specifically designed for educators, we mention it in the Purpose section of the activity.

Create Opportunities for Multidimensional Sharing

Opportunities for multidimensional sharing are those occasions, from introduction exercises to personal anecdotes to classroom rituals, that provide a chance for people to see one another as complete and evolving human beings who have similar needs, emotions, and experiences. These opportunities give a human face to a class, break down assumptions and stereotypes, and support each individual's identification of herself or himself with another person.

There are many ways to provide opportunities for multidimensional sharing, depending of course on the history, makeup, and purpose of the group. If there is a caution, it is to guard against intrusiveness, providing ways for people to self-disclose personal information only to the extent it feels appropriate and comfortable. There are many students in our classrooms who come from cultures that value modesty. Further, many of us have learned hard lessons about the untrustworthiness of "trust" that is developed in artificial ways. Multidimensional sharing should always be approached with respect for the privacy of others.

Meals and extracurricular activities can offer individuals opportunities to be themselves and can reduce self-consciousness. Activities that help people to learn each other's names and to laugh together can also be worthwhile. As facilitators of adult learning or as teachers of younger students, not taking ourselves too seriously can reveal our humanity and suggest that we are open to a range of feelings and perspectives.

Following are some specific exercises and activities for sharing that work well with just about any group. They offer ideas for routines and rituals that can establish classrooms where everyone feels she or he belongs and can safely offer personal perspectives and take risks in order to learn.

Activity 1. Venn Diagram Sharing

PURPOSE
To learn about each other, identify commonalities and differences, and personalize the concept of culture; to identify options for instruction that support the intrinsic motivation of all students.

TIME
Thirty minutes.

FORMAT
Triads and large group.

MATERIALS
Newsprint and markers.

PROCESS
Step 1. Ask the entire group to consider the concept of culture and to name factors that might influence individuals' cultural identities. People will normally suggest such possibilities as gender, socioeconomic class, ethnicity, language, music, religion, food, and home of origin. Emphasize that culture is a complex concept and cannot be reduced to a

simple list of nouns or adjectives but that for the purpose of this exercise a list is a way of helping people to select topics that they can easily explore together. Write down approximately seven to ten words that people call out.

Step 2. The large group divides into groups of three, and each group draws a Venn diagram, as shown in Figure 5.1. Each triad member selects one of the three circles to represent herself or himself. Triad members then select topics from the list that the large group has generated and begin to identify ways in which they are similar to and different from one another in regard to each topic. Unique qualities, such as languages spoken or ethnicity, are entered on the portion of the person's circle that does not overlap anyone else's circle. Qualities that are shared by two triad members—for example, gender—are entered in the space created by the intersection of the circles of the two people who have the quality in common. When all three triad members have a quality in common, they locate it in the in the center of the diagram, where all three circles intersect. Participants are encouraged to share information only on those topics that are comfortable for everyone in the triad.

Step 3. After fifteen to twenty minutes, participants take a short time to publicly reflect on something that they have learned as a consequence of participating in the exercise. Some generalizations occur more frequently than others: for example, "We realized that we had more in common than we might have predicted"; and, "The more information people have about each other, the more open their conversations become." This activity is often a good beginning for establishing a sense of community.

Activity 2. *Two Wishes and a Truth*

PURPOSE

To personalize the concept of culture; to identify options for instruction that supports the intrinsic motivation of all students.

TIME

Thirty minutes.

FORMAT

Triads and large group.

PROCESS

Step 1. Ask each participant to write down three statements about himself or herself—one that is true and two that he or she might wish to be true. For example, a person might state that he or she once climbed Mount Fuji, once met the Pope, and regularly parachutes out of an airplane. Triad partners take turns listening to each other's statements and trying to guess which of the statements is the truth.

Figure 5.1. Venn Diagram for Sharing.

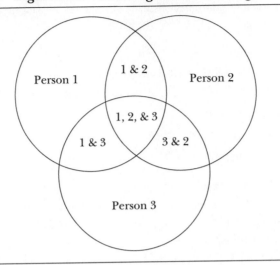

Step 2. In seminars with teachers, the debriefing includes these questions: What occurs to you as a consequence of participating in the activity? How does this activity relate to issues of cultural diversity? How might you adapt this activity for use in the classroom?

Activity 3. Decades and Diversity

PURPOSE
To personalize the concept of culture; to learn more about other people and their perspectives.

TIME
Forty-five minutes.

FORMAT
Small groups and large group.

MATERIALS
Overhead projector and a slide or a chart showing the five questions listed in the activity.

PROCESS
Step 1. Ask participants to group themselves according to the decade in which they graduated from high school (1950–1959, 1960–1969, and so on). Large decade groups can

be subdivided so people can work in more manageable groups. Each group brainstorms responses to the following five questions about their decade, listed on an overhead slide or large sheet of paper.

BRAINSTORMING QUESTIONS

1. What did you do on Saturday night?

2. What was some of your favorite music or what were your favorite musical groups?

3. What was the latest fashion?

4. What were some current world events?

5. What were some of the "no-no's"?

Step 2. Groups report out question by question, beginning with the youngest group and continuing to the oldest group. For example, the 1990–1999 group reports on what its members did on Saturday night. Next, the 1980–1989 group shares what it members did on Saturday night, and so forth.

In seminars with teachers, these debriefing questions are included: What occurs to you as a consequence of participating in this activity? What connections can you make between this activity and issues related to cultural diversity? How might you adapt this activity for use in the classroom? What does this activity help us understand about making generalizations about people?

In classrooms, students can be asked to interview an older family member and then to combine the data they gather and to chart or graph the responses according to categories. Similarly, students might interview adults in the school and creatively share their findings. Another alternative might be to ask students to identify "the place I have lived that has had the greatest influence on me" and then to group themselves by region according to their answers. The five questions can be easily adapted as well, asking, for example, What were our favorite nearby places to visit? What did we wear? What food did we eat that other people might not have tried? What important or fun community events did we have?

Activity 4. Think-Pair-Share Exercises

PURPOSE

To learn more about each other and each other's perspectives through reflection and sharing.

TIME

Fifteen to twenty minutes.

FORMAT
Dyads and large group.

MATERIALS
Overhead projector and transparencies or newsprint and markers.

PROCESS
Select *one* of the following questions and ask each participant to write a brief response on a piece of paper, pair with someone nearby, and share the response with that person. During the large-group debriefing, participants summarize shared and new ideas, and their responses are recorded on the newsprint or overhead transparencies.

THINK-PAIR-SHARE QUESTIONS

1. What is the significance of any part of your name to you?

   Debriefing question: What are one or two thoughts that occur to you as a consequence of reflecting on this question? What can we learn about ourselves and each other from this exercise?

2. What is one interesting thing about your classroom, school, or community that an outsider might not realize at first glance?

   Debriefing question: What are the implications of this exercise for our classroom or school? What are the implications of this exercise for you?

3. Draw a metaphorical illustration of yourself as a teacher [or as a student]. (The facilitator may create a *gallery* on a spare wall so that after the small-group exercises these illustrations can be viewed by everyone.)

   Debriefing question: How do you understand the picture that you drew? What can we say about our group as a whole when we reflect on the illustrations that were shared?

Activity 5. "Ask Me About . . ." Posters

PURPOSE
To learn more about each other and each other's perspectives.

TIME
Thirty minutes.

FORMAT
Triads and large group.

MATERIALS

Construction paper, markers, Scotch tape, and glue sticks.

PROCESS

Ask participants to share something about themselves or an experience they have had that they value, by creating individual posters that elicit others to ask them about the personal meaning of their drawing, symbol, or attached item. For example, the middle school counselor in Hessen, Germany, who taught us this activity, had recently traveled to a particular part of Italy. She modeled the activity by showing us a bean that can be found only in that region. She had glued it to a piece of paper, and the only other thing on her paper was what she had written in large letters across the top: "Ask me about . . ."

This activity is a good way for students to share experiences and projects.

Activity 6. Multicultural Inventory

PURPOSE

To learn more about each other, and to gain respect for the diversity one finds within any group.

TIME

Thirty minutes.

FORMAT

Large group.

MATERIALS

Handout (Multicultural Inventory).

PROCESS

Distribute the following multicultural inventory, and then ask participants to move around the room, introducing themselves to each other and initialing any statements on the other individual's inventory that they identify as personal qualities the statements describe.

MULTICULTURAL INVENTORY

Please see if you can identify people who have attributes that correspond to the following statements.

1. Speaks a language other than English.

2. Was born in a country other than the United States.

3. Was raised by someone who was born in a country other than the United States.

4. Has more than two siblings.

5. Lives with someone with a different ethnic or cultural background.

6. Has children with a different ethnicity or cultural background.

7. Is good at (or enjoys) something that isn't typical of his or her gender.

8. Is friends with someone who is elderly.

9. Reads books about cultural diversity (give an example of a good one).

10. Has contributed to a project that promotes cultural understanding and respect.

11. [Create an attribute of your own].

Activity 7. Bio-Poems

PURPOSE

To learn about other people while simultaneously expressing one's own needs and concerns. A bio-poem is a formulaic structure that expresses what the writer sees as significant or meaningful about the subject's life

Source: Gere, 1985, p. 222.

TIME

Forty-five minutes, including presentations.

FORMAT

Individuals and small or large groups (small groups if there are many participants).

MATERIALS

The bio-poem handout.

PROCESS

Discuss how the participants are going to use bio-poems to build community among themselves. Mention that the method is particularly useful in helping students in upper elementary, secondary, and postsecondary settings to see the personal dimensions of important figures. For example, students could write bio-poems about Rosa Parks, Eleanor Roosevelt, Julius Caesar, or Frankenstein's monster. Or students could visit a nursing home or a homeless shelter and create a bio-poem that lets others enter the life of a person in those environments. In math or science, students could write a bio-poem about an equation, a formula, or an approach to solving a problem (Bean, 1996). The following handout contains the formula for the bio-poem for educators in a professional development setting.

BIO-POEM FORMULA

Line 1: First name

Line 2: Four traits that describe the character of the poem's subject (in this case yourself)

Line 3: "Relative of . . ." ("Brother of," "Sister of," and so on)

Line 4: "Who feels . . ." (three items that relate to how you feel in this class)

Line 5: "Who needs . . ." (three items that express what you need to be successful)

Line 6: "Who fears . . ." (three items related to this class—or to your experiences as a learner)

Line 7: "Who gives . . ." (three items that indicate what you can contribute to others or to the class)

Line 8: "Who would like to . . ." (three items related to goals for this class)

Line 9: Last name

Activity 8. *Interpretative Community Maps*

PURPOSE

To personalize the concept of culture, especially as it relates to participants' experience in the community; to identify options for instruction that supports the intrinsic motivation of all students.

TIME

Thirty minutes.

FORMAT

Dyads, triads, or small groups.

MATERIALS

Newsprint, colored markers, and masking tape for posting maps.

PROCESS

Ask participants, in dyads, triads, or small groups, to think of the history, places, people, services, customs, and resources in their communities that have supported learning about and appreciating multiculturalism. Ask participants to propose a list of possibilities to include on a comprehensive community map. Because time constraints are generally a concern, ask participants to narrow their lists to a few key "sites." On a mural-size sheet of paper, use colored markers to construct a collectively designed interpretative map. It does not need to conform to a standard scale or geographical directions. Participants may, however, want to develop symbols or landscaping to enhance their contributions.

To extend the activity, divide the collective map into sections. Ask participants to divide into groups to design the sections of a guidebook for the sections of the map. Guidebooks might include descriptions, lists, stories, illustrations, interviews, and so forth. In addition to information on various sites, they might offer community history, a community time line, personal time lines, a local language survey, oral histories, discussions of social issues, and the beliefs of different people about various community issues.

Source: This exercise was inspired by Tiedt and Tiedt, 1995, pp. 119–156.

Activity 9. Dialogue Journals

PURPOSE

To enhance peer dialogue on issues related to a course or any other learning experience.

TIME

As needed.

FORMAT

Dyads.

MATERIALS

A journal or notebook.

PROCESS

Participants pair themselves (or are asked to pair) with another person. At least once a week, partners are asked to write a reflective response to a question or experience as framed by the facilitator. For example, the facilitator may say to teachers, "Please use your dialogue journals this week to reflect on your experience of visiting a colleague's classroom to observe instruction." At a designated time each week, dialogue partners exchange journals, read each other's entry, and respond in writing in the part of the partner's journal that is reserved for such responses. Some people wish to have their partner write a response on the same page. Others reserve a section in the back of the journal— or in a separate journal—for their partner's response.

Activity 10. Response Cards

PURPOSE

To provide an opportunity for all participants to express their responses to a perspective, statement, or minilecture.

TIME

One to two minutes.

FORMAT

Individuals.

MATERIALS

Three three-by-five-inch cards—one yellow, one red, and one blue—for each participant.

PROCESS

Ask participants to write "Interesting!" on the yellow card, "I have a different perspective" on the red card, and "I'm confused" on the blue card. When asked to hold up the card that best reflects their personal response to a perspective, statement, or minilecture, participants hold up the yellow card if what has just transpired is interesting, or the red card if there is a different perspective to consider, or the blue card if clarification is needed. This provides the facilitator with a way of respecting the perspectives of a group and of learning whether a presentation needs to be modified to respond to people's interests or concerns.

Activity 11. Fist-to-Five

PURPOSE

To check in with the perspectives of a group by asking participants to use the five fingers of one hand to give a scale response to a question. This strategy avoids forcing people to respond with a simple yes or no answer.

TIME

One to two minutes.

FORMAT

Individuals.

MATERIALS

None, except one's hand. Individuals who are physically unable to use a hand as a scale, may wish to write—or have someone else write—a number from one to five on a piece of paper and position it on their desk where the facilitator can see it.

PROCESS

Ask participants to raise the number of fingers on one hand that reflects their response to a question. For example, five fingers might mean "absolutely," four fingers "yes," three fingers "so-so," two fingers "caution," and one finger "no," and a fist might mean "I feel so opposed that I would encourage resistance." Thus, a facilitator might say, after much discussion, "Please raise the number of fingers—with five fingers being high and one finger being low—that reflects your opinion right now on whether or not we should focus on teaching reading and writing across the curriculum." (Another example of a set of fist-to-five values is presented in Chapter One.)

Activity 12. Class Historian

PURPOSE

To provide a record of topics and issues that have been examined, along with learning activities, assignments, and resources, so that participants who were not in attendance have reliable information about what occurred in their absence, so that all students can check the accuracy of their notes and records, and so that instructors have a portfolio that reflects the course as a whole.

TIME

As needed.

FORMAT

Individuals, who rotate in the assignment.

MATERIALS

A journal or notebook.

PROCESS

At the beginning of a course or institute, participants sign up to serve as class historian on a specific date. The format of the class record that is kept can vary, but class historians use their notes and handouts provided by the facilitator as a guide. In some instances a class editor reviews and compiles the submissions of the class historians to achieve enhanced reliability and consistency. A sample format follows.

CLASS RECORD

    Date:

    Topics discussed:

    Key points:

    Learning activities:

    Handouts:

    Resources:

    Assignments due:

Upcoming assignments:

Personal comments:

For additional information, contact [name of class historian].

Activity 13. Class Review

PURPOSE

To provide group memory and perspectives about topics and issues from the previous session; to support all participants in verifying that they have a reliable record of prior learning upon which to build.

TIME

Fifteen to thirty minutes.

FORMAT

Triads and large group.

MATERIALS

Notes from the prior session.

PROCESS

At the beginning of the learning experience, ask each participant in each triad to identify two to three of the most important points, concepts, or ideas from the previous session. Then a reporter from each triad joins a "panel of experts" at the front of the room and presents a key point discussed in his or her triad. Two volunteer scribes take turns recording the contributions of the panel of experts so that there is a written record to which any student may refer for additional information.

Activity 14. Bean Experiment

PURPOSE

To provide a context in which participants can examine whether or not all participants have had an opportunity to comfortably participate.

TIME

Ten minutes.

FORMAT

Small groups of five to six persons.

MATERIALS

A small container with twenty to thirty beans.

PROCESS

Ask each member of the group to take a bean each time she or he speaks. At the end of the learning experience, group members discuss how many beans each person has as well as the implications of any disparity in numbers. They set personal and team participation goals in order to support the opportunity for all group members to make meaningful contributions.

Activity 15. Class Agreements or Participation Guidelines

PURPOSE:

To provide an environment in which participants feel respected by each other as well as by their teacher and can comfortably offer their perspectives.

TIME

Thirty minutes.

FORMAT

Individuals, triads, and large group.

MATERIALS

Handout (Class Agreements).

PROCESS

Ask participants to work individually to review the following sample guidelines and to select, modify, and add other kinds of classroom agreements or guidelines that might help people construct a positive and productive learning environment. If participants are classroom teachers, ask them to discuss their recommendations for working with students to create class agreements.

CLASS AGREEMENTS

1. Listen carefully to others.

2. Share airtime.

3. Respect confidentiality when a person indicates that he or she is sharing something sensitive and personal.

4. Speak from one's own experience, saying, for example, "I think . . ." or, "In my experience I have found . . ."—rather than generalizing one's experiences to others with comments like, "People say . . ." or, "We believe . . ."

5. Diminish the temptation to blame others by focusing on offering constructive insights and ideas.

6. Contribute respectfully to the learning of others.

Some schools have schoolwide agreements intended to promote respect throughout the school. Horizons K–8 Alternative School in Boulder, Colorado, for example, has had consistent success with a communication agreement developed by the Horizons Council that reflects the values of parents, teachers, and students and that is posted in every classroom (see Exhibit 5.1).

Activity 16. Creating a Schoolwide Professional Agreement

PURPOSE

To create inclusion and cohesiveness among faculty members who work in schools that are making significant changes in order to become increasingly responsive to all students. Working on inclusiveness among faculty is especially important, because as schools or organizations make substantive changes, conflict increases. Professional agreements can help educators maintain their focus on renewal. This activity is particularly good to practice with teachers in schools or institutions actively engaged in a renewal or restructuring process. It goes beyond participation guidelines and class agreements because it helps educators make their decisions and interactions consistent with shared beliefs and values about school change.

TIME

Twenty minutes.

FORMAT

Dyads or triads.

MATERIALS

Handout (Sample Restructuring Agreement).

PROCESS

Present the information in the following handout about creating a professional agreement to participants for their consideration, revision, and adoption before they address restructuring goals. Request that participants identify two to three handout items that they believe to be especially important and might wish to include in their own schoolwide professional agreement. Then ask for volunteers to share their responses with the large group.

CREATING A PROFESSIONAL AGREEMENT

1. We commit to using meaningful and comprehensive data to make decisions.
2. We commit to creating and sustaining a culture of continued self-examination, extensive and continual professional development, and experimentation.

Exhibit 5.1. Sample School Communication Agreement.

We agree to

- Ask for help
- Be clear about our concerns
- Listen and understand the speaker's message
- Carry through with our stated responsibilities
- Believe other people's messages/views are real for them
- Encourage others to go to the appropriate person with ideas/ concerns
- Set up a communication structure for the school that is known by all members of the school community
- Be respectful
- Work together to meet challenges

. . . in a way that . . .

- Builds our relationships
- Works to find a win/win outcome
- Keeps a disagreement problem-based
- Is blame free
- Keeps the well-being of children first
- Acknowledges that all parties have the same educational goal
- Supports/upholds the philosophy of Horizons
- Creates a shared solution

Source: Horizons Alternative School, Boulder, Colorado. Used with permission.

3. We commit to helping *all* learners succeed.

4. We commit to viewing children and youths as human beings first, students second.

5. We commit to learning and implementing a broad range of instructional methods and curricular materials.

6. We commit to discarding what does not work or is no longer relevant.

7. We commit to respecting parents, family, and community members as equal partners in the education of children.

8. We commit to creating opportunities for broad-based staff involvement in decision making clearly focused on change.

9. We commit to establishing a shared vision of education in the school.

10. We commit to assisting adults who are threatened or challenged by changes occurring in the school. In return, all adults in the school agree to be supportive or constructively critical.

Source: Adapted from Conley, 1993.

Activity 17. Note Cues

PURPOSE

To provide an opening for participants who are cautious about speaking in class, so they can begin to participate in a discussion group.

TIME

Variable.

FORMAT

Individuals.

MATERIALS

Three-by-five-inch note cards with sample questions and comments.

PROCESS

Note cues tell participants *what* they might say in class discussion, leaving them to think only about *when* they might say it. Give each of certain participants a note card with a question or comment that might be made during class discussion. For example, a note card might have the question, Would you please provide an example to clarify that point? The person with the note card then decides at what point he or she will make this contribution to the discussion. The reading of facilitator-prepared notes may seem like mindless parroting, but it can help students feel more competent by helping them practice situationally appropriate ways for discussion participation. This strategy can also be designed to foster progressively greater forms of independence in question posing—for example, once the person is comfortable with asking prepared questions, the facilitator might supply a note card that supplies not a question but a direction for a question; for example, it might ask the participant to ask a certain kind of question, such as a question that asks for another perspective (Wilson, 1995, p. 29).

Source: Adapted from Manzo and Manzo, 1990.

Activity 18. Cooperative Groups

PURPOSE

To provide a setting in which educators or students can construct and extend their understanding of a topic through group discussion, joint resolution of a problem, or feedback about how effectively procedures are performed. An example of this strategy is cooperative peer editing, in which each person looks for specific attributes in the written work of group members.

Cooperative learning also has the potential to

- Provide individuals with social support and encouragement for taking risks in increasing personal competencies.
- Encourage accountability among peers for practicing and learning procedures and skills.
- Offer individuals new attitudes.
- Help individuals establish a shared identity with other group members.
- Assist individuals to find effective peers to emulate.
- Provide a means for individuals to validate their own learning.

TIME
Variable, according to the task.

FORMAT
Typically groups of two to five people.

MATERIALS
Variable, according to the task.

PROCESS
The process will vary according to the task or lesson the cooperative group is undertaking. Exhibit 5.2 lists some of the many different types of groups that can be structured as cooperative learning groups. One way to start the process with any group is to plan the task or lesson using a guide like the following.

COOPERATIVE LESSON PLANNING GUIDE
1. Select an activity and desired outcomes(s).
2. Make decisions.
   a. Group size
   b. Method of assignment to groups
   c. Room arrangement
   d. Materials needed for each group
   e. Roles of group members
3. State the activity in language your participants or students understand.
   a. Task description

Exhibit 5.2. Types of Cooperative Learning Groups.

- *Special interest groups:* Groups organized according to categories of participants' interests for the purpose of sharing information and experiences and exploring common concerns.
- *Problem-solving groups:* Groups organized to develop solutions to substantive problems of any nature.
- *Planning groups:* Groups organized to develop plans for activities and tasks such as field trips, guest speakers, use of resources, and so forth.
- *Instructional groups:* Groups organized to receive specialized instruction in areas of knowledge or skill, in such settings as a science laboratory, human relations seminar, or machine operation training course. Typically the instructional task cannot be taught on a large-group basis.
- *Investigation or inquiry groups:* Groups organized to search out information and report their findings to a larger learning group.
- *Evaluation groups:* Groups organized for the purpose of evaluating learning activities, learner behaviors, or any issue that requires feedback or decision making on the part of the learning group or teacher.
- *Skill practice groups:* Groups organized for the purpose of practicing any set of specified skills.
- *Tutoring or consultative groups:* Groups organized for the purpose of tutoring, consulting, or giving assistance to other learning group members.

---

    b. Importance of positive interdependence (that is, how each person is invaluable to completing the task)

    c. Role of individual accountability

    d. Role of collective accountability

    e. Criteria for success

    f. Specific behaviors or agreements to be encouraged among group members (this point especially important for heterogeneous groups, in which status issues may interfere with shared respect and learning)

4. Encourage participants or students.

    a. Evidence of cooperative interactions to look for

    b. Assistance that might be needed

- *Operational groups:* Groups organized to take responsibility for the operations of activities important to the larger learning group, such as room arrangements, refreshments, materials preparation, equipment operation, and so forth.
- *Learning instruction groups:* Groups organized to take responsibility for learning all they can about a particular content unit and instructing themselves and sometimes the rest of the larger learning group.
- *Simulation groups:* Groups organized to conduct some intergroup exercise, such as role-playing, a game, or a case study review, to increase knowledge or build skills.
- *Learning achievement groups:* Groups organized to produce a learning product that develops group members' knowledge, skills, or creativity.
- *Cooperative base groups:* Cooperative learning groups that last for the duration of a course, have a stable membership, and foster individual accountability as they provide support, encouragement, and assistance to group members in completing course responsibilities. For example, cooperative base groups might meet regularly to share challenges related to completing homework assignments (Johnson, Johnson, and Smith, 1991).
- *Learning communities:* Groups organized to work over a period of time on a set schedule as study groups.

5. Evaluate outcomes.

   a. Goal achievement

   b. Group functioning

   c. Ways to strengthen support for individual students

   d. Feedback to offer

6. Note suggestions for next time.

Source: Adapted from Johnson, Johnson, and Smith, 1991, pp. 4:35–4:36.

To help members of cooperative groups work together most productively, facilitators need strategies for enhancing individual accountability, negotiating conflict, and dealing with resistance.

The next three sections of this chapter discuss such strategies, which apply to many of the activities in Chapters Five through Eight.

Enhancing Accountability

Educators and staff developers using cooperative groups for any activity need to ensure that all individuals are benefiting from and contributing to the group process. Here are some specific ways to enhance individual accountability.

- Keep the size of the groups small. Keep the role of each learner distinct. Typical group size is two to four members.
- Assess learners individually as well as collectively.
- Observe and encourage groups while they are working.
- Randomly request individuals to present what they are learning to you or another group.
- Request periodic self-assessments and outlines of responsibilities from individual group members.
- Randomly or systematically ask individual learners to teach someone else or yourself what they have learned.

Note that a simple and positive way to support individual accountability and prevent conflict among group members is to brainstorm answers to these questions: How would I like to find out if someone in our cooperative learning group thought I was not doing enough to contribute to the total group's benefit? What are some acceptable ways of letting me know? Write the possible actions on the chalkboard, and discuss them. Such a procedure can go a long way toward avoiding suspicion, frustration, and embarrassment in group work (Wlodkowski, 1999, pp. 108–109).

Negotiating Conflict

As educators strive to make teaching more culturally responsive, conflict is inevitable. Believing that justice and equity inhabit a hopeful perspective about the potential of human beings, and knowing that it is easier to destroy a dream than to create it, all groups need ways to respectfully negotiate the harsh statements and accusations that sometimes arise. These statements may be directed at a person, a group, or the subject matter. Regardless of their targets, they can create an environment that is so reactive that the people within it violate their most fundamental beliefs about respectful human interaction. Fortunately, conflict can also be an opportunity to learn. Two strategies in particular come to mind. One is for interpersonal conflict, and one is for classroom conflict. The following examples involve a facilitator and an angry participant but can be adapted to interactions between any two people.

When a blameful or hurtful statement is directed toward a facilitator after class or in the hallway, especially one that catches the person off guard, it is tempting for the person to respond in ways that caricature his or her role as a facilitator of learning. For example, the facilitator might offer an analytical response, replying to the rebuke as an intellectual exercise. This approach can result not only in two ships passing in the night, because the facilitator avoids responding directly, but then in two ships colliding in the night, because such responses generally exacerbate the tension, especially when the situation is charged and the individuals are highly emotional.

The facilitator can foster a more effective and compassionate interaction in such a situation by offering an invitation to talk preceded by a sincere expression of empathy. Two examples of empathic statements are: "I can imagine how angry you must be," and, "I know that you are not alone in your perspectives." The invitation to talk about the issue at hand can be straightforward: for example, "Would you like to sit down a moment and talk?" This approach, when sincere, acknowledges the other person's perspective and diffuses the polarity that heightens anger. The invitation to sit down together and talk, respectfully and indirectly asks the other person if he or she is willing to share responsibility for engaging in dialogue directed toward understanding. These are important first steps that can lead to new ways of understanding and learning together.

When a blameful or hurtful statement is made in class, it is also tempting for the facilitator to respond in ways that can exacerbate discomfort, anger, and resentment. A helpful strategy in such instances is to offer a statement that removes the issue from the individual realm and positions it in a way that allows others to make meaning of it. For example, the facilitator might say, "This is an issue that represents the thinking of some people or groups, and it obviously causes a strong response." Next, the facilitator asks participants to pick up a pen and write what they are thinking at this moment. When we do this, we generally ask for five minutes of silence for those who need some quiet to think deeply about the issue. After five minutes or so (often we ask if anyone needs another minute before we proceed), the facilitator asks class participants to turn to a person next to them and talk about what they have written. This provides a situation in which everyone is heard. It also frequently diffuses any tendencies toward a purely emotional response. Finally, the facilitator asks for volunteers to share their perspectives.

It is important to acknowledge that truth in a multicultural world is not entirely indeterminate. Nurturing freedom of expression does not have to be confused with having an obligation to facilitate every point of view (Wlodkowski and Ginsberg, 1995). Purpose plays a pivotal role. If the goal is to deepen understanding of *what the truth may be*, rather than *who knows the truth*, then a real dialogue, a "thinking together," is more likely to occur. Under such circumstances people have a much better chance to discover insights not attainable individually (Senge, 1990).

Dealing with Resistance

This is probably a good place to say a few words about resistance in a group when it occurs at the beginning of a course or any other kind of learning experience. At times, resistance occurs because the learning experience is required or people believe they have been unfairly mandated to attend. The group feeling then tends to be some version of, "We don't need this," or, "This is going to be a waste of time." It is usually best for the facilitator to openly acknowledge the resistance and the feelings the group may be experiencing. The next step is to plan or engage in learning that emphasizes *immediate* relevance and choice (discussed in the next chapter) for participants. These procedures have a good chance of moving the group forward.

Of course resistance can occur at any time during a learning experience. Most resistance appears to stem from apprehensions about vulnerability or control. For example, this book advocates changing conventional teaching practices. However, many people have formed habits and expectations that run counter to some of our suggested approaches. To label their reluctance to buy in or their failure to recognize the need to approach teaching and learning in different ways as *resistance* is usually ineffectual. It can divert the facilitator's attention from real goals and from concerns such as providing emotional safety and greater clarity about learning goals and processes. Further, it may be incorrect, and incorrectly labeling other people can lead to thinking that immobilizes a facilitator's creativity.

We try to think of resistance as a concern about facing difficult realities. For example, if a participant in a learning situation maintains that there is not enough time to discuss a controversial topic when the time is actually available, he or she is probably being resistant. However, there may really not be enough time for an adequate discussion, and the person may be judiciously expressing a realistic concern.

We do not have a formulaic set of guidelines for dealing with resistance. We have found it to be so contextually determined (by who, what, where, when, and so forth) that employing a recommended series of steps would fly in the face of the complexity and variation we see. However, we have found that focusing on the positive meanings and functions of resistance is more informative than focusing on the negative ones. For example, perceiving that indirectly we are being told to proceed more slowly or cautiously, to make the situation safer, or to provide concrete results is more constructive than thinking only that participants wish to avoid a task, are cynical about the class, or don't want to do the work. Respectfully listening and soliciting information about the nature of learner concerns usually provides insights. It can also be helpful to request examples and evidence of the problem participants say they see and suggestions for courses of action to resolve the problem. One approach to communication is to use "suppose" or similar words to introduce ideas, to probe a comment, or to keep a conversation more open: "Suppose we ask . . ." or "Suppose we think . . ."

Conclusion

In closing this chapter on establishing inclusion, we acknowledge that a mere strategy does not create a milieu of emotional safety and respect. Inclusion is the result of complex interactions. The following checklist is a guide to key facilitator considerations in creating the conditions in which all learners feel respected by and connected to each other and to the facilitator or teacher.

Establishing Inclusion

How does the learning experience contribute to the development of students as a community of learners who feel respected by and connected to one another and to the teacher?

- Routines and rituals are visible and understood by all.
  - __ Rituals are in place that help all students feel that they belong in the class.
  - __ Students have opportunities to learn about each other.
  - __ Students and facilitator have opportunities to learn about each other's unique backgrounds.
  - __ Class agreements or participation guidelines and consequences for violating agreements are negotiated.
  - __ The system of personal and collective responsibility for agreements is understood by everyone and applied with fairness.

Describe the evidence:

- All students equitably and actively participate and interact.
  - __ The teacher directs attention equitably.
  - __ The teacher interacts respectfully with all learners.
  - __ The teacher demonstrates to all students that she or he cares about them.
  - __ Students share ideas and perspectives with partners and small groups.
  - __ Students respond to lessons by writing.
  - __ Students know what to do, especially when making choices.
  - __ Students help each other.
  - __ Work is displayed (with students' permission).

Describe the evidence:

The challenge we all face as facilitators and teachers is to model respectful practices consistently from the beginning to the end of every class session, course, and personal interaction. However, we all have personal challenges and contradictions that can interfere with the perfection we would like to achieve. When necessary, we can demonstrate the importance of being willing to learn from one's own mistakes, and in that way we can still be courageous leaders. Among the attributes of a great teacher is surely the refusal to allow personal contradictions to thwart a vision of humanity that is kind and just.

Activity Guide for Establishing Inclusion

Following is a list of the activities from this chapter. They are organized according to the audiences for which they are intended, that is, K–12 students or educators focused on professional development and pedagogical and school renewal strategies. Repetition between the lists is a consequence of the approach to professional development that we use. We model for professional development what we suggest teachers try both in their classrooms and throughout their schools. It is a parallel process, a form of walking the talk.

Establishing Inclusion: Classroom Activities for Students

Venn Diagram Sharing (Activity 1)

Two Wishes and a Truth (Activity 2)

Decades and Diversity (Activity 3)

Think-Pair-Share Exercises (Activity 4)

"Ask Me About . . ." Posters (Activity 5)

Multicultural Inventory (Activity 6)

Bio-Poems (Activity 7)

Interpretive Community Maps (Activity 8)

Dialogue Journals (Activity 9)

Response Cards (Activity 10)

Fist-to-Five (Activity 11)

Class Historian (Activity 12)

Class Review (Activity 13)

Bean Experiment (Activity 14)

Class Agreements or Participation Guidelines (Activity 15)

Note Cues (Activity 17)

Cooperative Groups (Activity 18)

Also, strategies described in the sections on opportunities for multidimensional sharing and negotiating conflict

Establishing Inclusion: Professional Development Activities for Educators

Venn Diagram Sharing (Activity 1)

Two Wishes and a Truth (Activity 2)

Decades and Diversity (Activity 3)

Think-Pair-Share Exercises (Activity 4)

"Ask Me About . . ." Posters (Activity 5)

Multicultural Inventory (Activity 6)

Bio-Poems (Activity 7)

Interpretive Community Maps (Activity 8)

Dialogue Journals (Activity 9)

Response Cards (Activity 10)

Fist-to-Five (Activity 11)

Class Historian (Activity 12)

Class Review (Activity 13)

Bean Experiment (Activity 14)

Class Agreements or Participation Guidelines (Activity 15)

Creating a Schoolwide Professional Agreement (Activity 16)

Note Cues (Activity 17)

Cooperative Groups (Activity 18)

Also, strategies described in the sections on dealing with resistance and negotiating conflict are particularly applicable to school renewal activities, as are Activity 16, the communication agreement in Activity 15, and the cooperative lesson planning guide in Activity 18. Also see Activity 6 in Chapter Six, which addresses the strategy of reframing.

Developing a Positive Attitude

You cannot shake hands with a clenched fist.
INDIRA GANDHI

As addressed in Chapter One, schools today serve many students who have histories and day-to-day challenges that can impede their development of positive beliefs about the significance of school. Yet a favorable predisposition toward a learning environment, a teacher, or a course is a significant precondition to academic success. It supports individuals' ability to find ways to safely and effectively interact with unfamiliar people and diverse approaches to learning. It strengthens individuals' determination to make sense of things.

Nonetheless, *developing a positive attitude* is a motivational condition that is frequently overlooked by educators. Some of us assume that students simply ought to be "ready to learn" when they enter the classroom. Others try to talk students into learning by accessing their own enthusiasm or ability to persuade. And still others believe that as soon as students experience success, a positive attitude will follow. Unfortunately, these notions often accomplish little of any lasting value in contemporary classrooms.

All students benefit from relevance and choice, two of the attributes, or criteria, that significantly influence a positive attitude. When relevance and choice are present most students perceive learning to be appealing and valuable (Clifford, 1986; Deci and Ryan, 1991). Relevance is the degree to which students can identify their own perspectives and values in the content, discussion, and methods of learning. Relevant learning processes are connected to who students are, what they care about, and how they perceive and know (Wlodkowski and Ginsberg, 1995).

Choice, the second criterion for developing a positive attitude, is in many ways wedded to the notion of relevance. When students find learning relevant, they are more naturally interested in what they are learning, and they then pursue answers to questions of authentic concern. Such self-determination, or choosing, contributes to a heightened sense of self-endorsement and self-satisfaction. Global history and social science merge to support this observation: people consistently struggle for the power to determine their lives as an expression of their beliefs and values. Learning is no exception to this desire.

In order to provide equitable opportunities for diverse students, educators need to offer relevant learning experiences, multiple ways for students to access and demonstrate knowledge, and opportunities for genuine choice. Although there are generally certain nonnegotiable expectations in the classroom, there are also many options for shared decision making and independent choice. Examples of choices include having a voice in how to learn, what to learn, where to learn, when a learning experience is considered complete, how learning will be assessed, with whom to learn, and how to solve emerging problems.

An unfortunate reality for many of us who teach is that early in our work we had limited knowledge about ways to encourage choice. For some of us, offering choice was seen as equivalent to saying "anything goes." Unfortunately, given that belief it was not infrequent that the dominant voices in the classroom were often the least democratic. What many of us have since come to understand is that choice is not a value in and of itself. Its value is determined by the purposes it serves.

As educators, we continually grapple with the tension between listening to the perspectives of others and maintaining a strong, clear agenda of our own. For culturally responsive educators, the challenge is to provide choices that are in harmony not only with high-quality learning opportunities for all students but with a powerful vision of a pluralistic democracy. In other words, the framework within which choices occur must be one that protects the inseparability of academic success and caring for others.

Being clear about nonnegotiables avoids confusion and mistrust. Similarly, it is essential that we consistently demonstrate respect for the authority of students—both as learners and as architects of democracy. The process of establishing class agreements, as detailed in the previous chapter, can help us clarify the framework within which shared and autonomous decisions are encouraged.

Following are a number of considerations and activities. Often an activity is preceded by an explanation of the theory that supports it. Our intention is to provide enough theoretical understanding so that educators can construct activities of their own. The activities we provide are among those that students have consistently identified as the activities they believe have strongly contributed to their positive attitude toward working with us in our area of study and practice. This attitude has helped students develop their sense of curiosity and imagination. Our hope is that it will assist them all through their lives to take the moment and make the best of it. Without a doubt one of the most powerful things that teachers do is to help students to develop attitudes that are positive toward learning and toward themselves as artful decision makers and designers of opportunity.

Make the First Experience with the Subject Positive

The first time students experience anything that is new or that occurs in a different setting, they form an impression that will have a lasting impact (Scott, 1969). In learning, first impressions are important, and it is essential that we make them as positive and motivating as possible. We achieve this effect when a learning activity meets the following five criteria.

Safe. There is little risk that students will suffer any form of personal embarrassment from lack of knowledge, personal self-disclosure, or a hostile or arrogant social environment.

Successful. There is some form of acknowledgment, consequence, or product that shows that the students are effective or at the very least that their effort is worthwhile.

Interesting. The learning activity has some parts that are novel, engaging, challenging, or stimulating.

Self-determined. Students are encouraged to make choices that significantly affect the learning experience (deciding, for example, what they share, how they learn, what they learn, when they learn, with whom they learn, where they learn, or how they are assessed), basing those choices on their values, needs, concerns, or feelings. At the very least students have an opportunity to voice their perspectives.

Personally relevant. The teacher uses students' concerns, interests, or prior experiences to create elements of the learning activity or develops the activity in concert with the students. At the very least a resource-rich learning environment is available to support students in making selections based on personal interest (for example, they have access to a library, the Internet, and community facilities and opportunities).

Brainstorming a new topic or essential question in small groups is an example of making a first impression positive because this process is

Safe. All answers are initially acceptable.

Successful. A list is created and acknowledged.

Interesting. Creative examples from personal experience are usually given.

Self-determined. Answers are voluntary and self-selected.

Personally relevant. The topic is selected because it is relevant.

The KWL process, originated by Donna Ogle (1986), is another example of this strategy. It helps students construct meaning for a new topic or concept based on their prior knowledge. In the first phase of this process students identify and list what they think they *know* about the new topic, anything from phobias to fractions. This safe and successful approach results in an interesting array of perspectives and historical contexts. It can be elaborated upon by asking students to express their ideas outside the conventions of oral and written discourse. For example, students may relate their experience with the new topic through drawing and storytelling. Or they may create metaphors that depict how they see themselves in relation to the topic.

In the second phase of the process, the students suggest what they *want to know* about the topic. This self-determined and relevant information may be recorded as questions or considerations for exploration and research. In the last phase the students identify what they have *learned*. This learning may respond to their initial questions, but often it also includes unanticipated discoveries and additional questions based on new insights. Powerful learning experiences have qualities that lead to and guide future learning. A simple KWL matrix (Figure 6.1) can help students organize their initial thinking about a topic.

Every learning activity the authors create has to meet the five criteria. When an activity does not go well, we use the criteria to critique, refine, and improve it. Often we do so with a trusted colleague. We have learned to resist the temptation to simply throw away new ideas when they are not immediately successful.

It generally takes a good deal of practice to use a new strategy effectively. This is one of the reasons collegial support is so important. As reasonably successful teachers, many educators have become self-protective. The need to look good, appear

Figure 6.1. KWL Matrix.

What We Know	What We Want to Know	What We Learned

smart, and sound capable can overwhelm their own opportunities to learn. A good peer coach, as discussed in Chapter Seven, can help all of us construct a "humility-friendly" environment (Garmston and Wellman, 1999) in which we can reflect upon our own intentions and make decisions that demonstrate our fidelity to the goal of encouraging a positive attitude toward learning.

Activity 1. Carousel Graffiti

PURPOSE

To share common, different, and multiple perspectives about a particular topic in a way that is safe, successful, interesting, self-determined, and personally relevant; to brainstorm ideas in ways that activate prior knowledge and create shared understandings as a foundation for learning.

TIME

Forty-five minutes.

FORMAT

Small groups.

MATERIALS

Newsprint, markers, and tape for posting newsprint pages.

PROCESS

The questions used in the following process will vary according to educators' purposes. This example shows how staff developers can use the process to build a positive attitude in staff toward forming school-based teams of teacher leaders and professional developers to support their colleagues schoolwide in motivating and culturally responsive instruction. We call these teams *schoolwide instructional leadership cadres,* or simply leadership cadres. They are explained in Chapters Eight and Nine.

Step 1. Select approximately four questions that you believe to be most relevant to participants of leadership cadres. Here are some examples.

QUESTIONS FOR DEVELOPING A POSITIVE ATTITUDE IN TEAMS

1. How might having an instructional leadership cadre benefit your school?

2. What might instructional leadership cadre members gain?

3. How can instructional leadership cadre members foster genuine collegiality between themselves and the rest of the school?

4. What might a school want to know about itself to inform the process of creating and implementing schoolwide innovations?

5. How can instructional leadership cadres know if they are serving their school well?

Using bright markers, write each of the questions you have selected for group dialogue on a separate piece of newsprint. Each piece of newsprint should contain only one question.

Step 2. Ask members of the large group to count off so that they can form four small groups. (The number of groups must correspond to the number of questions selected.) Give each group one of the questions written out on newsprint. Explain to the groups that in just a minute they will be asked to collectively address their questions. The process is called *graffiti* because group members may record their responses to their question in any way they choose, even with symbols or other artistic representations, as long as others can understand their thinking. After each group has had approximately five minutes to discuss and respond to its question, it passes its question clockwise to the next group (the carousel). Each group then considers its new question, adding to the graffiti of the previous group. After five minutes, the groups again pass the questions clockwise. This process continues until each group has had an opportunity to respond to all the questions.

Step 3. Finally, each group ends up with its original question. Its task then is to briefly summarize all the contributions. Because all the groups have had an opportunity to think about each of the questions, the summaries ought to be *concise* statements or artistic representations that express identifiable themes or that draw a conclusion. One member of each group takes the role of reporter and shares the group's summary with the larger group, limiting the report to approximately two minutes. If space permits, graffiti responses may be posted around the room. Later the information can transcribed for further study.

Additional notes. The carousel graffiti activity might also be used to open a dialogue about school renewal and cultural diversity in a nonthreatening way. Use the previously described process, employing four to five of the following questions or similar questions. It is a good idea to check first that all participants interpret the questions in the same way and that their interpretations are consistent with your own.

QUESTIONS ABOUT CULTURAL DIVERSITY

1. What beliefs and values prevail within your school or community that reflect the dominant European American culture and that might be inconsistent with the experiences and values of staff or students with a variety of backgrounds? (These values might concern a preference for working alone or a tendency to think primarily in terms of personal gain.)

2. What is one valuable lesson you have learned—either directly or indirectly—from a person with a background that is different from your own?

3. What, in general, are some attributes or components of schools that demonstrate respect for cultural pluralism?

4. What is one lesson you have learned about a successful school renewal planning process?

5. How might a school build commitment to imaginative and substantive continuous school renewal?

6. What might your school do to examine school renewal decisions and their impact on student learning and on the school as a whole?

The carousel graffiti activity also works very well with students in mid-elementary through high school. For example, a teacher who is introducing a new book might use carousel graffiti with prediction questions about the book.

Use Assisted Learning to Scaffold Complex Learning

Vygotsky (1978) demonstrated there were many problems and skills a person could solve or master when given appropriate help and support. Activity 2 is an example of assisted learning. It provides *scaffolding*, giving clues, information, prompts, reminders, and encouragement at the appropriate times and in the appropriate ways. This gradually supports independent learning.

Most of us naturally scaffold when we teach someone to drive a car, play a card game, or learn to use a personal computer. By making the implicit explicit, we can provide similar support to students who are learning to solve a math problem, conduct an experiment, or write a clear and cohesive paragraph. The key is to assess where a student needs assistance and to structure related scaffolding for ongoing success.

Historically, classrooms in the United States have been highly competitive, favoring students who are independent learners with a high tolerance for abstraction and ambiguity. These attributes can be an asset, especially in a rapidly changing world in which previously unquestioned truths are being effectively challenged at an exponential rate. However, many talented students have not had adequate opportunity to participate in academic discourse or even to construct a well-written paragraph. To do these things they require opportunities to access, demonstrate, and develop confidence in their rich capacities to learn. They often appreciate assisted learning because the support it offers is concrete, immediate, and relevant to their obvious needs and perspectives.

Following are some of the methods specific to assisted learning that can be used to build scaffolding for more complex learning (Association for Supervision and Curriculum Development, 1990). The description of each method concludes with an example that shows how we use the method to assist students to learn to write a research report.

Modeling. The teacher demonstrates the skill while students observe, or the teacher offers actual examples of learning outcomes, such as completed papers or solved problems.

> We often ask the students to read two previously submitted research reports by others, one that is excellent and one that is satisfactory.

Thinking out loud. The teacher states her or his thought processes while performing the demonstration.

> We talk to ourselves out loud about some of our goals related to writing the report. We also think out loud about the features of a strong report and ways in which we can create one. This is often a good time to check in with students and ask why they think one of the reports they read might be considered excellent and the other only satisfactory. We supplement the students' perceptions with our own.

Anticipating difficulties. Next, the teacher and students discuss areas in which mistakes seem most likely to occur and in which support may be needed.

> Because the sections of reports that discuss findings and analyses seem most challenging to students, we discuss how these sections were done in the two reports, and we arrange for prompt feedback on students' initial drafts of these sections in their own reports.

Providing prompts and cues. As students comprehensively examine other students' work (or the teacher's work), the teacher highlights critical features of these reports and structures personalized procedural steps that respond to students' individual strengths and challenges. Being careful not to overwhelm, the teacher helps students clearly identify accomplishments and their importance to the learning goal, limiting suggestions to two or three key opportunities for improvement.

> We provide an outline for writing a research report, with exemplars from previous student reports to increase clarity and the likelihood of initial success.

Regulating the difficulty. The teacher introduces a more complex task and may offer some practice with it.

> We give students a very basic research scenario, a hypothesis, data, and an analysis scheme, and ask them to write a brief research report with this information.

Using reciprocal teaching. The students rotate playing the role of teacher with one another.

> While we observe and provide support when needed, students pair off and one in each pair presents his or her brief research report to the learning partner, who acts as the teacher and gives supportive feedback, identifying specific accomplishments and making no more than two or three suggestions. Then the students reverse roles.

Providing a checklist. Students use self-checking procedures to monitor the quality of their learning.

> When the topic is research papers, we generally give students a checklist of questions and criteria to consider as they write their reports. But with other tasks, we often create the criteria for success with the students; they base their ideas for criteria on their comparisons of an excellent and a satisfactory example of the work to be done or on their analysis of what three excellent but different examples of student work have in common.

Consider the possible metaphors for the provider of assisted learning: sensitive tutor, experienced coach, wise friend—all are people who tell learners just enough, what they need to know when they need to know it, and who trust learners themselves to chart the rest of their journey toward accomplishment. Strong learners need not be rugged individualists or solitary explorers.

Assisted learning embraces a vision of every student as a confident, creative, and intelligent learner, nurtured in a caring community.

Activity 2. Scaffolding for Success, or the 360-Degree Turnaround

PURPOSE
To elicit participants' different perspectives and ways of understanding related to a learning experience; to teach educators how to apply the five criteria for making the first experience with a subject positive; to provide an opportunity for participants to share their own motivational practices.

TIME
One hour.

FORMAT
Large group and small groups.

MATERIALS
Criteria checklist and four movable chairs.

PROCESS
Step 1. Begin by referring to a previous learning activity, such as one of the multidimensional sharing activities in Chapter Five, a brainstorming activity, or carousel graffiti, and clearly describe how it met each of the five criteria: safe, successful, interesting, self-determined, and personally relevant (this step uses the scaffolding methods of *modeling* and *thinking out loud*).

Step 2. Provide a checklist with the five criteria defined (see the list earlier in this chapter), thus *providing prompts and cues* for all participants. Ask three volunteers to join you in front of the group. One represents the safety criterion, one represents the successful and interesting criteria, and one represents the self-determined and personally relevant criteria. *Regulate the difficulty* by narrating another example from your own teaching (showing a video example would be great!) that illustrates the five criteria, but never use the words *safe, successful, interesting,* and so forth. Then ask each volunteer to tell you and the rest of the group how the criteria he or she represents were met by the activity you described. Facilitate a large-group discussion afterward to emphasize and elaborate insights from this round-robin process.

Step 3. Ask participants to form small groups (no more than four people) in which they will repeat the process they have just observed. They begin by taking some time to reflect on learning activities they already use that meet these five criteria and then to construct an original learning activity that meets the criteria. Each person takes a turn to share his or her learning activity, and the other three participants assign criteria to themselves (as in Step 2) and offer feedback on the criteria each represents. By rotating the role of teacher, each participant can give and receive *reciprocal teaching,* or feedback, about a learning activity in his or her own subject area. This entire process should be very supportive, with everyone having a chance to apply and refine his or her understanding of the five criteria.

Step 4 (optional). Ask participants to work in pairs to revise or create a learning activity that meets the five criteria for a subject they will soon teach. They share the completed activity with another dyad for reciprocal feedback.

Additional notes. This round-robin activity can be used for different teaching purposes when a teacher wants to facilitate the sharing of different perspectives for commonly experienced phenomena. For example, students might listen to or read a story about a historical event and offer different perspectives on various characters (father, mother, child), political views (Republican, Democrat, Socialist), or ethnic groups (Latino, Chinese Americans, African Americans); in science, students might review an ecological event and offer a possible analysis from the perspective of chemistry, biology, or physics.

Activity 3. Scaffolding Minilectures with Human Highlighters

PURPOSE

To provide opportunities for participants to strengthen their recall of lecture material and strengthen their understanding by reflecting upon the key points and interpretations offered by other participants; to learn about the meanings designated participants give to lecture material and about their perspectives; to support note-taking skills.

TIME

Variable, according to the length of the minilecture.

FORMAT

Large group.

MATERIALS

None, unless the highlighters wish to write down key points with markers on newsprint. (Writing the key points benefits English language learners and those who learn best with visual aids. However, it can slow down the process. If visuals are desired, it may be preferable for a volunteer scribe to jot down the summaries on newsprint as highlighters present them.)

PROCESS

Prior to a brief lecture, four to five volunteers are solicited to serve as periodic summarizers, or *human highlighters,* for the whole class. Periodically, the facilitator pauses in delivering the lecture and asks a highlighter to illuminate what she or he believes to be most important to remember. Generally it is best to pause for a highlighter's summary every five to ten minutes (Conyers, 1998), depending on the density or complexity of the lecture material. Highlighters can also be invited to enrich their summaries with insights or examples of their own.

Following is an outline of a minilecture for introducing the Motivational Framework for Culturally Responsive Teaching. The places where we generally pause for a human highlighter to summarize are designated by a star (*).

KEY POINTS FOR INTRODUCING THE MOTIVATIONAL FRAMEWORK
FOR CULTURALLY RESPONSIVE TEACHING

- *The concept of culture.* The motivational framework uses the term *culture* broadly to refer to race, ethnicity, gender, social class, and a host of other influences on the ways in which we all are socialized, but the focus of the Motivational Framework for Culturally Responsive Teaching, especially as it relates to school renewal, is students who have been historically underrepresented in education.

- *Macrocultural framework.* The motivational framework is supported by research about what works within and across cultural groups. It is not a group-specific approach.

- *Intrinsic motivation—a point of synthesis for research.* Individuals are intrinsically motivated when they feel wise, capable, creative, joyful. These are the emotions of intrinsic motivation. This is what educators want *all* students to experience as they learn. The principles and practices of intrinsic motivation provide a synthesis that can be used in research on culture and learning (see, for example, the work of Gloria Ladson-Billings, James Banks, Jim Cummins, Sonia Nieto, Lisa Delpit, and John Ogbu) and in research on specific methodologies such as cooperative learning, multiple intelligences, brain-based learning, authentic assessment, learner-centered principles, experience-based learning, language acquisition, and emotional intelligence.

- *Intrinsic motivation—why it is important.*

  Intrinsic motivation presumes that all people are naturally curious and want meaning in their lives and that *all people are motivated* to do something (even if it is not what we want them to do). People own their own motivation. When we act as if motivation is something we *do to* others, we put them in a one-down position, a position of dependency. What we as educators do is to create the conditions in which people can access their motivation. To avoid using phrases like, "I motivate students to learn," we might say, "I encourage students' motivation to learn," or, "I help to elicit students' motivation."

  Intrinsic motivation is cognitively more effective than extrinsic motivation for problem solving, persevering in creative tasks, and avoiding behavior that makes it necessary to cram for tests later.

Respect for intrinsic motivation diminishes power issues in the classroom and helps students see themselves as the agents of their own learning.

However, intrinsic motivation can work alongside extrinsic motivation if the extrinsic reward is culturally valued and highly informational about performance toward a goal (as an Olympic gold medal might be, for example).

*

- *The Motivational Framework for Culturally Responsive Teaching has four conditions that are interdependent and each of which can be defined by two criteria (or critical attributes).* One condition without the others does not provide consistent motivation and may actually undermine motivation (as an example, cooperative learning may be ineffective in settings where educators use competitive grading and only a few can excel). A good metaphor for the interactions among the four conditions of the motivational framework is jazz.

- *First condition: establishing inclusion.* (Note: refer to the Partnership Guide for Culturally Responsive Teaching, Exhibit 8.1, throughout the following introduction of the four conditions.)

  Criteria: respect and connectedness.

  A strong sense of belonging and respect contributes to emotional safety—to an environment in which it is *safe* to take risks and to learn.

  Provide a reflective question: for example, ask participants to recall a time when they worked hard to learn something of value. How did they feel? What kind of emotional safety nets were they able to access?

  Ask participants to review the section on establishing inclusion in the Partnership Guide for Culturally Responsive Teaching. Ask participants to try to identify their own strengths and the teaching challenges that are associated with establishing inclusion.

*

- *Second condition: developing a positive attitude.*

  Criteria: choice and personal relevance.

  We can't assume students have a positive attitude toward school, a particular teacher, or a particular subject. As an example of how quickly attitudes form, there is evidence that many jurors make up their minds about guilt or innocence within the first ten minutes. First impressions are often lasting impressions.

  Provide a reflective question. For example, ask participants to recall a time when they had a bad attitude toward a learning experience. To what extent did they feel a sense of personal choice? To what extent did they feel that the subject matter and learning methods were personally relevant?

Choice does not imply a wide-open free-for-all. It occurs within a framework that asks individuals to respect agreed-upon norms for working together as a community of learners in which everyone has an opportunity to learn.

There are several kinds of choices—what to learn, when to learn (does everyone have to learn the same thing at the same time?), where to learn, how to learn, with whom to learn, how one will assess one's accomplishments, how one will be assessed by others.

Ask participants to review the section about developing a positive attitude in the Partnership Guide for Culturally Responsive Teaching. As they review the guide, ask participants to try to identify their own strengths and the teaching challenges that are associated with developing a positive attitude.

*

- *Third condition: enhancing meaning.*

  Criteria: challenge and engagement.

  Introduce the concept of *flow* and the need for a high-challenge, low-threat environment in order to achieve flow (see Chapter Seven). Flow is the state that occurs when a person is so completely absorbed in an experience that he or she may lose track of time or may even lose his or her appetite.

  In education, we often hear talk of *expectations*. People say things like, "Shouldn't we be realistic about our expectations of certain groups of kids?" or, "Everyone ought to be able to perform according to standards that signify high expectations for all students." The critical issues are challenge and safety nets. *All* students ought to experience academic challenge. However, if they are to meet this challenge, we need to provide multiple kinds of safety nets. Then, *all* students will have a genuine chance to successfully challenge themselves. Safety nets might take the form of cooperative base groups in which students regularly meet during class time to support each other in solving problems associated with completing homework assignments. Another safety net might be for teachers to resist the temptation to average grades—especially if they believe that grades ought to represent what students know and can do at the end of a learning experience—and to understand that averaging can penalize students who are cautious starters or who need more time to learn but who can meet high standards if given the necessary support and flexibility.

  Projects, critical inquiry, and learning through the arts are examples of the kinds of activities most likely to give students opportunities to experience challenge and engagement.

  Ask participants to review the section on enhancing meaning in the Partnership Guide for Culturally Responsive Teaching. As they review the guide, ask participants to try to identify some of their strengths as well as some of the teaching challenges that are associated with enhancing meaning.

*

- *Fourth condition: engendering competence.*

Criteria: authenticity in and effectiveness at what students value. (This personal value is integrated with what is of value to society.)

More than anything else, students need to believe that they are implicitly and explicitly connected to a hopeful future. Every time we help students clearly identify their success we help them link themselves to a hopeful future. This can occur in both small and large ways. An example of a small way is the *door passes* activity, which asks students to reflect upon a question and write their response on a three-by-five-inch card. Each student hands this card, as a ticket to leave, to the teacher at the classroom doorway. This activity has the added benefit of ensuring that the teacher makes contact with every student. Questions to which students might respond include: What is one way in which you challenged yourself today? and, What is one way in which you assisted the learning of another person this week? An example of a large way to promote students' sense of their success is to examine grading policies from the perspective of equity.

Ask participants to review the section on engendering competence in the Partnership Guide for Culturally Responsive Teaching. As they review the guide, ask participants to try to identify some of their strengths as well as some of the teaching challenges that are associated with engendering competence.

*

- *The framework may be used as a template for a single strategy (such as cooperative learning) and to design a lesson or unit.* The goal is to hit on all four conditions as simultaneously as possible. Consistency is key.
- *Good lesson planning is motivational planning.* Refer to the form for creating a lesson plan illustrated in Activity 22 of Chapter Eight. Ask participants how they might use it.

Source: © 1998 by Margery B. Ginsberg; use with permission only.

Help Students Accurately Attribute Their Success to Their Capability and Strategically Focused Effort

Students frequently think about the consequences of their behavior. If they experience success, they often reflect on a reason or cause for that success, telling themselves, for example, "I think I did well in this debate because I put a lot of work into preparing for it." Cognitive psychologists call these inferred causes *attributions* and have created a body of research to demonstrate their significant effects on human behavior and attitudes (Weiner, 1992).

When students experience success—complete a fine project, solve a challenging problem, earn a high score on a test that provides evidence of learning that they value—their attitude toward learning is generally enhanced when they believe the *major causes* of this success are their capability, effort, and knowledge. That is, there is a positive effect on their motivation because they feel they have personal control or possession of the causes of their success. Unlike other possible causes such as luck or an easy task, these causes tell academically successful students that when they exert effort *in strategic ways* they will become more knowledgeable. Because capability has a stable quality to it (it lasts), students tend to feel more confident when approaching similar learning experiences in the future. Also, attribution of success to effort and capability fosters realistic hopes even when learning outcomes are not successful. These students are more likely to believe that trying harder and seeking new strategies for learning will make a positive difference.

We emphasize the importance of effort that is *strategic* because many students, from all backgrounds, who view themselves as academically unsuccessful have come to believe that they are not bright and that their effort is to no avail. They see themselves as working hard and so tend to attribute lack of success to lack of capability as well as to other factors that they consider to be outside their control. This contrasts with the attitude of academically accomplished students, who, regardless of background, rarely attribute personal failure to lack of ability (Bempechat, Graham, and Jimenez, 1999). What students who see themselves as unsuccessful often do not realize is that successful students do not just apply effort. They have *strategies* to *focus* their effort in ways that generate knowledge and lead to success. Successful students typically believe that effort and strategy work together in accomplishment of a goal.

Here are some ways to help students attribute their success to their own capability, effort, and knowledge.

- Provide or create with students learning experiences suitable to their current levels of skill. "Just within reach" is a good rule of thumb. Such experiences challenge students' current capabilities, and in applying knowledge and effort in ways that are successful, students can come to see that ability is not a fixed state.

- Before initiating a learning experience, speak with students about the importance of strategic effort and about ways to apply knowledge that can lead to success.
- At the conclusion of verbal and written messages, make sincere comments that help students positively connect capability, effort, and knowledge to their success: say, for example, "This is a skillful performance"; "Great to see your hard work pay off"; or "This work clearly demonstrates your strength in applying new information in powerful ways."
- When students experience a sense of failure or make mistakes, help them develop strategies to overcome disappointment. You might say, for example: "I realize you might be feeling quite bad about how this assignment turned out, but there is clear evidence in this assignment that you have what it takes to experience significant improvement. Let's talk about ways you might build on what you know and demonstrate your real potential."

Activity 4. Finding Numbers

PURPOSE

To help students and teachers realize the importance of knowledge and strategies for effective learning and performance; to facilitate a dialogue about the meaning of *working smarter* as compared to *working harder.*

TIME

Twenty minutes.

FORMAT

Large group.

MATERIALS

Three copies per participant of previously prepared random number sheets.

PROCESS

Step 1. Prior to meeting with participants, prepare a sheet of paper with numbers from one to fifty on it. Begin by folding the paper in half and then in half once more. You now have four quadrants. Write the number one in the first upper left quadrant, and then, following clockwise, the number two in the upper right quadrant, the number three in the lower right quadrant, the number four in the lower left quadrant, the number five in the upper left quadrant, and so on up to the number fifty. Write the numbers at different angles so that they appear random and scattered. Make enough copies of this page so each participant can receive three.

Step 2. Pass out three copies to each participant and explain the exercise, along these lines: "This is an exercise that provides an opportunity to examine our beliefs about what it takes to be academically successful. Let's see how talented we are when it comes to quickly circling numbers from one to fifty. Please take out your first sheet, and do not begin until I tell you. We'll see how many numbers you can *consecutively* circle, starting with one, then two, then three, and so forth, in thirty seconds."

After the thirty seconds are up, take a few moments to identify participants with the highest amount of numbers consecutively circled, but do not discuss why. The authors often do this by asking, "Who was able to circle numbers up to at least ten? Fifteen? Twenty? Higher than twenty?"

Step 3. Now tell the participants that the first try could be considered a practice round and that you would like participants to once again circle numbers in order, but that you would like them to "try harder." Proceed as before, timing the round at thirty seconds, and seeing which participants had the highest amount of numbers consecutively circled. Ask how many people improved (had more numbers consecutively circled) as a result of "trying harder." Usually, a few people will actually do less well. Note this, but at this point don't discuss it.

Step 4. Now, ask participants to prepare for a third round. State that you would like everyone to be successful. Ask participants to fold the third sheet in half, lengthwise and then widthwise, so that it has four quadrants. Show them how numbers are organized in a circular pattern on the paper, with one in the first quadrant, two in the second quadrant, and so forth. Now that they have this knowledge, ask participants to again consecutively circle as many numbers as they can in thirty seconds. Afterward, ask how many improved their performance and by how much. The improvement should be vast for most people.

Step 5. Conclude with a whole-group discussion of how this activity on working smarter versus working harder relates to academic success. Perhaps ask where working smarter has made a difference in their own lives and how attributing their success to knowledge and effort has helped them believe in their own capabilities. With educators, you may want to extend the debriefing to address the ways this exercise applies to school renewal.

Following is another activity that helps students see themselves as capable of being wise, able, creative, and joyful. It is also useful

as a precursor to learning about the Motivational Framework for Culturally Responsive Teaching, because it helps participants (students or educators) recall experiences and feelings associated with being intrinsically motivated.

Activity 5.   Identifying the Emotions and Conditions of Being Intrinsically Motivated

PURPOSE

To recall experiences and feelings associated with being intrinsically motivated.

TIME

Thirty minutes.

FORMAT

Dyads and large group.

MATERIALS

Overhead projector and transparencies or newsprint and markers.

PROCESS

Step 1.   Using the think-pair-share structure (as described in Activity 4 in Chapter Five), the facilitator asks participants to think silently about a time in which they were learning and felt capable, creative, and joyful at the same time. Request that participants also think about the situation in which this occurred: with whom, where, when, and under what conditions.

Step 2.   After one to two minutes, ask participants to share their experience with a partner, focusing on the *conditions* that supported them in feeling capable, creative, and joyful.

Step 3.   Then, working with the whole group, ask participants to list some of these conditions that contributed to their success. Chart them as people volunteer responses: for example, "I didn't feel threatened," or "I was involved in a task that was really a challenge." After compiling a list of these conditions, mention that this exercise helps people to identify from their own experiences the conditions that support intrinsic motivation and to remember that everyone is capable of learning in powerful ways. When the conditions exist that individuals need for support, intrinsic motivation emerges.

Also ask participants to consider what this means with respect to creating classrooms or learning environments in which all students feel motivated to learn. This activity can serve as a segue to a deeper discussion of the difference between intrinsic and exclusively extrinsic motivation and as a segue to introducing the motivational framework.

Create a Learning Environment with a Nonblameful and Realistically Hopeful View of People and Learning

Justice and equity inhabit a hopeful consciousness. They resist cynicism and accusation. Often when people experience frustration or difficult challenges they attribute the responsibility for these circumstances to others rather than to themselves. This is commonly known as *blame*. Although the tendency to blame, especially when one is frustrated, is tempting, it reduces one's personal sense of responsibility, drains energy away from problem solving, and is damaging to relationships among people, especially culturally different people with relationships built on fragile trust.

The blame cycle in Figure 6.2 graphically represents the series of outcomes that seem to emerge automatically and with a devastating

Figure 6.2. The Blame Cycle.

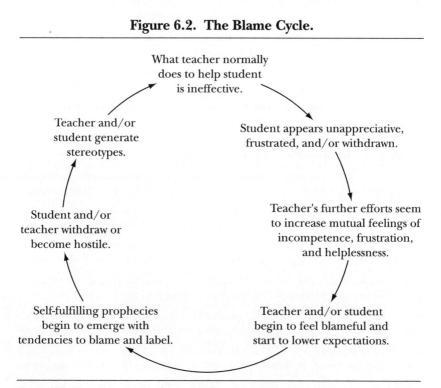

Source: Wlodkowski and Ginsberg, 1995, p. 71. Used with permission.

impact on people's relationships. In this instance the cycle is shown occurring in the relationship between a teacher and student.

Let us say that in this case the student has done poorly on a weekly quiz. At the top of the cycle the teacher wants to help because the student appears to be struggling and sincerely wants to improve. The teacher's normal procedure is to encourage persistence, greater effort, and study habits that might include reviewing notes and outlining chapters. The student sees the problem differently. She thinks the quizzes contain irrelevant material that she has to memorize, with no meaningful context or personal application. The teacher acknowledges the student's comments but offers little empathy or validation and continues to emphasize his previous advice. As the student departs, her frustration is noticeable.

When the student again comes to see the teacher because her quiz scores have not improved, the teacher offers only a variation on his former advice, telling the student to join a study group. As her performance still does not improve, both the teacher and the student feel more incompetent and frustrated. Each feels justified in blaming the other, with the student's continued poor performance confirming their reasons for simply lowering their expectations of each other. Now both teacher and student begin the search for ways to label each other—"lazy," "unprepared," "unfair," "insensitive." They have become hostile, allowing themselves to stereotype and dismiss each other with such comments as, "He just doesn't get it. I've seen this before with people like him." And so the cycle maintains itself. It can be quite disturbing to listen to faculty talking about students who do not perform well in their classes and to students in those classes talking about the faculty with whom they are frustrated. The conversations are mirror images of blame.

In difficult matters between people who do not know each other well, blame often occurs after only one negative encounter. People are particularly vulnerable when they have not had a chance to develop ways of understanding each other and interacting. This is one of the primary reasons some school reform programs, such as the one pioneered by James Comer (1993), have a *no-fault agreement*. In these schools, meeting time is not used to blame others. *The focus is on solving problems and taking advantage of opportunities.* The blame cycle is prevented by simply not allowing blame to occur. Teachers can model this approach, teach it to their students, and support it as a norm for behavior in the classroom. Similarly, schools engaged in a renewal process often create professional agreements that discourage blame and hold an entire faculty to a set of agreed-upon ideals (see Activity 16, Creating a Schoolwide Professional Agreement, in Chapter Five).

Ridding a learning environment of blame does not mean people must stop telling the truth or avoid confronting another person about unethical or contradictory behavior. What it does mean is that students and teachers accept that the purpose of disagreement is to gain perspectives that lead to shared understanding, to finding common ground, and to establishing a clearer path to open communication in the future. The goal is for each person to agree that even though I may see it differently from you, I do not withdraw my support from you as a person.

Activity 6. Reframing

PURPOSE
To teach students (from the upper elementary grades through high school) and educators an effective way to promote change in problematic relationships in which the cycle of blame may have occurred, eroding trust and mutually supportive problem solving. This example focuses on working with teachers.

TIME
Forty-five to sixty minutes.

FORMAT
Large group and small groups.

MATERIALS
Newsprint, markers, and handout (Reframing).

PROCESS
Step 1. Give participants copies of the following handout about reframing.

REFRAMING
• Reframing is based on the view that human behavior can be legitimately interpreted in a variety of ways and that people tend to view their behavior as appropriate to the situation as they perceive it (Molnar and Lindquist, 1989). Consider this example. A teacher regards a student as too aggressive and sees the student's repeated blurting

out answers in class as proof of this estimation. The student considers it necessary to blurt out answers because he believes the teacher ignores him. Their perceptions are mutually reinforced when the student suddenly raises his voice to get the teacher's attention, and the teacher ignores the student to discourage his behavior. And on it goes, with the likelihood of consequent labeling and stereotyping by both individuals.

- Reframing means realizing that people with whom we have a problematic relationship may hold an idea about their experience different from the one we hold. If the teacher in our example were able to interpret the student's blurting out answers as impassioned involvement in the learning experience instead of a hostile act to gain attention, then responses other than ignoring the student would suggest themselves, along with a change in the teacher's demeanor. This might even be an opportunity for disarming humor.
- Reframing requires finding a plausible, positive alternative interpretation of the problematic behavior and then acting in ways consistent with that interpretation.

Step 2. Tell participants that the first stage in reframing is "awareness of your current interpretation of what you consider to be the problem behavior." Ask for a volunteer to describe a recurring problem that she is having with a particular student and to offer her interpretation of the reasons why the student acts as he or she does.

Step 3. Tell the group that the second stage of reframing is the "creation of positive alternative interpretations of the behavior." Then ask the participants to form small groups to brainstorm plausible, *positive* alternative interpretations of the behavior of the student just described. These interpretations are then listed for the whole group.

Step 4. Tell the group that the third stage is "selection of a plausible positive interpretation." Then ask the teacher who volunteered the example to indicate which of the brainstormed positive interpretations might hold some truth and why. Then she selects the one that seems most realistic and truthful.

Step 5. The next stage is "formulation of a sentence or two that describes the new positive interpretation." The teacher offers in her own words the new positive interpretation that she will use. This interpretation is recorded.

Step 6. The final stage is "action that sincerely reflects this new interpretation." Ask the group to brainstorm possible action strategies for the new interpretation. These are listed and then the teacher selects from among them to create a plan to use with the student.

Source: Adapted from Molnar and Lindquist, 1989, p. 61.

By avoiding blame, reframing offers a process to generate effective solutions to teacher-student conflicts. Part of this method's success is due to how well it invites the creativity of teachers. It also can invite the creativity of students. An example of reframing follows that involves a sixth-grade student trying to come to terms with his mother's attempts to help with homework. (This example could be used by educators who would like to teach reframing to younger students).

Step 1. Think through a series of interactions with another person and map them. What did or does someone do? How did or do you respond? What happens next? Then what happens? and so forth. You are trying to describe what happens in the problem situation, how you respond, and what the usual result is.

> My mother tries to help me understand a math homework problem. But the way she explains it is confusing. I respond by telling her I am still confused. She tries to teach me another way, but it is a lot like the first time. I get very frustrated. I stop listening and tell her she is no help at all. She gets angry and says that I have a bad attitude, that I need to care enough to patiently figure things out. I start to think that my mother doesn't know much about how to figure out math. I get mad at her for just making my life more complicated. I go to my room and close the door.

Step 2. Explain your current understanding of why the person behaves this way.

> My mother is nervous about my future. She thinks if I am not a perfect student then I won't have a good life.

Step 3. Determine what positive alternative explanations there might be for this behavior.

> My mother cares about me and wants to help. My mother wants me to have more choices about my future than she had. The fact that we get angry at each other shows that we are really comfortable with each other and know that deep down we love each other.

Step 4. Figure out how you can respond differently than you have previously, working on the basis of one of your positive explanations. What might you actually say or do differently?

> When I feel myself getting frustrated I am going to try to count to ten in order to stay calm. Then I will tell her that I know she is trying but it isn't working even though I really do care about

doing well. I will tell her that I am going to try Plan B, which is to call a friend. I will tell her that I will try to learn the math so well that I can teach her.

Use a Variety of Entry Points for Learning a Subject to Develop Diverse Students' Multiple Intelligences

When we understand intelligence as the capacity to solve problems or to fashion products that are valued by one's culture or community, we realize intelligence cannot be conceptualized apart from the context in which people live. There is always an interaction between the students' personal inclinations and the opportunities for learning that exist in their cultural milieu. Thus there exist multiple ways to be capable and to demonstrate intelligence. According to Howard Gardner (Checkley, 1997), people have the capacity for at least eight intelligences. And people differ in the strengths of their various intelligences. For example, some students perform best when asked to manipulate symbols such as words and numbers, whereas others demonstrate their understanding best through a hands-on approach, building or creating a concrete representation or product. Rather than possessing a single intelligence, students have a *profile* of intelligences that combine to perform different tasks.

Although the theory of multiple intelligences includes the idea that people will have preferences for ways of learning as the concept of learning styles also does, multiple intelligences theory locates intellectual processing in a specific location of the brain and across a much wider context of experiences. Gardner (1993) proposes that any concept worth teaching can be approached in numerous different ways that allow *all* students relevant access. Let us look at each of the eight intelligences to understand its meaning (Gardner and Hatch, 1989), related career choices, and relevant action words to inspire lesson planning.

- *Logical-mathematical.* Sensitivity to and capacity to discern logical and numerical patterns; ability to handle long chains of inductive and deductive reasoning

  Careers: scientist, accountant, engineer, economist, physicist, and programmer

Action words: sequence, rank, prove, conclude, judge, assess, critique, analyze

- *Verbal-linguistic.* Sensitivity to the sounds, rhythms, and meanings of words; sensitivity to the different functions of language written and spoken

  Careers: author, journalist, teacher, salesperson, actor, translator, politician

  Action words: write, speak, read, narrate, talk, e-mail, script, translate, create a metaphor

- *Visual-spatial.* Capacities to perceive the visual-spatial world accurately and to effectively transform one's initial perceptions and images

  Careers: designer, navigator, sculptor, cartographer, architect

  Action words: imagine, draw, dream, graph, design, visualize, videotape, create

- *Musical.* Abilities to produce and appreciate rhythm, tone, pitch, and timbre; appreciation of the forms of musical expressiveness

  Careers: musician, composer, disc jockey, music critic, dancer, sound engineer, singer

  Action words: wing, rap, play, rhyme, compose; create a jingle, beat, melody, opera

- *Bodily-kinesthetic.* Abilities to know, use, and control one's body movements and to handle objects skillfully

  Careers: athlete, actor, juggler, physical therapist, dancer, coach, performance artist

  Action words: express, enact, perform, dance, mime; create a game, play, drama

- *Interpersonal.* Capacities to discern, intuit, and respond appropriately to others; to communicate the moods, temperaments, motivations, and desires of other people

  Careers: therapist, politician, teacher, manager, executive, salesperson

  Action words: collaborate, process, communicate, empathize, lead; create a plan, interview, policy, law

- *Intrapersonal.* Access to one's own feelings and inner states of being with the ability to discriminate among them and draw on them to guide behavior; knowledge of one's own strengths, weaknesses, desires, and intelligences

   Careers: philosopher, spiritual leader, inventor, researcher, author, computer expert

   Action words: plan, envision, reflect, write, invent, propose, investigate, study; create a philosophy, credo, new way, research plan, software package

- *Naturalist.* Capacity to recognize, classify, and use plants, minerals, and animals, including rocks, grass, and all variety of flora and fauna

   Careers: botanist, farmer, oceanographer, park ranger, geologist, zookeeper.

   Action words: classify, grow, develop, find, search; create a terrarium, aquarium, field trip, classification system

Notice that for each intelligence there are action words concerning creating something especially relevant to that intelligence. In teaching any topic or concept we can use a variety of approaches to respect and accommodate the wide range of profiles of intelligence found among diverse students. For example, rather than presenting the concept of photosynthesis only as a series of steps reflecting chemical changes (logical-mathematical), we might also ask students to examine relevant transformative experiences in their families and communities and to compare them with the process of photosynthesis (interpersonal), or ask students to look for musical transformations that parallel photosynthesis. In such ways we can improve the chances that diverse students with different ways of knowing can find engaging ways to learn.

Activity 7. Using Multiple Intelligences to Learn

Purpose

To help students become aware of and apply their multiple intelligences to learning; to help teachers become aware of their own profile of intelligences and practice creating learning activities to accommodate that profile

Time

Sixty minutes.

FORMAT

Large group and small groups.

MATERIALS

Handout defining the multiple intelligences.

PROCESS

Step 1. Ask participants to peruse the handout that defines the eight intelligences (drawn from the list given previously), and then tell an interesting story (linguistic intelligence) from your own history (that is, concerning yourself or a child, student, friend, or relative) about someone who exemplifies and thrives on using his or her multiple intelligences (at least three of them). Then narrate (linguistic intelligence), draw (visual-spatial intelligence), or enact (bodily-kinesthetic intelligence) how you know which four intelligences are dominant in your own profile.

Step 2. Ask participants to work individually to analyze the handout (logical-mathematical intelligence) and to determine which four intelligences dominate their own profile of intelligences. Then, as you modeled in step 1, ask participants to narrate, draw, or enact to a partner how they know which four intelligences are dominant in their own profile.

Step 3. Ask each participant to find one or two other people in the group who have the same or nearly the same four intelligences in their profile as he or she does. After these groups have assembled, request that they each choose one relevant concept or topic they have to teach. Each group then brainstorms and invents ways (intrapersonal intelligence) to teach this topic or concept in a manner that compellingly accommodates their four intelligences.

Step 4. Groups report out, post on the wall, or dramatize the activities that teach their concept or topic.

Activities Primarily Focused on Developing a Positive Attitude Toward School Renewal

Many of the following exercises are adaptable for use as classroom activities that develop a positive attitude among students. However, they have been particularly useful for helping adults acquire a positive attitude toward school renewal work. Like some of the activities located elsewhere in this chapter, such as carousel graffiti, these activities have helped school-based educators to creatively share perspectives. Such sharing is especially important in the initial stages of a school renewal process, when commitment to change is understandably influenced by the extent to which people believe they will have ownership in the process.

Activity 8. Story Posters

PURPOSE

To reflect on prior experiences and learning in order to develop shared understandings as well as a foundation upon which to build.

TIME

One hour.

FORMAT

Small groups.

MATERIALS

Newsprint, glue sticks, precut symbols, and handout (Symbols for Story Posters).

PROCESS

Step 1. Participants review a handout like the following, which defines visual symbols such as a heart, a jagged heart, and fog in terms of questions about the issues in which participants are most interested. For educators working on school renewal, topics might include cultural diversity, motivation, or schoolwide change. This handout focuses on motivation.

SYMBOLS FOR STORY POSTERS

Heart. What holds particular value for you when you think about the potential of your school?

Jagged heart. What aspects of your work disappoint you?

Fog. As you reflect on ways to support student motivation, what are some of the things that cause confusion or leave you puzzled?

Gift. What are some treasured times of celebration or success related to your work with students families, and staff?

Green people. Who are some of the people you personally know who currently inspire your commitment to the success of all students?

Blue people. Who are some of the people you have personally known who have inspired you even though they are no longer present in your life?

Thunder clouds. What are some of the storms you have had to endure and learn from in seeking to improve teaching and learning on behalf of *all* children?

Lightning. What are some unexpected things that have happened as a consequence of working with and learning from students?

Sun. What helps you to sustain your sense of hope?

Step 2. As members of the groups share their experiences related to the specific symbols they select, they glue precut symbols on their newsprint in whatever way they like. Groups also summarize their dialogue related to the symbols they have selected and write a few words on the poster to clarify the meaning of the symbols. In this way, other people looking at the finished story posters will understand more about the dialogue that took place while symbols were being posted. Some groups paste their symbols on the poster randomly, whereas others prefer a more deliberate way of representing their thinking. The facilitator encourages each group to proceed in its own way.

Step 3. Groups hang their posters gallery-style on a wall and elicit a reporter to share one or two features of the poster with the whole group.

Activity 9. Blue Skies

PURPOSE

To create a vision of an ideal school and to use that vision to imagine changes that could make a powerful difference for a particular school or for schools throughout a district. This is a good staff development exercise. But it is also a good exercise to use with students to learn how they imagine the ideal classroom for learning in and supporting their success, and to use with parents to learn more about their ideas of an ideal school, classroom, or learning experience.

TIME

One hour.

FORMAT

Individuals or small groups (depending on the size of the group as a whole).

MATERIALS

Newsprint, colored markers, masking tape, and a large sign that says "Draw, map, or use words to describe an ideal school for working in, for having your own children attend, and for supporting the success of *all* students."

PROCESS

Step 1. Ask participants to use the large paper to draw, map, or use words to describe an ideal school for working in, for having their own children attend, and for supporting the success of *all* students. The goal is to be as creative as possible. Each poster ought to have a few descriptive words beneath the drawing or map to clarify the illustrator's ideas. Some captions we have seen are "all kinds of literature everywhere"; "a publishing center"; "a room where students can go at any time to build, paint, or create something using lots of different media"; "a student-run teahouse for relaxing and studying near the media center"; "personal coaches/mentors who support students until they gradu-ate"; "ongoing community work"; "learning by doing"; "a parent center with washing machines and dryers"; "Lots of time to work with and learn from other teachers."

Step 2. Hang all the posters around the room and ask people to stroll, gallery-style, identifying and jotting down themes that they would most like to see represented in a shared vision statement.

Step 3. Work with the group to shape a few sentences that represent the themes in which the group most believes. Here, for example, is a vision statement built on the cap-tions just quoted: "Our school will be a place where students, faculty, and student advo-cates and mentors work together to create learning experiences that build strong literacy skills in ways that are meaningful to students and provide multiple ways for students to creatively express themselves. In addition, our school will maximize the use of commu-nity resources, encouraging parent involvement throughout the school and facilitating service learning as an integral part of the academic program. We will resist labeling stu-dents if they are not succeeding and will, instead, consistently work together to examine our school and classrooms in order to support the motivation and success of all stu-dents." After a rough draft has been generated, participants work in small groups to sug-gest any revisions that might make the vision more representative or stronger. Finally, their suggestions are integrated into a final draft by a small committee nominated by the group. (This usually occurs while participants take a brief break). Participants respond to the final draft by using the fist-to-five method, in which the fingers are used as a scale (five is high, one is low, and a fist means "I can't live with it").

Additional notes. Vision statements ought to be reflected throughout a school plan. One way to ensure that this occurs is to create subgroups according to the themes represented in the vision statement. For example, given the sample vision statement, one subgroup might be "literacy across content areas." Another group might be "creativity and self-expression." Another group might be "student advocates," and yet another, "col-laborative, job-embedded professional development that helps us strengthen classroom practice." Subgroups review the school plan to ensure that it is rich with the goals and ideas manifested in the vision statement.

Activity 10. Examples and Indicators of a Successful School

PURPOSE
To examine school strengths as well as new opportunities for school renewal.

TIME
Forty-five minutes.

FORMAT
Individuals and dyads.

MATERIALS

Handout listing strategies already in place, an ideas matrix, sticky dots in three colors, three-by-five-inch cards, and tape for posting cards.

PROCESS

Ideally, prior to determining which school renewal themes to offer in the exercise, the facilitator works with a team of teachers and administrators to review data indicative of school renewal (for example, test scores of different student groups, attendance records, retention rates, drop-out rates, graduation rates, conflict reports, and parent or family surveys). The facilitator also interviews teacher, student, and parent representatives. This makes it possible to identify which of the following themes are most relevant to the school or how they might be rewritten to be more relevant.

SCHOOL RENEWAL THEMES

- Collaboration and trust throughout the whole school
- Highly motivating teaching and learning for *all* students
- Meaningful parent and family involvement for *all* families
- Professional development that matters
- Supporting literacy in every possible way
- Making school a safe and healthy place

Step 1. Ask participants to count off by sixes, so that there is at least one group for each of the six themes. Distribute a handout with three columns. The left-hand column lists strategies that are already in place in the school. The middle and right-hand columns are blank. In the left-hand column, each group identifies examples of the strategies that are already in place that support the group's theme. In the middle column, participants list ways in which they know that each of the strategies they identified is effective (or promising). In the third column, participants list new ideas related to their group's theme that they think could make a real difference.

Step 2. Each group selects two to three of the new ideas that it believes could make the greatest difference for the school as a whole and for student success. Participants write the ideas on individual three-by-five-inch cards and post the cards on a *reading wall* labeled "Ideas!" There are several possibilities for next steps. We offer two.

Step 3a. Volunteers create a matrix that lists all the ideas. It may simply be a series of rows, as in the following example.

IDEAS FOR SCHOOL RENEWAL

Design groups for highly motivating lessons and units

Peer coaching

Service learning once a week for all middle school students

Student demonstrations once a quarter to share best work

Or the matrix might look more like a table, with staff members' names written vertically and ideas listed horizontally, as in this example.

IDEAS FOR SCHOOL RENEWAL

	COLLABORATIVE LESSON PLANNING	PEER COACHING	SERVICE LEARNING
Joan			
Ray			
Mario			
Wilma			
Leticia			

At a staff meeting, staff place sticky dots next to the row or in the appropriate cell of the table to demonstrate their level of interest. The first method allows people to make their choices anonymously. A green dot signifies their first choice, a blue dot their second choice, and a red dot their third choice. Each person is given one dot of each color and places all three dots on the matrix.

Next, staff identify the choice preferred by most. The school then determines an approach to learning more about and perhaps experimenting with the idea. For example, one school agreed to try three rounds of peer coaching over a six-week period. Each faculty member teamed with a trusted colleague and, using the Partnership Guide for Culturally Responsive Teaching (Chapter Eight), each visited the other's classroom for one class period every other week (thus they rotated visitation weeks). Using the guide, they agreed to only look for strengths. Their goal was to create a common language to inform motivating instruction and to develop trust in the peer coaching process. Interestingly, almost every team began—on its own—to brainstorm ways to overcome self-identified challenges. At the end of six weeks the faculty met to evaluate what worked, what needed to be improved, and how they might proceed.

Step 3b. An alternative way to work with the ideas on the cards that have been posted on the reading wall is to cluster cards according to similarities and work with the group to identify five ideas that participants would like to learn more about. Participants then form *inquiry groups* to collect articles, visit model programs or demonstration sites, arrange for guest speakers, and so forth, according to the focus of each group's inquiry. Time for teams to meet can be provided in many ways. Sometimes it can be as simple as hiring four or five substitutes to free up several teacher teams over the course of a day. Sometimes teachers pair with other teachers, and members of each pair free each other at agreed-upon times. This works because there are times when it is appropriate for an educator to work with a very large group of students, just as it is also necessary at times to work with small numbers of students (creating time for collaboration is discussed later in this chapter). The inquiry groups use staff meetings to share resources and insights with the entire faculty, supporting decision making for schoolwide implementation. Whatever the idea selected, it ought to be one backed by trustworthy evidence that if implemented well it can substantively contribute to student motivation, support academic accomplishment, and encourage students, parents, and staff to see school as a good place to be.

Activity 11. Metaphorical Ecosystems

PURPOSE
To recognize strengths in order to identify needs.

TIME
Thirty minutes.

FORMAT
Small groups.

MATERIALS
Newsprint and colored markers.

PROCESS
Step 1. Ask participants to examine the *whole picture* within which their role in implementing change in their school or district occurs. Have them work collaboratively in teams to design and draw a metaphorical illustration that highlights the conditions and situations that have, continue to, and will affect their work as it relates to cultural diversity. The picture may use the following symbols and definitions.

   Blooms. What programs are in place in your school or district but still need tending in order to increase staff skill and ownership?

   Seeds. What are the ideas for substantive change that seem most interesting or important to you?

   Nutrients. Keeping in mind current programs and other ideas you find interesting or important, what would need to happen for teaching and learning to improve for *all* students throughout your entire school or district?

   Clouds. What challenges might schools face as they work toward whole school change, and how might those challenges be overcome? Consider what you might need to let go of in your school.

   Sun. How might you sustain your energy as you continue to ask hard questions and move toward substantive change?

Step 2. A spokesperson for each group displays and briefly explains the group's poster. Afterward, the entire group responds to these questions: What insights do you have from the process of creating your illustration or from thinking about what other teams have created? What can you recommend as a follow-up to this exercise? How might you adapt this activity for use in your classroom?

Activity 12. Creating Time for Collaboration (Professional Learning Teams)

PURPOSE
To encourage educators to engage in collaborative planning, teaching, examining of student work, and other forms of reflective practice.

TIME
Thirty minutes.

FORMAT
Triads.

MATERIALS
Handout (Strategies for Expanding Time for Collaborative Planning, Teaching, and Reflection)

PROCESS
Ask school staff, working in groups of three, to read the handout at the end of this activity, which shows strategies for allocating time for enhanced collaborative learning. Then ask them to respond to the following questions about working in collaborative learning teams and creating the time for collaboration and to add any additional questions they would like to consider.

QUESTIONS ABOUT COLLABORATION
1. What norms or traditional ways of organizing time make it challenging for educators in your school to learn and plan together?
2. How do you currently tap into the expertise and resources of school personnel, members of students' families, or community members?
3. How might more flexibility with scheduling help members of your school community plan and work together in ways that support highly motivating classroom practice?
4. What is one idea you would like to try in support of greater collaboration?
5. What would you need to do to make your idea a reality?

Additional notes. There are several valuable articles that address the significance of adult collaboration and the ways that schools are finding and using time to meet the goal of strengthening student learning. For example, the entire Summer 1999 issue of the *Journal of Staff Development*, published by the National Staff Development Council, is dedicated to this topic and provides informative and practical articles on powerful designs for adult collaboration.

STRATEGIES FOR EXPANDING TIME FOR COLLABORATIVE PLANNING, TEACHING, AND REFLECTION

- Ask staff to identify with whom and when they need to collaborate and to redesign the master schedule to accommodate these needs.
- Hire *permanent substitutes* to rotate through classrooms to periodically free up teachers to attend meetings during the day rather than before or after school.
- Institute a community service component in the curriculum; teachers meet when students are in the community (for example, one afternoon a week).
- Schedule *specials* (for example, art and music classes), clubs, and tutorials during the same time block so teachers have those one or two hours a day to collaborate.
- Engage parents, family members, and community members to plan and conduct half-day or full-day exploratory, craft or hobby (for example, gourmet cooking, puppetry, photography), theater, or other experiential programs, leaving teachers free. Partner with colleges and universities; have their faculty teach in the school or offer distance learning lessons, demonstrations, and on-campus experiences to free up school personnel.
- Rearrange the school day to include a fifty- to sixty-minute block of time before or after school for collaborative meeting or planning. Faculty already often leave school later than the students. When faculty add forty-five minutes to their school schedule one day a week—and leave earlier on another day of their choice as compensation—they have a nice block of time to work together.
- Lengthen the school day for students by fifteen to thirty minutes, allowing students to spend the same amount of time in school but to be dismissed early occasionally, providing time for teachers to meet.
- Earmark some professional development days for collaborative meetings.
- Use existing time for small-group faculty meetings to solve problems related to issues of immediate and long-range importance.
- Build into the school schedule at least one *collaboration day* per marking period or month.
- Lengthen the school year for staff but not for students, or shorten the school year for students but not for staff.
- Institute year-round schooling with three-week breaks every other quarter; devote four or five of the three-week intersession days to teacher collaboration.

In considering these ideas, note that parents and family members are frequently assumed to be opponents of scheduling changes. However, schools that elicit support from parents and family members in planning needed changes and schools that explain changes in terms of how students will benefit have reported widespread support for new ideas.

Sources: The strategies for expanding time for collaborative planning, teaching, and reflection are adapted from Villa and Thousand, 1995, p. 67. The exercise is adapted from Ginsberg, Johnson, and Moffett, 1997, p. 40.

Activity 13. Creating a Statement of Purpose for a Schoolwide Instructional Leadership Cadre

PURPOSE

To define the purposes of a schoolwide instructional leadership cadre in ways that honor the perspectives of those who have been asked or who have volunteered to serve. This activity is best facilitated at an introductory work session with the cadre.

TIME

Fifteen minutes.

FORMAT

Individuals and large group.

MATERIALS

Handout (Draft Statement of Purpose).

PROCESS

Step 1. Ask cadre members, working individually, to review the following draft statement of purpose for the cadre. Request that they add, delete, and modify items on the draft statement as they desire.

DRAFT STATEMENT OF PURPOSE

The purpose of the schoolwide instructional leadership cadre is to inform, demonstrate, and encourage your school to apply information and methods of instruction that respond to the needs and interests of *all* students. The leadership cadre supports its school in applying the Motivational Framework for Culturally Responsive Teaching to lesson and course design. In addition, it works with its school to create, schoolwide, the conditions in which all students experience

- Respect and connectedness to each other and to their teachers
- Curriculum and instruction that is relevant, challenging, and engaging
- Assessment that is meaningful to students, promotes learning, and clearly identifies

the ways in which students are becoming competent at what they value and at what is of value to their communities

The leadership cadre will work with its school in a way that promotes positive involvement of all school community members (parents, school staff, and students); helps build collaborative schoolwide norms; facilitates ongoing, job-embedded adult learning through the development of professional learning teams and peer coaching; and collects data so that the school can identify its accomplishments and make informed decisions for continuous schoolwide improvement.

Step 2. Have participants share their recommendations, as you note them on a piece of newsprint. Facilitate a process of reaching agreement on the changes that work well for everyone. Together, participants integrate the agreed-upon changes into the draft statement.

Activity 14. Establishing Norms for Teamwork

PURPOSE

To define how the members of the schoolwide instructional leadership cadre will work together. This activity is best facilitated at an introductory work session with the team.

TIME

Thirty minutes.

FORMAT

Individuals, triads, and teams of six.

MATERIALS

Handout (Profile of an Effective Organizational Team) and sticky notes.

PROCESS

Step 1. Ask participants to review the handout containing the profile of an effective organizational team (Exhibit 6.1). Each person notes the three most important items in the *entire* matrix that she or he needs to have happen in order to serve effectively on the leadership cadre. Participants then write each item on a sticky note, one item per note.

Step 2. Ask participants to form triads. (When staff developers are working with several leadership cadres at one time, they need to be sure that members of school-specific cadres work together throughout this activity). Members of each triad lay their sticky notes out on a tabletop and group them according to similarities. The matrix has quite a bit of redundancy among the categories. For example, the norm of collaboration is represented in several different ways. So it is quite easy for triad members to find overlap among their priorities and to group them.

Exhibit 6.1. Profile of an Effective Organizational Team.

The categories as well as the items for consideration are an integration of research on effective teams and themes and needs pertinent to creating change in institutions. Please rate your responses in terms of the team's highest and lowest priorities.

General Direction of the Team

	Low		Middle		High	Examples
1. The team has a shared vision and mission that focuses on students and highly motivating instructional practice.	1	2	3	4	5	
2. The team develops a manageable work plan with clear goals.	1	2	3	4	5	
3. The team focuses on activities that have a significant impact on *all* students.	1	2	3	4	5	
4. The team participates in the development and implementation of the schoolwide plan.	1	2	3	4	5	
5. The team ensures that the diversity elements of the schoolwide plan are substantive and well integrated.	1	2	3	4	5	

Meetings

	Low		Middle		High	Examples
1. The team meets at least once a month.	1	2	3	4	5	
2. Team meetings are scheduled in advance and participants are notified of meeting times.	1	2	3	4	5	
3. Team members have an opportunity to contribute to the formation of the agenda.	1	2	3	4	5	
4. Team members are in regular attendance.	1	2	3	4	5	
5. Minutes are kept of all meetings and, when appropriate, are made available to key constituencies.	1	2	3	4	5	
6. Team members conduct work as needed between meetings, with the necessary support to make professional decisions that effectively and efficiently respond to the needs of their school.	1	2	3	4	5	

(Continued)

Exhibit 6.1. Profile of an Effective Organizational Team. (*Continued*)

Ability to Work as a Team

	Low		Middle		High	Examples
1. Team members effectively communicate with each other.	1	2	3	4	5	
2. Team members use consensus decision-making skills and all members fully participate in discussions as well as decisions.	1	2	3	4	5	
3. The team uses members' skills and areas of expertise.	1	2	3	4	5	
4. Team members support each other in fulfilling responsibilities.	1	2	3	4	5	
5. Team members resolve conflicts and problems effectively.	1	2	3	4	5	
6. The team works to ensure that all members feel included and valued.	1	2	3	4	5	
7. The team regularly assesses itself.	1	2	3	4	5	

Leadership

	Low		Middle		High	Examples
1. The leader works with team members to clarify respective roles and responsibilities.	1	2	3	4	5	
2. The leader works collaboratively with all team members.	1	2	3	4	5	
3. The leader acts as a facilitator in team decision making.	1	2	3	4	5	
4. The leader ensures that all team members have the timely information they need to make decisions.	1	2	3	4	5	
5. Members of the team share leadership and responsibility for the team's work.	1	2	3	4	5	
6. The leader encourages diversity of opinion and ideas.	1	2	3	4	5	
7. The leader encourages creativity and risk taking.	1	2	3	4	5	

(Continued)

Exhibit 6.1. Profile of an Effective Organizational Team. (*Continued*)

External Communication

	Low		Middle		High	Examples
1. The team seeks input equally from school staff, administrative personnel, students, community members, and other constituencies.	1	2	3	4	5	
2. The team effectively communicates with staff for all professional development initiatives about relevant issues.	1	2	3	4	5	
3. The team fully informs school constituencies of its activities and outcomes.	1	2	3	4	5	
4. The team uses an external as well as internal communication plan, communicating with the communities at large as well as with those within the institution.	1	2	3	4	5	

Source: Adapted from Hirsch, [no date].

Step 3. Ask each triad to merge with another triad to form a six-person team. Members of this team repeat the grouping process. They then prioritize the norms they have found in order to identify the top three to five norms they would like to have in place.

Step 4. Ask cadre members to work together on a final statement that contains norms that will guide their teamwork. Then ask them to create a procedure for regularly assessing and strengthening their fidelity to their agreed-upon norms. A volunteer scribe writes the cadre norms and the procedure for assessing them on two three-by-five-inch cards, along with the names of two people who will serve as cochairs for the cadre. The scribe gives one card to the facilitator, and the cadre saves one card for itself.

Activity 15. Roundtable Dialogue on Change

PURPOSE

To share insights and lend perspectives related to the process of school change.

TIME

Thirty minutes.

FORMAT

Individuals and small groups.

MATERIALS

Handout (Caveats About School Change), newsprint, and markers.

PROCESS

Although the process of change is complex and an examination of it is most relevant once a renewal process is under way, it is a good idea to *normalize* some of the caution and ambiguity people feel as they begin to work together on a course of sustained study and action.

Step 1. Distribute the handout containing the caveats about school change (Exhibit 6.2), and ask participants to underscore or mark with sticky notes the issues that speak to their own experiences—or that make sense for other reasons. Next, ask participants to identify a challenge that they feel because of their involvement in this process and one or two strategies for productively addressing the challenge.

Step 2. Ask participants to count off by fours to form small groups in which they will hold dialogues. Request each group to identify a facilitator (who poses dialogue questions and keeps things moving), a recorder (who records key points), a reporter (who will provide a one- to two-minute summary for the large group by noting *insights* and *recommendations*), and a process observer (who will help participants remember to share airtime so that all people have an opportunity to comfortably participate and

Exhibit 6.2. Caveats About School Change.

School change is a complex, nonlinear process that requires an open exchange of literature, practices, and ideas; participation from as many representatives of the school community as possible; validation of important work; planning time as a part of everyday work; and support at all levels within the school district. What caveats might the schoolwide team members consider in advance of their work as change agents in order to be better prepared? On this topic the research of Carl Glickman, Richard Hayes, and Frances Hensley (1992) with the League of Professional Schools is particularly informative:

- Conflict will increase when members of shared governance teams take their responsibilities seriously. (This is also true of schoolwide instructional leadership cadres.)
- Assessment information will cultivate dissatisfaction and possibly blame if it does not match up with the *cardiac approach* to student learning and attitudes—"in our hearts we're doing fine" (Wolfe, 1989).
- Without new information, decisions will be made that reinforce the status quo.
- With immediate school success, pressure for more short-term success will increase at the potential cost of long-term student gains.
- Decisions about the content of dreams will be easier than decisions about how to attain those dreams.
- Criticism will develop from the outside, especially as a school attains success and recognition.

Rosabeth Moss Kanter, in *The Challenge of Organizational Change—How Companies Experience It and Leaders Guide It.* (1992), helps us examine why people resist change. Among the frequently mentioned reasons are

- Loss of control
- Excess uncertainty
- Concerns about competence
- More work
- Past resentments

We also know that

- Change is a process that occurs over time (some theorists indicate that at a minimum, school change is a three- to five-year process).
- Ultimately change is an individual act.

- The more complex a new idea or behavior, the longer it takes for change to occur.
- Change efforts must be directed not only toward the new idea itself, but also toward individuals and the time and assistance they need to implement a new idea.

Here is what some of the leading theorists say:

Most organizations today have mission statements, purpose statements, official visions, and little cards printed with the organization's values. But precious few can say that our organization's mission statement has transformed the enterprise. (Peter Senge, p. 59)

Leaders who take the same risks they ask of others—changing their own behavior and giving up a measure of comfort and control—truly inspire and energize others. When leaders are learning and growing, everything about them communicates the same opportunity to other people. (Douglas K. Smith, p. 101)

I believe that hope is an absolute moral imperative, because if we don't have it we have become part of the problem, ourselves, not part of the solution. (Steven R. Covey, p. 224)

Old ways die hard. Amid all the evidence that our world is radically changing, we cling to what has worked in the past. (Margaret Wheatley, p. 151)

Leaders are necessary to foster experimentation, to help create connections across the organizations, to feed the system with rich information from multiple sources—all while helping everyone stay clear on what we agreed we wanted to accomplish and who we wanted to be. (Margaret Wheatley, p. 158)

If we've learned anything in the past twenty years it is that there are no quick fixes. (Margaret Wheatley, p. 159)

There is a limit of foresight. Even when foresight is nearly perfect, a distinction remains between the clarity of the vision and the proximity of the goal. The end target may be clearly visible—"I want to climb that mountain"—but much of the route may be invisible from the starting point. The only way you are going to see the path ahead is to start moving. Thus strategy must be as much about

(Continued)

Exhibit 6.2. Caveats About School Change. *(Continued)*

experimentation as it is about foresight. (Gar Hamel and Jim Scholes, p. 93)

Biographical sources for understanding school change include the following:

Allen, L., and Lunsford, B. *How to Form Networks for School Renewal.* Alexandria, Va.: Association for Supervision and Curriculum Development, 1995.

Goodman, J. "External Change Agents and Grassroots School Reform: Reflections from the Field." *Journal of Curriculum and Supervision,* 1994, *9,* 113–135.

Journal of Staff Development, Summer 1998, *19* (entire issue 3, *Strategies to Move Hearts and Minds*).

McLaughlin, M. "The Rand Change Agent Study Revisited: Macro Perspectives and Micro Realities." *Educational Researcher,* Dec. 1990, *19,* 11–16.

Miles, M., Saxl, E., and Lieberman, A. "What Skills Do Educational 'Change Agents' Need?" *Curriculum Inquiry,* 1989, *18,* 157–192.

Olson, L. "Critical Friends." *Education Week,* May 4, 1994.

Snyder, J. S., Giella, M., and Fitzgerald, J. H. "The Changing Role of Central Office Supervisors in District Restructuring." *Journal of Staff Development,* 1994, *15,* 30–34.

Source: Quotes are from *Leader to Leader* (Hesselbein and Cohen, 1999).

who will also be the timekeeper). Ask the groups to discuss these questions, which you have written on newsprint and posted.

QUESTIONS ABOUT SCHOOL CHANGE

1. As you reflect on the caveats in the handout, what are some of the issues that have particular meaning for you?

2. What is a challenge that occurs to you because of your involvement in this process, and what are one or two ways a person or a team could effectively address that challenge?

3. As you think about what we have discussed, what are some of your most important insights?

4. What are some of your most important recommendations as they relate to the challenges we may face?

Conclusion

In this chapter we have presented several strategies for developing a positive attitude, the second motivational condition in the Motivational Framework for Culturally Responsive Teaching. Many of the strategies are classroom focused and contribute to students' positive attitude toward learning across content areas. When applied to adult learning, especially to the preparation of school-wide instructional leadership cadres, they have helped, amid the skepticism that is and *ought to be* part of any renewal initiative, to facilitate open-minded dialogue and learning. All of the activities are based on respect for the existing professional and personal expertise of experienced educators and a concern for providing adults with relevant information to guide them in their work.

As you tailor the resources to the needs of your own setting—whether it be a classroom, the preparation of schoolwide instructional leadership cadres, or whole faculties, we once again caution that mere strategies, in and of themselves, do not create a positive attitude toward learning. A positive attitude, as most educators are well aware, is the result of complex interactions involving sincerity and integrity. The following checklist is a guide to key facilitator considerations in creating the conditions in which meaningful choices and personally relevant content and methods contribute to learners' positive attitude.

Developing a Positive Attitude

How does the learning experience offer meaningful choices and promote personal relevance to contribute to students' positive attitude?

- The teacher works with students to personalize the relevance of course content.
  - __ Students' experiences, concerns, and interests are used to develop course content.
  - __ Students' experiences, concerns, and interests are addressed in responses to questions.
  - __ Students' prior knowledge and their learning experiences are explicitly linked to course content and questions.
  - __ The teacher encourages students to understand, develop, and express different points of view.

__ The teacher encourages students to clarify their interests
and set goals.

__ The teacher maintains flexibility in the pursuit of *teachable
moments* and emerging interests.

Describe the evidence:

- The teacher encourages students to make real choices.

  __ Students choose how to learn (multiple intelligences).

  __ Students choose what to learn.

  __ Students choose where to learn.

  __ Students choose when a learning experience will be considered to be complete.

  __ Students choose how learning will be assessed.

  __ Students choose with whom to learn.

  __ Students choose how to solve emerging problems.

Describe the evidence:

We end this chapter with a comment directed toward those
educators who struggle with the relevance of working for change
in such a cynical time, those whose own positive attitudes are, at
times, reduced to such thoughts as, "Should I wait for greater wisdom, a time when the issues will be clearer and our supporters
more steadfast? Should we even bother?"

The process of school renewal is technically and morally complex. In spite of the rather large body of research that exists on the
topic, we lack a *perfect standard,* one that proves, with absolute certainty, that ordinary human beings will make a critical difference,
maintain moral consistency, and express themselves eloquently
under pressure. Even when we are equipped with years of teaching experience, college degrees, and wonderful memories of the
moments when we most mattered to a child, it can seem far easier
to justify detachment than to voice our convictions.

Unfortunately, there is no perfect time for getting involved in
any form of social change, in our schools or anywhere else. A positive attitude toward gaining the knowledge and confidence we
need to strengthen educational opportunity for *all students,*
requires a tolerance for doubt, humility, and often contradictory
motives. Uncertainty, however, is not an insurmountable obstacle.

Even Gandhi called his efforts "experiments in truth," because results could come only through trial and error.

However, even though there is no perfect standard for educational change, research and experience can help us as we try to offer choices that are meaningful. And we can listen carefully to others so that even if we have to do things a bit differently than we prefer, learning has an increased likelihood of being relevant to all of us. Still, the effectiveness of any learning experience or change initiative is context dependent and as unpredictable as the children we teach. Therein lies the fascination. We discover how much our actions matter only by working together as caring human beings. What could be more relevant at this time?

Activity Guide for Developing a Positive Attitude

Following is a list of the activities in Chapter Six. As in Chapter Five, they are delineated according to the audiences for which they are intended, that is, participants or educators focused on pedagogical and school renewal strategies.

Developing a Positive Attitude: Activities for Students

Carousel Graffiti (Activity 1)

Scaffolding for Success (Activity 2)

Scaffolding Minilectures with Human Highlighters (Activity 3)

Finding Numbers (Activity 4)

Reframing (Activity 6)

Story Posters (Activity 8)

Also, the discussion of the KWL process

Developing a Positive Attitude:
Professional Development Activities for Educators

Carousel Graffiti (Activity 1)

Scaffolding for Success (Activity 2)

Scaffolding Minilectures with Human Highlighters (Activity 3)

Finding Numbers (Activity 4)

Identifying the Emotions and Conditions of Being Intrinsically Motivated (Activity 5)

Reframing (Activity 6)

Using the Multiple Intelligences to Learn (Activity 7)

Story Posters (Activity 8)

Blue Skies (Activity 9)

Examples and Indicators of a Successful School (Activity 10)

Metaphorical Ecosystems (Activity 11)

Creating Time for Collaboration (Activity 12)

Creating a Statement of Purpose for a Schoolwide Instructional Leadership Cadre (Activity 13)

Establishing Norms for Teamwork (Activity 14)

Roundtable Dialogue on Change (Activity 15)

Also, the discussions of the KWL process and of ways to help students attribute their success to capability, effort, and knowledge

Chapter Seven

Enhancing Meaning

. . . now the eyes of my eyes are opened.
E. E. CUMMINGS

Of all the challenges we face as educators, student indifference to carefully developed plans for learning is especially disheartening. One thing, however, is certain. For learning to matter to students it must hold meaning. Meaning is the portal to our hearts and minds, to the "eyes of our eyes." This chapter examines an essential question: What is meaning? In addition, it provides examples of learning experiences that students and teachers with whom the authors have worked have consistently found compelling.

One way to think about meaning is as the ordering of information in ways that provide basic understanding. For example, when we say the word *castle*, we know it means a large fortified residence. When our telephone number is in a listing, we can discern it from others. This kind of meaning contributes to our awareness of how things operate or are defined but in a way that does not deeply touch us. In the words of Whitehead (1979), this is "inert knowledge," sometimes necessary but often of little emotional importance.

When meaning provides a connection or pattern that links our perceptions to important goals or questions, it intensifies motivation for *all* of us because there is obvious relevance. This deeper meaning accesses strong feelings that are intertwined with the ways in which we have been socialized in our families, communities, ethnic affiliations, genders, and so forth. Thus, even though, as philosopher Susanne Langer (1942) has posited, there is a basic and pervasive human need to invest meaning in one's world, to search for and find significance everywhere, this meaning cannot be separated from who we are as cultural beings. Nor can it be separated from our sense of purpose. Across many cultures, achieving purpose is fundamental to a satisfying life (Csikszentmihalyi and Csikszentmihalyi, 1988).

To exalt the significance in students' lives, to assist students in realizing and enhancing what is truly important in their communities and world, educators generally rely on language. Language can serve as a powerful mediator between deep meanings, awareness, and expression. But it is not the only mediator. There appear to be deeper structures in human beings that process meaning (Caine and Caine, 1991). These connections are made through creative, artistic, spiritual, and manual experiences involving music, dance, theater, the visual arts, meditation, and service to others. Creative and contemplative forms of cognition contribute in pivotal ways to students' interest in and interpretation of opportunities to learn. In essence, they help students experience harmony in their feelings, thoughts, intentions, and actions. This fusion of feeling, wishing, and thinking has been described as *flow* (Csikszentmihalyi, 1997), *being in the zone,* or at times as *ecstasy.*

Flow is the feeling and concentration that often emerge when a musician is playing a challenging score, a weaver is designing a complex tapestry, or athletes are experiencing a closely contested athletic competition. But flow can also occur while we are reading an appealing book or having a deep conversation with an old friend. In such activities we feel totally absorbed. Often we are in a state of exhilaration in which time quickly passes.

Flow occurs in learning when the students' goals are desired and clear, feedback is relevant, and the level of challenge is in balance with the required skills or knowledge. A visual representation of this phenomenon might be a student absorbed in creating a photographic journey of her neighborhood or solving a compelling math problem. Because flow can be found across cultures, it may be a sense that humans have developed in order to recognize patterns of actions that are worth preserving and transmitting over time (Massimi, Csikszentmihalyi, and Delle Fave, 1988). When it occurs as part of the process of learning, it makes learning an end in itself. Students who experience flow have not only a better chance of learning but also a better chance of wanting to learn more. All of the activities that follow in this chapter are structured to elicit flow in the learner.

Flow requires *engagement* on the part of the student, an action that might involve searching, evaluating, constructing, creating, or organizing some kind of learning material into new or better ideas, memories, skills, values, feelings, understandings, solutions, or decisions. Critical to engagement are the voices of the students and teacher in dialogue with one another, creating meaning as they develop and meet a learning *challenge*. This challenge often has a goal-like quality, such as solving a problem or completing a project, and requires some degree of capacity, skill, or knowledge on the part of the student. At its core, motivating instruction is the co-creation by teachers and students of challenging learning experiences in engaging formats about relevant topics. The following activities are designed to serve this aspiration.

Use Metaphors and Stories to Encourage Different Perspectives and Deepen Relevance and Meaning

Metaphors allow us to create meanings with students and educators in ways that are often not possible through academic language. For example, to say that being the principal of a large high school is enormously challenging is logically clear, but to say that being the principal of a large high school may at times give you the feeling you're steering the *Titanic* adds insight and expands meaning to a deeper and more emotional level. When we encourage students to find and use their own metaphors, they not only build their own knowledge but contribute additional perspectives to classroom dialogue and learning. Such was the case when one of the authors asked high school students to create metaphors to sum up the Revolutionary War, and one of them responded, "Peewee's Big Adventure."

Metaphors may be illustrated as well as written. At leadership institutes, for example, we have asked principals to share a metaphorical illustration of themselves as administrators as part of their initial introductions. At the end of a class period we have asked students to draw a metaphorical illustration of a concept that the class has studied. To illustrate the concept of blame, for example, one student drew a desert oasis with poisoned water and another sketched a pin in search of a balloon.

Stories are a way for people to give meaning to their lives. Ask anyone to tell a favorite family story or how he or she celebrated birthdays as a child, and you may gain personal understanding of that individual that exceeds the abstract principles of textbook psychology. When people tell stories about what matters to them, their authentic voice becomes discernible, and they are able to shape a *whole* that gives understanding to the particular (Shor, 1992). Whether the issue is an academic problem, a political event, or a childhood memory, when people tell how it mattered in their family, their community, or in their world, their narrative provides a context for the fundamental desire to make meaning.

Activity 1. Where I'm From

PURPOSE

To examine how personal metaphors, poems, and stories provide unique perspectives and enhance the meaning and understanding of events; to share unique perspectives about our lives and enhance the meaning of particular events.

TIME

One hour.

FORMAT

Individuals and large group.

MATERIALS

The poem "Where I'm From."

PROCESS

Step 1. Read George Ella Lyon's poem "Where I'm From," out loud with participants (Exhibit 7.1). Note that some poems use a hook, such as a repeating line, to "link the poem forward" so it builds momentum.

Step 2. Ask participants to use the line "I am from" (or to create another phrase) to think about their past. Ask them to write lists like the lists of details that Lyon remembers about her past. They may share their memories as they think, if they wish. They can try to make the lists sound like home, using the names and languages of home, family, neighborhood. They can let sounds, smells and languages emerge—for example, bubbles of chicken fat on hot soup, pink tights crusted with rosin. They might use the following list as a guide.

Exhibit 7.1. Where I'm From.

Where I'm From

George Ella Lyon

I am from clothespins, from Clorox and carbon-
    tetrachloride.
I am from dirt under the back porch.
(Black, glistening
it tasted like beets.)
I am from the forsythia bush,
the Dutch elm
whose long gone limbs I remember
as if they were my own.

I am from fudge and eyeglasses,
    From Imogene and Alafair.
I'm from the know-it-alls
    And the pass-it-ons,
from perk up and pipe down.
I'm from He restoreth my soul
    With a cottonball lamb
    And ten verses I can say myself.

I'm from Aretemus and Billies' Branch,
fried corn and strong coffee.
From the finger my grandfather lost
    to the auger
the eye my father shut to keep his sight.
Under my bed was a dress box
spilling old pictures,
a sift of lost faces
to drift beneath my dreams.
I am from those moments—
snapped before I budded—
leaf-fall from the family tree.

(Continued)

Exhibit 7.1. Where I'm From. (*Continued*)

Excerpts from student poems written after reading Lyon's poem:

I am from bobby pins, doo rags, and
    wide tooth combs.
I am from prayer plants that lift their
    stems
and rejoice every night.

I am from chocolate cakes and deviled
    eggs
from older cousins and hand-me-downs
to "shut-ups" and "sit-downs."

I am from Genesis to Exodus,
Leviticus, too.
church to church, pew to pew
I am from a huge family tree that begins
with dust
and ends with me.

Source: Christensen, 1997, pp. 22–23. Used by permission.

PROMPTS FOR DETAILS

- Items found inside whatever you called "home" when you were a child (for example, bobby pins, stacks of newspapers, discount coupons for a Mercedes—you can use your imagination as well as your memory)
- Items found in your yard if you had one (for example, hoses coiled like green snakes, dog bones, broken rakes)
- Items found in your neighborhood (for example, the corner grocery store, the "home-base" tree)
- Names of relatives, especially ones that link you to your past (for example, Uncle Charlie and Aunt Selma)
- Sayings (for example, "If I told you once . . .")
- Names of foods and dishes that recall family gatherings (for example, matzoh ball soup, black-eyed peas, tamales)
- Names of places you kept your memories (for example, diaries, boxes, the family Bible)

Step 3. Ask participants to share their lists out loud as everyone brainstorms. Once everyone has specific lists of words, phrases, and names, participants begin writing, using a phrase like "I am from . . ." to weave their poems together. They end the poem with a line or two that ties their past to their present, that ties them to their family history. For example, Lyon ends her poem with "Under my bed was a dress box/spilling old pictures, . . . I am from those moments. . . ."

Step 4. After participants have written their first drafts, they join in a *read around* to share poems. As they listen, they write comments about each reader's piece. Ask them to "pull out a piece of paper, write the name of the reader, then as each person reads, write what you liked about the poem. Be specific. Write down what words or phrases made the poem work. Did the writer use a list? A metaphor? Humor?")

Step 5. Participants sit in a circle, and each person reads his or her final poem. After each poem is read, participants raise their hands to comment on what they liked about it. The writer calls on people to speak.

Source: This activity was created by Linda Christensen, coeditor of *Rethinking Our Classrooms: Teaching for Equity and Justice* (1997). The website for further information is www.rethinking schools.org.

Use Thought-Provoking Questions and Critical Thinking to Facilitate Student Engagement and Learning

John Dewey (1933) wrote that thinking itself is questioning. If teachers and students are to engage realistically in the construction of knowledge, they must be capable of thinking about information in ways that transform it into new knowledge. In many instances this transformation occurs when thought-provoking questions prompt critical thinking and reflection about contradictions between what is known and what is presented. This critical questioning stimulates students and teachers to use their own information, perspectives, and experience to become involved, deepen learning, and transform ideas and concepts into new meanings. Most definitions of critical thinking find that it involves the actions of analyzing, inferring, synthesizing, applying, evaluating, comparing, contrasting, verifying, substantiating, explaining, and hypothesizing (Beyer, 1987).

Unfortunately, there is research to show that fewer than 5 percent of teacher questions request students to think critically and that the frequency of student-generated questions is infinitesimally low, averaging 0.11 per hour per student in classrooms (Dillon, 1988). Moreover, most of those questions seek only factual answers. As educators we need procedures that challenge us and our students to pose relevant, thought-provoking questions more frequently.

Alison King (1994) has developed an approach we ourselves have found very effective. Once learned, this procedure can become a classroom thinking strategy that students can use with their teacher, independently, or in peer groups. The teacher provides students with a written set of question starters, or *stems,* such as, "What would happen if . . .?" and, "How does . . . apply to everyday life?" Students then use these generic questions to guide them in formulating their own questions pertaining to a passage of material or class discussion on any given topic. Exhibit 7.2 contains a list of question stems that students use by filling in the blanks with information relevant to the subject at hand. The critical thinking skills these questions elicit are also listed.

To the list in Exhibit 7.2 we would also add our adaptation of five question types that Paul (1990) associates with Socratic dialogue.

1. *Clarifying:* What do you mean by . . . ? Could you give me an example?
2. *Probing for assumptions:* What are you assuming when you say . . . ?
3. *Probing for reasons and evidence:* How do you know that . . . ? What are your reasons for saying . . . ?
4. *Seeking other perspectives:* What might someone say who believed that . . . ? What is an alternative viewpoint for . . . ?
5. *Probing for consequences:* Because of . . . what might happen?

Activity 2. Fishbowl Questioning Procedure

PURPOSE

To examine and strengthen participants' understanding of an issue by using thought-provoking questions; to practice the use of thought-provoking questions and realize their value for achieving deeper understanding and multiple perspectives about relevant issues.

TIME

Thirty minutes.

Exhibit 7.2. Guides for Thought-Provoking Questions.

Generic Question	Specific Thinking Skill Induced
What is another example of . . . ?	Application
How could . . . be used to . . . ?	Application
What would happen if . . . ?	Prediction; hypothesizing
What are the strengths and weaknesses of . . . ?	Analysis; inference
What is . . . analogous (or similar) to	Creating analogies and metaphors
What do we already know about . . . ?	Activating prior knowledge
How does . . . affect . . . ?	Analysis of relationship
How does . . . relate to what we learned before?	Activating prior knowledge
Explain why . . . or Explain how . . .	Analysis
What is the meaning of . . . ?	Analysis
Why is . . . important?	Analysis of significance
What is the difference between . . . and . . . ?	Compare-contrast
How are . . . and . . . similar?	Compare-contrast
How does . . . apply to everyday life?	Application to real world
What is a possible argument against . . . ?	Rebuttal argument
What is the best . . . and why?	Evaluation and identifying evidence
What are some possible solutions to the problem of . . . ?	Synthesis of ideas
How do you think . . . would see the issue of . . . ?	Taking other perspectives
What do you think causes . . . ? Why?	Analysis of relationship
Do you agree or disagree with . . . ? Support your answer.	Evaluation and identifying evidence

Source: King, 1994, p. 24. Reprinted by permission of Jossey-Bass, a Wiley company.

FORMAT

Small and large group simultaneously.

MATERIALS

Newsprint and markers.

PROCESS

Step 1. One-third of the large group sits in a circle (the fishbowl) and discusses with the facilitator a relevant topic, using the list of question stems in Exhibit 7.2 to stimulate dialogue. Ask each fishbowl member to choose an appropriate time to extend or deepen the dialogue by using at least one higher-order question. A couple of relevant questions for faculty dialogue are: How do we allow multiple perspectives on change in our school and still maintain a clear and focused direction? and, How can we help our kids and our school more effectively confront and overcome racial prejudice? The rest of the group (the remaining two-thirds) sits in a circle around the fishbowl group. Members of this larger group listen and take notes, recording their own ideas for thought-provoking questions that extend or deepen the discussion. In addition, two people act as scribes, recording material for group memory on newsprint. One scribe records the higher-order questions that are asked. The other is content focused, noting ideas for further consideration.

Step 2. After the smaller group has had approximately fifteen minutes to discuss the topic, there is a dialogue among all participants, with questions and comments initially coming from the larger group.

Step 3. The facilitator debriefs the group by asking questions like these: What are some of the ways we as educators can work with students to encourage the integration of higher-order questions in academic discourse? What are some of the group's ideas about the *content* discussed that warrant additional examination?

Activity 3. Guided Reciprocal Questioning

PURPOSE

To model and stimulate use of higher-order questions for meetings as well as instructional purposes.

TIME

Thirty minutes.

FORMAT

Dyads or small groups.

MATERIALS

List of question stems and articles or other source materials.

PROCESS

Step 1. Explain that *guided reciprocal questioning* (King, 1994) is a way for students to use thought-provoking questions among themselves in pairs and small groups when discussing any subject matter. After activities such as observing a project presentation, listening to a short lecture, or reading an article or a book, ask students to use the generic question stems and work independently to generate two or three questions based on the material. Next, in pairs or small groups, they engage in peer questioning, taking turns to ask their questions of a partner or small group and to answer the others' questions in a reciprocal manner. This approach encourages a deeper dialogue and helps students check their understanding as well as learn from other students' perspectives.

We applied this procedure, for example, in a class that had just read Ralph Ellison's *Invisible Man.* They agreed that each student would bring along two questions, based on the list in Exhibit 7.2, regarding any aspect of the book that they found applicable to their own lives. Breaking off into pairs, each student placed two questions before his or her partner. One dyad had formulated these questions.

> "How does the last line of the book, 'Who knows but that, on the lower frequencies, I speak for you?' apply to our everyday lives?"

> "What is the 'brotherhood' analogous to in our communities?"

> "The book has many strengths but, from your perspective, what were some of its weaknesses?"

> "Are there examples of invisibility in our school?"

With these questions the students had an opportunity to relate ideas from the novel to their own knowledge and experience. Each had a chance to guide, to some extent, the thinking that occurred. This process provides opportunities to infer, compare, evaluate, and explain, all of which can lead to a fuller awareness and better understanding.

Step 2. Distribute one of your own favorite literary passages or a brief article on some aspect of cultural diversity, teaching and learning, or school renewal. The April 1999 issue of *Educational Leadership,* titled "Race, Class, and Culture," offers many good articles to use with educators. A particular favorite of ours is Joan Montgomery Halford's interview with Ronald Takaki, in which she discusses the direction of multicultural education in the complex racial and ethnic climate of the United States (Takaki, 1999).

Step 3. Ask participants to generate two to three question stems based on the article. Then they form pairs or small groups and engage in peer questioning, taking turns asking their questions of their partner or group and answering each other's questions in a reciprocal manner.

Step 4. Debrief participants by asking them how they might use this exercise in their own work.

Questioning, of course, is not the only way to encourage critical thinking. Beyond the more extensive activities elaborated in the pages that follow, there are numerous learning activities that can stimulate critical thinking. The following list (adapted from materials provided by the Center on Learning, Assessment, and School Structure, 1991) offers a range of performance verbs to inspire the design of tasks that require critical thinking.

Discern a pattern	Infer a relationship
Teach someone	Create a model
Pursue an alternative answer	Disprove a notion
Reveal the limits of a theory	Creatively exhibit findings
Design an experiment	Evaluate a performance
Judge the accuracy of a superficially appealing idea	Explore and report fairly on a controversy
Complete a cost-benefit analysis	Assess the quality of something
Graphically display and illuminate a complex idea	Find common elements in diverse items or ideas
Rate proposals or candidates	Develop (and implement) a plan

For example, a group of science class students might *design an experiment* to *assess the quality* of their school's water supply and *present the results* to the student council. A history class might illuminate a complex idea by having teams of students, recruited from many different student groups, paint murals based on a relevant historical incident. A psychology class might collect and *graphically display data* related to increased or decreased indicators of care for school facilities. Higher-order performance verbs stimulate imaginative problem-solving opportunities that encourage students to develop and apply their own unique perspectives.

Activity 4. Learning Activities That Stimulate Critical Thinking

PURPOSE

To encourage educators across the school to share and develop best practices by using performance verbs; to encourage interdisciplinary dialogue about pedagogy.

TIME
Thirty minutes.

FORMAT
Dyads or small groups.

MATERIALS
List of performance verbs and course syllabi.

PROCESS
Step 1. Ask participants working in interdisciplinary pairs or small groups to review the list of performance verbs presented in the introduction to this activity and then to design tasks for critical thinking and to identify an activity they have done with students that corresponds to one of the ideas in the list. Next, ask participants to think about some content that they will be teaching and with the assistance of others in their group to outline a new idea for teaching that topic, using the performance verbs to prompt imagination.

   Step 2. Ask group members to rearrange themselves in discipline-specific groups to share their ideas. Next, ask the whole group to identify the benefits of working in inter-disciplinary and discipline-specific groups and the ways this method might influence collaborative lesson planning at their schools.

Use Relevant Problems to Facilitate Learning

A *problem* may be broadly characterized as any situation in which a person wants to achieve a goal but for which an obstacle exists (Voss, 1989). If relevant and within the range of an individual's capacity, problems are by definition engaging and challenging. Further, some of the processes people employ to solve problems are to a certain extent culture bound (Hofstede, 1982). Differences in perspectives and social codes influence how people conceive and approach a problem, from decorating a room to solving a dispute. The remarkable variety among students in terms of how they perceive and resolve a problem can contribute to a wonderful learning experience.

   Education has enjoyed a long history of using problem solving as a procedure for learning. The use of ill-structured problems (those not solvable with certainty) and problem posing (Freire, 1970) dates back to ancient times. Today, *problem-based learning* is a widely accepted approach to learning across multiple disciplines (Wilkerson and Gijselaers, 1996).

Although the basic steps used in problem-based learning may vary, they generally constitute a self-directed, constructive learning process. Problem-based learning is characterized by working at understanding and solving real-world problems as a means for students to learn critical thinking, problem-solving skills, and the essential concepts of the particular discipline in which the problem is set. In most instances, methods of questioning or brainstorming with students help to draw forth a relevant problem based on student concerns and interests. Students then immerse themselves in research to learn concepts and develop skills for finding insights and ideas that may contribute to a problem resolution. For example, students may question a popular historical viewpoint and need to become historians themselves, reading primary material and writing their own historical accounts. Or students may distrust the media's presentation of a "social problem" and investigate the issue themselves, through interviews, literature reviews, statistical analysis, and so forth.

Another approach is to place the student *in* a relevant problem. In courses in math or accounting, for example, a problem might be stated in this form: You are the treasurer of a community organization and you are losing *x* amount of money per month. With these assets, liabilities, dues, and so forth, what do you do? In a course in government, social issues, economics, or math a posed problem might state: You are a seventeen-year-old African American female. You have your first automobile accident, for which you are not at fault. Although you have no driving violations your insurance is canceled. Please review your options, using as a part of your investigation actuarial records and predictive statistics.

A problem-posing activity for educators' professional development follows.

Activity 5. Problem Posing Using Personal Challenges

PURPOSE

To help educators recall the potential of problem posing, using professional challenges as a context.

TIME

Thirty minutes.

FORMAT
Triads.

MATERIALS
Newsprint and markers.

PROCESS
Step 1. Ask participants, gathered in triads, to think of a problem or challenge on which they are working. A volunteer from each triad presents to the larger group the problem the triad has selected. Next, group members check for clarity.

Step 2. Once the problem is well understood, a round of suggestions follows (with a scribe listing the suggestions on a sheet of newsprint). Each suggestion begins with the stem, "What might happen if you . . ." Finally, the person who posed the problem originally selects or modifies a suggestion that he or she can use to develop a form of action to guide additional inquiry or experimentation.

Step 3. Ask the participants how they might adapt or expand this exercise for student use.

Use Case Study Methods to Enhance Learning

A *case study* is a narrative of real events that presents provocative questions and situations in a way that compels students and teachers to analyze, deliberate, and then advance informed judgments that integrate an array of perspectives and concepts (Shulman and others, 1990). The hallmark of cases is their authenticity. They provide a realistic context for otherwise abstract concepts. Because cases often present dilemmas and are open ended, they tend to stimulate diverse reactions in and propositions from a group.

The case study method enhances meaning and is ideal for motivating, culturally responsive teaching for the reason that it fosters "an ethos of critical inquiry that encourages multiple interpretations, conflicting opinions, and equal participation" (Mesa-Bains and Shulman, 1994, p. 7). Further, especially when the situation is someone else's, the case study produces this effect in a manner that permits students in classrooms and teachers in professional development courses to be more open and less defensive. With compelling cases participants can share uncertainty as well as knowledge, because thorny problems do not yield to glib resolutions. When individuals collectively face a relevant story or predicament with an opportunity to learn something important, solidarity often emerges. The ethos of inquiry—a group spirit that is not limited to opinions but that also involves imagination and vision—both results from and mediates this process.

As in our discussion of the previous procedures in this chapter, our goals are to be specific enough about the ways to use case studies that you can make use of this method in your own setting, and to offer guidelines that are general enough to work in different contexts. Most practitioners are dogmatic about only one thing with this method: having a thorough understanding of the case and its nuances before using it (Mesa-Bains and Shulman, 1994).

We recommend reading a case a few times so you can see if it merits selection by meeting such criteria as relevance, authenticity, narrative strength, and complexity. Some questions to reflect on as you read a case follow.

- What might be learned from using this case?
- What might be the different ways to interpret this case?
- What might participants find culturally and personally relevant about this case?
- Will participants be able to construct principles and applications from this case?

Please keep these questions in mind as you read the case in Activity 6, which was composed to stimulate the discussion and application of ideas in this book. Finally, note that individually or collaboratively, students and teachers in professional development situations are a great resource for constructing cases.

Activity 6. Case Study

PURPOSE
To understand the benefits of case study as a teaching strategy by applying learning from a professional development institute.

TIME
Forty-five minutes.

FORMAT
Individuals and small groups.

MATERIALS

A case study and a discussion outline.

PROCESS

Step 1. Distribute copies of the Ben Happier case study given at the end of this activity. (The names of persons and schools in all our case studies are pseudonyms.) Then explain the goals of the case study activity. Goals you might consider discussing include the following.

- To increase understanding of how to improve instruction, with particular attention to the four conditions for supporting the motivation of all students.
- To analyze and explore multiple perspectives on the issues found in the case.
- To improve understanding of multicultural issues—bias, fear of conflict, parental mistrust, creating community among diverse students—as they relate to teaching.

Step 2. Ask participants to free-write for a couple of minutes about issues that come to mind after reading the case, putting their pencils to paper in a flow of consciousness and keeping their pencils in motion at all times, even if they only make squiggles until thoughts emerge. This technique can help focus attention and is quite effective with diverse students—especially those whose attention might otherwise wander. After free-writing, participants will be prepared to offer reflective comments.

Step 3. Ask participants to talk with a partner for few minutes about the content of their free-writing, that is, their ideas on the key issues in the case. Then request individual responses. Ask each participant to remark about one element she or he felt was important in the case and record these elements on a piece of newsprint or chalkboard so everyone can see them. This lets everyone understand, before discussion begins, that there is a range of interpretations.

Step 4. Distribute a discussion outline, which might include questions like these.

CASE STUDY QUESTIONS

- What are some of Ben's strengths?
- What attitudes does Ben have and what actions has he taken that may increase tension and separation among his students?
- How might Ben's teaching suppress motivation to learn?
- What ideas in particular have you learned from our work together that might be of genuine assistance to Ben?
- What could Ben do to improve the sense of community among his students?
- If you were to help Ben transform his approach to teaching, where and how would you start?

- How might the school as a whole benefit from what you have learned about school renewal and job-embedded professional development?
- What would you say to Ben if he were to ask you to observe his classroom? (This question might be developed into a role-playing exercise.)

During the discussion, the kinds of questions the facilitator asks can serve different purposes—for example, to encourage further analysis, challenge an idea, mediate between conflicting views, and guide people to generate principles and concepts and to apply them. Creating a discussion outline for the case study and being open to addressing questions that participants offer keep the case study process flowing and relevant.

With case studies the pattern of learning usually moves from reflection and analysis to the surfacing of concepts and principles to the development of possible solutions and the application of action strategies to the real-world context. However, we have also used an approach in which, instead of distributing discussion questions, we draw three columns on a board or piece of newsprint. In the first column, we ask participants to delineate key issues. In the second column we ask participants to phrase key issues as researchable questions. And in the third column, we identify with participants resources for investigating research questions. This works especially well when you are teaching a course in which learners have an opportunity to select a question and research it.

Step 5. How a case study discussion is closed is critical. Many cases do not result in *the* answer or in a confident resolution. Nevertheless, you should provide some opportunity for people to reflect on what they have learned, to raise additional questions or unresolved thoughts, and to make plans for action. Here are some suggested approaches to closing a case study (Hutchings, 1993):

- Ask participants to spend some time writing answers to such questions as these: What new insights did you gain from this case study and its discussion? What new ideas would you like to try?
- Ask participants to brainstorm insights, personal changes in thinking, or new areas to explore as a result of the case study.
- Go around the group, and ask each person to provide one insight, question, lesson, change, or intuition that has emerged as a result of this process.

BEN HAPPIER CASE STUDY

Ben Happier is a second-year European American teacher at Jefferson High School, a large, ethnically diverse, low-income school in suburban Chicago. The student population is largely African American and Latino. Ben previously taught for two years in an upper-middle-class suburb in which the largest student group was European American and in which students were presumed to be similar in terms of academic skills and interests. Since joining the staff at Jefferson High, he regards himself as a conscientious teacher with a very challenging job.

Ben teaches language arts. His students seem to be divided between those who show little desire to succeed in school and those who want to earn grades just good enough to pass. A few students are particularly high achievers. Ben's general approach is to try to be fair to everyone and to treat all of his students the same way. He believes that ignoring differences as much as possible creates a classroom with more equal opportunities. Part of Ben's daily concern is to encourage students to be respectful to one another. Students seem to group themselves according to ethnicity and their interest in academic success. At times the different groups become hostile toward each other. Students who vent any inappropriate feelings are sent to after-school detention as punishment.

Given block scheduling, Ben's teaching approach is to use short lectures followed by short general discussions and silent reading. He borrows many videos from the library and frequently uses them so that those students who haven't read the assigned novels can at least understand the stories from watching videos. He administers a weekly quiz, which is graded and returned to students. When 70 percent of the class has completed the weekly assignment (answering questions at the back of a textbook chapter and handing them in), he rewards the class with an opportunity to watch a classic American movie such as *Gone with the Wind* or *Star Wars*. Most of his classes get to view these films and look forward to seeing them. Ben feels he has achieved a workable truce with his students and has made the classroom tolerable. However, on the language arts portion of a statewide standardized English test, his students have been scoring well below what he had expected. A few of his colleagues assure him that because so many students have limited motivation, he should not feel overly concerned.

One day during Ben's fourth-period class, which meets just after lunch, a group of students speaking loudly in the back of the room continued to do so even after Ben asked for their cooperation. Ben walked to the back of the room and spoke with them personally, requesting their attention so class could begin. They quieted but resumed speaking loudly as soon as he reached the front of the room. Ben again asked for their cooperation but without success. He wrote a discipline referral and asked the four students to report to the principal's office.

The next day Ben was called to the principal's office. Four angry parents were demanding an explanation for their children's discipline referral. They told Ben that their children had nearly given up on language arts because it was so boring to them. They also told Ben that word had it that the only time he paid attention to anyone was when the person was talking out of turn. The principal nervously suggested that Ben might benefit from two upcoming professional development seminars, "Ten Quick Ways to Capture Student Attention," and "Classroom Management for the Urban High

School." He assured the parents that he and Ben would discuss the merits of these opportunities.

Ben was insulted and angry that the principal implied that Ben's teaching was inadequate and that he did so in front of parents. He thought of quitting but was afraid he would not find an equivalent teaching position. Reluctantly, he sought the advice of a colleague known for her academic success and positive relationships with a broad range of students.

Activity 7. Case Study That Exemplifies the Motivational Framework

PURPOSE

To examine what an elementary, middle, or high school classroom might look like when it is implementing the four conditions of the Motivational Framework for Culturally Responsive Teaching; to deepen understanding of the framework by applying knowledge about the four motivational conditions.

TIME

Twenty minutes.

FORMAT

Individuals and large group.

MATERIALS

A case study, such as one of the sample case studies.

PROCESS

Ask participants to read one of the case studies given at the end of this activity and to be prepared to answer one (or more) of the following questions.

CASE STUDY QUESTIONS

- From your perspective, what are the best examples of how the teacher in the case study applies the four conditions of the Motivational Framework for Culturally Responsive Teaching?
- If you were the teacher, what else might you do?
- If you were a coach to the teacher, how might you provide support?
- What insights, personal challenges, or new areas to explore and learn about occur to you as a result of analyzing this case study?

BEVERLY HILLMAN CASE STUDY

Beverly Hillman is a fourth-year social studies teacher at Roosevelt Middle School, a large demographically mixed school in Orlando. The school is trying to recognize the talents of all students and create the motivational conditions to support their success. She regards herself as a conscientious teacher with a very challenging job.

Beverly's classes are two and one-half hours long because of Roosevelt Middle School's block teaching schedule. She begins each class with fifteen-minute cooperative base groups. The purpose for the group meetings varies, but a primary goal is to ensure respectful and productive peer support for all students. Beverly has worked with the students so that each base group member always has a clearly defined role—for example, facilitator, timekeeper, recorder, reporter, or process observer. Beverly has also worked with students to create consciousness about agreed-upon norms for collaboration and, in particular, positive ways to encourage all group members to participate in base group dialogue. Today's base group task is to solve problems that students may have had with last night's homework. Yesterday's task was to share notes from the previous class session and identify three key insights.

Beverly organizes all of her teaching around problems and issues. For example, seventh-grade students are studying how cities develop. The students have studied cities in ancient African kingdoms, Europe, and Asia. They have taken trips to city hall and have seen the city council in action. In fact, the mayor has visited their classroom. Groups of students have worked on solutions to problems specific to their city. These problems included the city's budget deficit, homelessness, the poor condition of some of the roads, and crime. They have written letters to the editors of local papers and presented their recommendations to different community representatives and task forces.

Each student is currently becoming an "expert" in some aspect of urban living. For example, students are studying the city's architecturally unique buildings, bridges, urban planning, recycling programs, and unique schools, and the contributions and challenges of local artists. Every Tuesday, instead of coming to class, students work in teams with a community mentor who is helping them learn about their area of expertise.

Students are working toward an exhibition night so that they can demonstrate to their parents, mentors, and other community members what they have learned. They will create multimedia presentations that use and develop strengths in their multiple intelligences. They are also keeping a process folio that chronicles their experiences, research, and contributions. Twice a month, Beverly meets with each student to review his or her process folio and to refine and update individual goals.

Students understand Beverly's scoring rubric, which is used for all their assignments. A 4 means "Outstanding job! You could teach this"; 3 means "Good. You are almost there"; 2 means "Practice some more. You can do it on your own with more attention to detail"; 1 means "Ask for help so that once you practice some more, you are going to really understand." For their demonstrations of what they have learned about their city, students will be rated on criteria such as "knows information in depth," "speaks clearly and is easy to understand," "uses visuals and other props," "demonstrates clear organization with introduction, major points, and summary," "stays focused," and "uses creativity in style of presentation." Beverly hopes that assessment will guide learning as well as assess it. She is hopeful about students' accomplishments because she has found that when students learn in ways that are natural to them, they experience increased academic achievement and confidence in themselves as learners and as people.

Regularly, Beverly talks or meets with parent volunteers who have been helping to coordinate the community mentor program. Parent volunteers also work with students to produce a monthly newsletter related to community issues and their learning experiences. Along with students, parents are currently working with a technology specialist to send a state-of-the-art newsletter worldwide on the Internet, using imaginative applications.

Next year, when these students are in the eighth grade, they will do a presentation for seventh graders to share what they have learned and to encourage the children in the new seventh grade to reach beyond their dreams.

Bill Hollins Case Study

Bill Hollins is a second-grade teacher at New Visions, a demographically mixed urban school. The school is trying to recognize the talents of all students and to create the motivational conditions to support their success. Bill is currently in his ninth year of teaching and regards himself as a conscientious teacher with a very challenging job.

Bill starts each school day at his classroom door with a personal greeting for each student. After putting their name cards in the attendance bucket, students sit in a circle for "class meeting." Bill always uses this time to recall the previous day's learning focus; recall significant activities, events, ideas, values, and assignments; and use group responses, calls, and claps to heighten the level of group participation and learning. In addition, he involves the whole group in acts of remembering, affirming, and valuing individual and group learning. Sometimes he initiates a group activity that helps students know more about each other and learn to work together well. Students play name games, use inside-outside circles to talk to each other, talk about how to handle put-downs from other people, tell a group story to learn to rephrase what the speaker before them said in order to become a good listener, and make gumdrop inventions to practice cooperative group skills. As much as possible, Bill shares the spotlight with his students so that each student has a chance to lead a class meeting. He uses the term *griot* (pronounced gre-o) for class meeting student leaders. Griot is a West African name for an oral performance expert. On Mondays, Bill reviews the class agreements, which are focused on self-respect and respect for others, responsibility (taking care of oneself and others), imagination (imagining goals, planning for them, and being persistent), effort, and humor that is positive.

At the end of the day, Bill asks students to make a circle, close their eyes, and visualize their day and their completed tasks. He then asks students to talk about what they learned that they are going to talk about at home or what they hope to learn more about because of something that happened today. Students write or draw their ideas on a card that becomes a door pass they give to Bill as they leave. This also ensures that Bill can say a personal good-bye to each student.

Bill also asks students to accept responsibility for classroom organization and management. They assume such roles as receptionists, timekeepers, couriers, distributors of work and materials, collectors of work, room inspectors, pet and plant care specialists, and board maintenance people. They take on a role for five days at a time. Students evaluate their performance in these roles through completing goal sheets, journal entries, and pre- and postevaluations.

Just as he believes in creating a safe and responsible environment for learning to occur, Bill believes in strong, effective support for academic learning. He uses small-group learning, peer tutoring, and heterogeneous groupings that resemble families. In addition, word tasks and other instruction provide students with opportunities for creative expression, for learning about the culture and traditions of all of the people in the United States—and the world—and for exploring their own community. Because the students like it when Bill plays music while they work, Bill regularly does so.

Bill is also creative with reading and writing. He has had students slide around the room to demonstrate how some letters and sounds blend together. Students then slide letters and sounds together. Bill also uses choral reading, singing, call and response techniques, demonstrations, and performances, and kinesthetic instruction. This is good for all students, but it is especially helpful to his students who are new to the English language.

To help students appreciate and comprehend literature, Bill involves them in writing, acting, and drawing some of the ways they are alike and different from a character in a book. Students have also written letters from themselves to a character in a book—and then they have pretended that the character writes back. Students have also written about something that they have made up about a character that others don't know. And at times students have pretended to be different characters, and they have written, drawn, and role-played these characters' different perspectives on a topic. Regardless of what students are learning and doing, they can see their work proudly displayed around the room.

When it comes to assessment, Bill works hard to provide opportunities for students to demonstrate what they have learned, with a clear understanding, up front, of what success looks like. In his scoring rubric 4 means "Outstanding job! You could teach this"; 3 means "Good. You are almost there"; 2 means "Practice some more. You can do it on your own with more attention to detail"; 1 means "Ask for help so that once you practice some more, you are going to really understand." For storytelling, students were recently rated on criteria such as "knows information in depth," "speaks clearly and is easy to understand", "uses visuals and other props," "demonstrates clear organization with introduction, major points, and summary," "stays focused," and "uses creativity in style of presentation." Before they began creating and telling their stories, students worked with Bill to understand what each of the criteria looked like. In all subjects, Bill tries to use real-life situations that are connected to students' experiences to help students create a product or demonstration. This approach guides learning as well as assesses learning. Bill has found that when students learn in ways that are natural to them, they experience increased academic achievement and confidence in themselves as learners and as people.

Source: Aspects of both cases adapted from Ladson-Billings, 1994; Shade, Kelly, and Oberg, 1997.

Use Simulations and Role-Playing to Enhance Meaning Through Realistic Contexts

When students experience perspectives, ideas, skills, and situations approximating authentic instances of life, they have an opportunity to enhance the meaning of what they are learning and to become more proficient. *Role-playing* is acting out a possible situation by personifying another individual or by imagining another scene or set of circumstances or by doing both. *Simulation exercises and games* are activities in which a whole group is involved, with students assuming different roles as they act out a prescribed scenario. These scenarios allow students to acquire or put into practice particular concepts or skills. Simulations often immerse students in another social reality, providing them the opportunity to experience what might otherwise remain abstractly expressed in textual materials—for example, power, conflict, or discrimination.

Because role-playing has broad applicability across subject areas and accommodates multiple perspectives, it can be a potent strategy to engage all students. The main goal of role-playing or simulation is to create an experience that genuinely involves the students' intellect, emotions, and physical senses so that this experience is as realistic as possible.

Role-playing gives students the opportunity to think in the moment, question their own perspectives, respond to novel or unexpected circumstances, and consider different ways of knowing. It is an excellent procedure for developing empathy, for example, by taking on the role of a person who has experienced a particular form of social injustice. When students have a chance to reverse roles, so that they find themselves in positions that conflict with their own perspectives (for example, when a student takes on the role of a teacher, and vice versa), they have a reason to think and feel in new ways. Role-playing is an excellent procedure for shifting perspectives, adding insights, and starting conversations that before the introduction of this strategy would have been unimaginable.

The following are some guidelines for conducting effective simulations and role-plays.

Make sure the simulation or role-play is a good fit. Nothing is worse than a role-play that feels contrived or trivializes an important issue.

Plan ahead. Students should be familiar and moderately proficient with the concepts or skills that will be practiced during the activity. Do they have a fair knowledge of the cultural or personal roles they may assume? If they are uncomfortable, can they excuse themselves or observe until they are more at ease about playing a role?

Be relatively sure students understand the roles and the scenario before you begin. Often it is helpful to write a script with a description of each role's attitudes, experiences, and beliefs. The students use the script to deepen their familiarity with their own role. For example, the role of new student might be described this way: "I'm a new student in the school. I come from a much poorer neighborhood than most of my new classmates. Although I am usually self-reliant, I feel intimidated by the way others talk and dress. . . ."

Set aside enough time for the simulation and the discussion that follows. The discussion and analysis are as important as the simulation itself. What are some different perspectives, reactions, and insights? What has not been dealt with that still needs attention? Have our goals for learning been accomplished? How do we know?

When role-playing seems potentially embarrassing or threatening to students, it is often helpful for the teacher to model the first role-play and discuss it. This may alleviate some initial hesitation and allow students to see how competent adults use potential imperfections and mistakes to learn.

Freeze the action during a role-play when you need to. A pause in the action can serve many purposes, giving students time, for example, to critique a perspective, to explore their reactions to a poignant comment, to make beneficial suggestions to the actors, and to relieve tension.

Plan follow-up activities for simulations and role-plays. This is extremely important. For example, a compelling next step after a role-play could be to create action plans to use what has been practiced and discussed.

For many students and teachers, simulations may be the only way to enter worlds apparently too distant or to try out actions initially too uncomfortable. In some instances this procedure may not only enhance meaning but also nurture courage and the ability to act with new understanding.

Activity 8. Teacher, Parent, and Student Role-Play

PURPOSE

To provide students with an opportunity to practice and apply new learning under near authentic circumstances and to make meaning from multiple perspectives; to provide educators with an opportunity to practice role-playing and to apply personal perspectives and ideas from this book in order to work more effectively with parents and students.

TIME

Forty-five to sixty minutes.

FORMAT

Small groups of four participants.

MATERIALS

Cards that explain the roles.

PROCESS

Step 1. After participants have divided into groups of four, ask each person in each group to choose one of four possible roles to carry out—teacher, parent, student, or observer. Explain that the role-play scenario is a conference being held at the teacher's request to intervene in the apparent decline in a student's academic performance. Distribute a card to each participant with a description of his or her role, attitude, experiences, and beliefs, as shown in the following examples. Explain to all participants that the observer facilitates role-playing and its consequent discussion.

ROLE DESCRIPTIONS

Observer's role. You are both the observer and the leader of this role-play. Make sure everyone has a chance to clearly understand his or her role before you begin the role-play. Participants mutually decide on subject area, grade level, and names to be used. Everyone is welcome to use notes. Help all participants stay focused on their roles and involved in the discussion that follows. Once the role-play begins, participants have about fifteen minutes to resolve the issue the role-play deals with. If the issue remains unresolved after fifteen minutes and no progress seems to be occurring, suspend the process and begin the discussion.

Teacher's role. You've seen this situation develop before—a highly capable student from a low-income, ethnic minority community, who as the quarter progresses experiences diminished interest and boredom in class, increasingly poor performance, and declining grades. This is a subject (for example, math, science, languages, writing, or music) in which student effort, regardless of natural skill, is essential.

You are worried and frustrated when this student, who demonstrated such strong potential at the beginning of the quarter, falls behind. You attribute what is happening to the fact that the student doesn't regularly do homework, is cavalier about in-class group work, is careless during independent practice time, and doesn't diligently study for tests.

You are hopeful because this student is socially skillful and articulate in class discussions and follows through with assignments that don't take a great deal of preparation.

You are concerned because the student seems to have other priorities and doesn't seem to "get it" that reasonable effort is needed simply to keep up in this course.

You frequently do not grade assignments, but the few you have marked for this student have received poor grades because they've been so incomplete. You want this conference to turn out well. You believe a collaborative effort on the part of the parent, yourself, and the student is necessary. You are prepared to be flexible, but you believe the student and parent have a responsibility to come partway as well.

Student's role. For you, life is very full. You have your job, your friends, and your other subjects—most of which you like better than this one. You have ambivalent feelings about this teacher. Some things you like about the teacher, and some things you don't like. For example, one concern for you is that the teacher, who is from an ethnic group and social class that is different from your own, typically uses examples that have little to do with your experiences and current interests. You see her as "distant" from most of her students.

You believe you are bright, and generally you do participate in the class. The teacher seldom gives feedback on coursework—just a checkmark and an occasional grade. Often the homework is too difficult or too much. Although you generally get it done, you feel it's a waste of your time. In fact, you don't really see how this class is going to matter for you one way or the other.

You view the conference as a hassle, but you'd rather not argue or get tense. However, you know you had better participate and offer your opinions because your parent is there and is very firm about school.

Parent's role. Here you go again—another parent-teacher conference where your child is the problem. You know school is important. You have paid a price for not completing high school yourself. But you believe the quality of teachers was—and still is—very uneven. Some are good, but from your perspective, a lot have been mediocre. They did not understand you or truly seem to care about you as a student, and the same seems to be true for your child. When they speak about caring, their words are often hollow.

Still, you do not want to take sides. You know your child is not perfect. You know your child often does not work up to his or her capability. You want your child to have a better life than you have had, and you believe grades are tied to opportunity.

You are a single parent with two other children. You work in a service job. You often feel overwhelmed and exhausted.

You want the conference to work out, but you don't want to be more stressed by some new task from the teacher because he or she can't keep your child involved. Yet you are willing to listen and might even have a few suggestions of your own.

Step 2. Follow the role-play with a discussion to explore insights, new learning, and the means by which different groups resolved (or did not resolve) the problem. Ask participants what they have learned in this session and from other experiences about the use of role-playing as a teaching and learning procedure.

Step 3. Ask educators to think about a topic they teach that lends itself to a role-play. Ask them to form teams of two. Each team selects one person's topic and thinks through a design for a related role-play. After approximately fifteen minutes, ask for one or two volunteers to share a role-play they hope to facilitate.

Use Imagination and Artistry to Render Meaning and Emotion in Learning

Imagination and artistry are forms of self-expression, responses to compelling interests, reactions to experiences, and the creation of connections between the known and the unknown, the worldly and the spiritual among all people. We all ought to consider artistry as an embedding of art in learning rather than as a separate and frequently disenfranchised experience ("Now we are going to do art!"). As Jamake Highwater (1994) has said, "Knowledge is barren without the capacity for feeling and imagination." Art is a fundamental part of life and learning across cultures. We believe the lack of meaning that is often attributed to academic learning is due to a significant extent to the separation of learning from imagination and artistry.

Imagination and artistry can be used in every subject area. Both processes are open ended and serve as kindling for creative possibilities and academic goals. One teacher, for example, in helping a class of students to prepare for service learning, approached them with the question, "What are the things we most deeply want to contribute to and accomplish in our communities?" After reflecting and then writing and sketching their responses to this question, they agreed to compose a mural depicting the theme of community, contribution, and learning. Using poster paints and a large roll of paper, the students created a mural that covered the bottom of the wall around the entire circumference of the classroom. During the creation of the mural, two of the students took photographs of the process and created a collage from them for the class. Each student wrote a reflective paper discussing the ideas represented in the mural. At the concluding class session, the students, encircled by the mural they created, summarized their responses to the process of creating the mural and of developing its content and made connections between their art and the work they intend to do in their communities. They then set personal goals and developed ways to eventually represent or demonstrate their accomplishments.

A further example of the role of imagination in learning can be found in a science teacher we recall, who was struggling to teach his students systems theory and who decided to work with them to invent games that could teach students in other classes the fundamental concepts and principles of this theory. He told his students that at a minimum, they would need to physically represent the planets and provide a way for participants to imagine, predict, coordinate, and simulate the movement of planets, either along a large cloth version of a solar system or through the use of computer technology. The games were so popular that, annually, the science teacher—in concert with students—develops an interactive solar gallery for parents and community members to explore.

Typically, students more than welcome the invitation to integrate academic work with imagination and artistry. In addition to projects that involve the visual arts, projects that include works of fiction, playwriting, musical composition, songwriting, video making, and other performance art as *essential* components of learning result in some of students' most profound understandings (and memories). There are myriad possibilities, several of which are listed in the section of Chapter Eight titled "Assessment Options Based on Gardner's Multiple Intelligences." An example of using dramatization to encourage the development of literacy skills across content areas (Activity 10) is provided at the conclusion of this section, following a professional development exercise that relies on creative mapping to help representatives of a school community—teachers, administrators, parents, and students—prepare for visits to other schools.

Activity 9. Visitation Maps

PURPOSE

To provide representatives of a school community with an opportunity to imagine and visually represent a visit to another school for developing ideas and engaging in dialogue related to school renewal.

TIME

Forty-five to sixty minutes.

FORMAT

Small groups of four.

MATERIALS

Newsprint, colorful markers, masking tape, and a sample agenda.

PROCESS

Step 1. Distribute a sheet of newsprint and several colorful markers to each group. Explain that the purpose of this exercise is to think through the way a visit to another school might look—from the moment the team of visitors awakes in the morning until it returns home at the end of the day. Explain that the visual representations ought to be as creative as possible and may even verge on the outrageous—as long as they ultimately represent what the team might actually wish to do once it reaches the school. For example, in a rural community, teachers pictured themselves traveling to the host school together via covered wagon equipped with digital technology. They imagined host faculty waiting to greet them with outstretched arms, followed by an introductory meeting that revealed fantastic accomplishments directly related to the visitors' aspirations. As exaggerated as this visitation map may have been, it allowed the educators to imagine the potential of a school visit to forge new relationships and to think through ideas worthy of a *genuine* visitation agenda.

We have found that it is helpful to provide illustrators with a sample agenda like the following to initially stimulate their thinking—even though their own conceptualization of the visit may significantly vary.

SAMPLE AGENDA

- An initial meeting between visiting and host representatives of both schools.
- An *icebreaker* to help representatives from both schools become better acquainted.
- Review and refinement of a preplanned, flexible agenda.
- An opportunity to review a campus portrait of the host school—to understand its vision, accomplishments, and challenges (the campus portrait might, for example, include a school portfolio, slides or a video, photographs, and so forth).
- Dialogue about what the visiting team might wish to know that they might not be able to observe: for example, how was the school's vision created? How does school governance work? How does the host school encourage parent, family, and community involvement? How is service learning facilitated? How do teachers support each other's professional learning? How is conflict mediated?
- Personal tours with student representatives serving as guides.
- Classroom visits.
- Interviews or focus groups with students, parents, media personnel, and so forth to elicit ideas and perspectives of relevance.
- An exit meeting to share what has been learned, discuss emerging interests and ideas, and consider opportunities for ongoing school-to-school interaction.
- A closure activity (for example, everyone might mention one thing he or she intends to recommend or further investigate at his or her own school).

Step 2. Ask the groups to post their maps, gallery-style, around the room. A docent from each group stands by the group's map to point out highlights or to answer questions that viewers (other participants) may have as they spontaneously wander. When participants are called back together as a large group, they consider two questions: What have you learned about school visits? How might you proceed?

Activity 10. Focal Point Performances (FPPs)

PURPOSE

To support diversified student interests and the enhancement of literacy skills across content areas.

TIME

Five minutes per student group.

FORMAT
Small groups of four.

MATERIALS
Literature such as newspaper articles, biographies, stories from different cultures, and portions of textbooks.

PROCESS
Explain to students that the first (or last) five to ten minutes of selected class periods will be reserved for small groups of students to bring a concept to life through a brief dramatic performance. Explain that students will have adequate time to prepare and will be able to sign up to present topics about which they are most interested. Their goal will be to make selected (or assigned) passages from different kinds of literature related to the course come to life through dramatic presentations. Depending on the course, the literature may include biographies, stories, newspaper or journal articles, or sections of a textbook that address key concepts. Explain that the class will appraise the success of each performance, with an opportunity for the performing group to self-assess. The final grade, for which the teacher is ultimately responsible, will incorporate but not be exclusively determined by peer and self-assessment.

We recommend that teacher and students together create approximately five criteria for success, and refine them over time. These expectations for a successful presentation might include: clear identification of the major themes, topics, or points in the material; active participation of all team members; thoughtful organization; interesting content; and creative delivery.

In addition, teachers may wish students to design presentations around resource materials that the students discover. Many teachers report the value of eliciting volunteers to collate presentation resources in a vertical file for ongoing student and teacher reference.

Use Action Research with Students to Investigate and Understand, Apply, or Evaluate a Relevant Interest

Action research is a form of disciplined inquiry used to investigate a problem or question of personal interest for which there is no satisfactory present answer. It is a cyclical process in which educators or students use primary resources and real-world information and data to inform new courses of action. Although such research can lead to valuable insights, results are almost never generalizable because the samples are typically very small. Action research can be conducted in any subject area or across disciplines. Through it, teachers and students come to know that their questions and perspectives matter, and they acquire the skills and knowledge to pursue investigations in a competent and critical manner.

When students are involved in action research, teachers often become co-researchers, acting as colleagues collaborating in the pursuit of knowledge. A popular form of action research involves clarifying the defining characteristics or important features of a concept, event, skill, intervention, or situation for which such characteristics are unknown, in question, or not readily apparent (Marzano, 1992).

In schools and society there are many concepts and events that have an emerging quality or debatable interpretation about which action research can make important distinctions and lead to student and teacher learning and action of social consequence. Examples of current social problems and areas of debate, for example, that students might explore are sexual harassment, welfare reform, immigration, standardized testing, affirmative action, environmental hazards, weapons in school, equality of educational opportunity, and multiculturalism. For teachers, questions might be focused to address student learning and performance, curriculum, instruction, teacher morale, professional development, and parent involvement. Learning to identify a concern, develop a researchable question, collect data, justify findings, and make action-oriented decisions is a powerful motivational force. Such a process is also empowering when, as a result of skillful design and implementation, those performing the research become able to more effectively critique everyday events and perspectives.

Action research can be as simple as raising a question about a school practice and collecting information to answer it or as complicated as applying a statistical test to determine whether the results from an experiment are significant. No matter what the process, action research is disciplined inquiry, a systematic and organized method of obtaining valid evidence.

In Glanz's model (1999), there are four basic steps in action research. We elaborate each of these steps with a research scenario adapted from the work of Grant and Sleeter (1998) of finding out what kids know about other ethnic groups. Many teachers with whom we work find this topic to be relevant because the issue is not *whether* students should learn about other groups, who are already a part of students' daily lives, but *what* the school should do to further develop (or perhaps correct) what students are learning elsewhere. Students are frequently concerned about this topic because of the bias and stereotypes they face as well as those they enact themselves. They are likely to be motivated to carry out this research to inform themselves, to contribute to their school's and community's goals, and ultimately to cement the belief that together we can make a difference (Glickman, 1995).

Step 1. Select a Focus

This step includes three subordinate steps: (1) know what you want to investigate; (2) develop some questions about the area you have chosen; and (3) establish a plan to answer these questions.

> Students in the fifth grade at Walker Elementary School are concerned about the ways they are stereotyped and the ways they may stereotype others. They decide that almost all fifth graders in their school appear to fall into four ethnic groups: African Americans, Chinese Americans, European Americans, and Mexican Americans. They think their class as well as their school would benefit from trustworthy information about how these groups are viewed by the fifth-grade students who do not belong to them. After a number of discussions and brainstorming sessions guided by the question, What information do we need to know and how should we collect it? they decide to use an interview approach to do their research and also to interview one another regarding all the groups identified except the one the person interviewed is a member of. They also agree upon four interview questions and organize them in the following order.

1. Have you had any personal contact with members of different ethnic groups in our school?

2. If I were a visitor from outer space trying to find out more about this school, how would you describe the different ethnic groups that go to school here?

   What have you heard?

   What have you seen?

What has your own personal experience taught you?

3. How certain do you feel the information you have is accurate?

4. Where did you learn most of your information? [*After the student has responded, probe to find out what was learned from each of the following sources.*]

Parents, family

TV

Movies

Books, magazines, comics

School

Friends, classmates

The computer

Music

Step 2. Collect Data

Once you have identified a specific area of interest, created relevant research questions, and agreed on how you plan to answer them, you are ready to collect the information (data) to answer your research questions. Before we return to the Walker Elementary example, let's look at an example of how teachers might proceed. Suppose a group of teachers decides to investigate their school's new math program. They are especially interested in achievement levels and students' attitudes toward math. They might thus agree to base conclusions about the program's effectiveness on data collected about students' achievement and attitudes. They might administer teacher-made or standardized tests, conduct surveys and interviews, or examine portfolios. Other data might be collected as well. They might plan to analyze the data according to meaningful categories such as age, grade level, classroom, participation in the free and reduced-price lunch program (to determine if there is a performance gap between low-income and upper-income students), ethnic affiliation, and gender. They might present their findings using graphs and pie charts.

Let's return now to our student example.

There are forty fifth graders at Walker Elementary. Each one interviews a classmate and organizes his or her interview sheet into the following data groupings.

Yes/No questions

Example   Have you had any personal contact with members of different ethnic groups in our school? *[Ask about one group at a time.]*

Lists

Example   What have you heard?
                     Cliquish
                     Smart
                     Strange food
                     What have you seen?
                       Usually nice to other people

Likert Scale

Example   How accurate do you believe your information is?
                     Very inaccurate   1 2 3   4   5 6   7 Very accurate

Rank Order from Most to Least (1 to 8)

Example   Where did you learn most of your information?
   1.   (Most) parents, family
   2.   (Second most) friends, classmates . . .
   8.   (Least) the computer.

     After the interviews have been completed, the interview sheets are collected and duplicated. They are then distributed to student research teams, which collate the data according to the particular research questions.

Step 3. Analyze and Interpret the Data

Once you have collected the data, the next step is to analyze and interpret them. Based on your analysis, report your findings, discuss your enhanced understanding of some phenomenon, arrive at an actual conclusion or decision, or explain the need for more research and exploration. During this step you describe or summarize the data clearly, identify consistent patterns or themes among the data, discuss and answer your research questions, and when possible, draw conclusions. When standards are applied, such as reliability coefficients or comparisons with national test results, these should be noted and appropriately discussed.

> A few of the important findings in the action research study conducted by Walker Elementary fifth graders were that most fifth graders thought their information about classmates from other ethnic groups was accurate (5.5 average on the Likert scale); the top three sources for information about other ethnic groups were, first, parents and family, second, friends and classmates, and third, TV; and the lists of what students had heard and of what they actually saw were more different than alike. The students concluded that most of them sometimes do stereotype and that they learn these images primarily from their families, other people they know and generally trust, and television.

Step 4. Take Action

You have reached the point where deciding what to do based on your analysis and a conclusion is appropriate. In the case of the new math program, teachers might continue the program as originally established, modify it (for example, by ensuring that lessons are consistent with principles of intrinsic motivation), or disband it. Such decisions can open up new avenues of research because there are new forms of action to examine. This is what we mean when we say that action research is cyclical and ongoing.

Let's return to the example of Walker Elementary School.

> Walker Elementary fifth graders were concerned about the number and kind of stereotypes that appeared to exist among them. They decided to list the most frequently cited stereotypes and then to do more research to understand the history of these views. They also decided to investigate approaches to increasing students' awareness about racism and other kinds of prejudice and to enhancing respect among all student groups. They will share their findings with the student council, with staff at a monthly after-school meeting, and with parents and teachers at a PTA meeting.

Activity 11. Dot Graphing

PURPOSE

To learn an approach to initiating action research for student learning or professional development. The following example focuses on professional development related to school renewal.

TIME

Forty-five minutes.

FORMAT

Individuals and large group.

MATERIALS

Newsprint, markers, and sticky dots.

PROCESS

Step 1. On separate sheets of newsprint, write different questions related to the topic at hand. In this discussion the topic is school renewal. Begin each question with the stem, "To what extent . . ." School renewal questions might include the following.

SCHOOL RENEWAL QUESTIONS

1. To what extent does our school have a shared purpose or vision?

2. To what extent is classroom learning highly motivating and relevant to *all* students?

3. To what extent do we systematically engage in collaborative adult learning?

4. To what extent does our school encourage diverse parents and community members to participate in meaningful ways?

5. To what extent do we have an effective way to negotiate conflict among ourselves?

   Step 2. As each question is written, create a Likert scale along the bottom of the sheet that spans from one to seven (seven is high and one is low), as in the following example.

- To what extent do we have an effective way to negotiate conflict among ourselves?

   1   2   3   4   5   6   7

   Step 3. Distribute as many dots as there are questions to each participant. Then ask participants to come up front and place one dot at the appropriate point along each Likert scale to represent their perspective on that question. Next, post two more sheets of newsprint. At the top of one sheet write "Observations." On a second sheet write "Questions." Ask for two volunteers to be scribes so that the observations and questions that arise can be collected for group memory.

Step 4. Next, ask participants to reflect on the Likert scales and note observations or questions that occur to them. For example, if there is a cluster of dots around the mid-point for question 2 and a cluster of dots around the low end for question 3, participants might ask whether it would help them to develop more motivating learning experiences if they collaborated more or they might observe that they don't really know what teaching looks like in rooms other than their own. Finally, participants examine all the questions and observations they came up with and rephrase them as researchable questions. Given the previous example, a researchable question might be: Can we improve student motivation by collaborating on lesson design using the motivational framework? or, Can regular visits to other people's classrooms inspire more effective teaching in our own classrooms?

Step 5. In teams organized according to interests, participants select a researchable question and work together (ideally, with an action research coach) to shape a research design. Once the large group reconvenes, each small group shares its design, its next steps, and its overall time line.

Additional notes. Action research teams need adequate time and support for their designs. Productive teams meet regularly with an experienced action research coach. In addition, they negotiate clear agreements for tasks team members will perform between meetings. Due to the rigor and duration of such a project, incentives such as college or professional development credits are often appreciated.

Conclusion

This chapter has described several practices that can help teachers create compelling learning experiences with students. But we emphasize once again that powerful and worthwhile learning can never be reduced to a formula or single strategy—no matter how creative or meaningful one believes that strategy to be. There is much subtlety to the order, connections, or patterns each of us needs to make meaning of an experience and to accomplish goals. One of the authors recalls giving a demonstration lesson not too long ago at an urban high school. It was designed with the motivational framework in mind and focused on using creative, small-group presentations to enhance meaning. At the conclusion of the ninety-minute lesson, students put their chairs in a circle, and the demonstration teacher asked them, "What is one word that you might use to describe your experience in this course today?" The words that different students chose complimented and supported the carefully executed lesson plan—until the last student, the person who may have been the most important one to engage, spoke up. This student, a person struggling in several courses, offered the word "weird."

After class ended, the demonstration teacher approached this student. Wondering if he would generalize his assessment to school as a whole, she inquired if weird was a word he would apply to other classes. After he said no, she asked him to help her understand. He explained that for him, science did not fit that description, that in science he knew exactly what to do.

Among the many ways that this information could be interpreted and applied to improve pedagogical practice, the author was clearly reminded of what can happen when "instructional creativity" interferes with another person's way of understanding. So rather than throw out ideas that seemed powerful for many students, she gave serious consideration to how she might provide better scaffolding for students inclined toward different ways of making meaning. The challenge of teaching in a way that matters to *all* students is the challenge of student and teacher voices in constant dialogue with each other.

The following checklist can serve as a guide for teachers and other facilitators of learning as they work to create the conditions in which challenge and engagement contribute to enhancing meaning.

Enhancing Meaning

How does the learning experience engage students in challenging learning that has social merit?

- The teacher encourages all students to learn, apply, create, and communicate knowledge.
  - __ The teacher helps students to activate prior knowledge and to use it as a guide to learning.
  - __ The teacher, in concert with students, creates opportunities for inquiry, investigation, and projects.
  - __ The teacher provides opportunities for students to actively participate in challenging ways when not involved in sedentary activities such as reflecting, reading, and writing.
  - __ The teacher asks higher-order questions of all students throughout a lesson.

___ The teacher elicits high-quality responses from all students.

___ The teacher uses multiple *safety nets* to ensure student success (for example, not grading all assignments, asking students to work with partners, designing cooperative learning experiences).

Describe the evidence:

Activity Guide for Enhancing Meaning

Enhancing Meaning: Classroom Activities for Students

Where I'm From (Activity 1)

Guided Reciprocal Questioning (Activity 3)

Learning Activities That Stimulate Critical Thinking (Activity 4)

Problem Posing Using Personal Challenges (Activity 5)

Case Study (Activity 6)

Role-Play (Activity 8)

Action Research (Activity 10)

Dot Graphing (an approach to initiating action research) (Activity 11)

Also, strategies described in the section on action research and the thought-provoking questions listed in Exhibit 7.2.

Enhancing Meaning: Professional Development Activities for Educators

Where I'm From (Activity 1)

Fishbowl Questioning Procedure (Activity 2)

Guided Reciprocal Questioning (Activity 3)

Learning Activities That Stimulate Critical Thinking (Activity 4)

Problem Posing Using Personal Challenges (Activity 5)

Case Study (Activity 6)

Case Study That Exemplifies the Motivational Framework (Activity 7)

Teacher, Parent, and Student Role-Play (Activity 8)

Visitation Maps (to prepare for school visits) (Activity 9)

Dot Graphing (an approach to initiating action research) (Activity 11)

Also, strategies described in the section on action research.

Chapter Eight

Engendering Competence

*In recognizing the humanity of our fellow beings, we pay
ourselves the highest tribute.*
THURGOOD MARSHALL

In recent years our profession has learned a great deal about different kinds of assessment and their purposes. We know, for example, that assessment ought to be used to enhance learning as opposed to simply auditing it. We understand the importance of having clear criteria for success and helping students to assess the development of competencies throughout a learning process. We know as well that grading practices such as averaging ought to be reexamined if we want grades to ultimately reflect what students know and can do. Nonetheless, the topics of educational assessment and grading can be particularly challenging to educators. They deal with issues that are politically charged, and compound an aspect of educational practice about which many educators feel tremendous ambivalence, having to evaluate students while serving as an encouraging and trustworthy facilitator of learning.

Assessment and grading practices influence student motivation in powerful ways, and providing opportunities for educators to examine their practices is essential. For this kind of teacher self-assessment to occur optimally, professional development needs to provide enough safety for teachers that they are willing to question their practice and enough time that they can examine and develop new approaches.

This chapter begins with a series of perspectives on assessment and motivation, followed by activities that facilitate self-assessment and closure, methods for providing feedback that matters, norms for safety as teachers talk about the politically charged topic of grading, procedures for *authentic assessment,* and staff development exercises that enable teachers to demonstrate their competence in designing motivating and culturally responsive lessons.

We believe that the essential purpose of assessment is to engender competence in ways that have value to *all* students and to society as a whole. Intrinsic motivation is elicited when people—within and across cultural groups—know they are competently learning from a meaningful activity that leads to a valued goal. The process and the goal are reciprocal and, to our way of thinking, indivisible—one gives meaning to the other. If someone wants to learn computer applications because this is a valued skill that will increase the likelihood of work-related opportunities, that awareness will evoke motivation as she or he learns. Further, the progress the person makes and competence she or he gains will influence the motivational value of the original goal. In other words, becoming more effective in pursuit of a goal often increases the value of the goal. With increased competence, computer skills and work-related opportunities may acquire even greater value. In this way, experiencing competence can construct a significant link to a future worth believing in.

Across cultures, the human need for competence is not acquired but already exists, and it can be strengthened or weakened through learning experiences. For some people competence is valued as a sign of individual proficiency and survival. For others its fundamental importance resides in a collective responsibility for learning about and demonstrating what is best for others—for future human and environmental well-being. An essential goal in achieving this motivational condition is to support personal competence while illuminating the socially redeeming aspects of an individual's increased effectiveness. Competence ought to be accomplished with consideration for the interdependence of all people and all things and with respect for each person's impact on the generations to come.

Competence and Self-Determination

Building competence and exercising self-determination go hand in hand. Mastery of complex content and development of reasoning skills ultimately require students of all ages to take responsibility for their own learning. In addition, the contexts in which most children and adults live, as well as the contexts in which they work or will work, increasingly require them to be capably self-directed. This does not imply a laissez-faire learning environment. Nor does it imply that all learners are equally prepared or have sufficient self-confidence to take responsibility for their learning. In fact, many students, of all ages, appear to be most comfortable when someone just tells them what to do. Their experiences have fostered an expectation of subordination, homogenized routines, and rigid approaches to grading. Independent thinking can signal uncomfortable shifts in personal authority and require a tolerance for ambiguity that may be initially problematic.

Strategies to support taking ownership of learning have been discussed in the prior chapters. When combined with the following strategies to engender competence, they offer a holistic system for *enhancing* the self-determination of *all* learners. Consistently applied, they enable K–12 students as well as adult learners who feel minimal control over their learning to grow in the realization that they have an important voice in the classroom and society. The strategies in this chapter contribute to the making of large and small decisions, in ways that enhance learning, respect for one's own opinion, and responsibility to others.

Relating Authenticity and Effectiveness to Assessment in Order to Engender Competence

For assessment to be intrinsically motivating it needs to be *authentic*, connected to students' life circumstances, frames of reference, and values. For example, for a case study to be used as an authentic assessment, it might ask learners to respond to a situation that mirrors their home or community life and its normal resources and conditions. A real-life context for demonstrating learning enhances students' perception that the learning is relevant, appeals to their pragmatism, and affirms their rich background of experiences (Kasworm and Marienau, 1997). In contrast, one can easily see how an impersonal multiple-choice exam might seem tedious and irrelevant, not only to historically underrepresented students but to all learners.

Learners' *effectiveness* is their awareness that in the *process* of learning or as an *outcome* of learning, they have understood or accomplished something they find important. Therefore, both the processes as well as the results of learning provide significant information. How well are we doing? and How well did this turn out? are a critical duet for learning activities. In the example of the case study, to judge the quality of their thinking, students would likely want to know the criteria for excellent case study analysis and understand what different excellent analyses might look like. They would also want feedback as they *process* the case to determine how well their responses relate to the issues found in the case study. In addition, upon resolution of the case, they would want to assess the quality of the *outcome* for its merits. It is in this manner that motivation is elicited, through students' realization that they are competently performing an activity that leads to a valued goal. This realization affirms the need of students across all cultures to adequately guide, develop, and assess their learning in pursuit of a valued accomplishment. Student effectiveness is not simply something that happens at the completion of a learning experience.

In the following pages are some exercises that though neither exhaustive nor absolute as solutions to the complex challenges of assessment, may expand educators' repertoire of ways to think about and assess academic growth so that all student groups have a better chance to experience and trust their competence.

Offer Opportunities for Self-Assessment

Self-assessment can be a valuable complement to feedback from an external source. Self-assessment allows us to validate our authenticity as learners and as human beings. It means reflecting and gaining perspective on how we understand ourselves in the process of learning, knowing, and participating as community members. Self-assessment can help us weave important relationships and meanings between academic or technical information and personal histories and experiences. By exploiting our surprises, puzzlements, and hunches we can launch a process of self-discovery and self-determination, even when self-assessment is primarily intended as a simple record of learning.

Caution with self-assessment is advised however. Too much ambiguity can overwhelm students of all ages. Students typically appreciate knowing what to focus on and what to try to learn in the assessment process. It is also a good idea for teachers to explain how they will use or evaluate self-assessments. Teachers do not need to comment on everything, but learners are more likely to strengthen their reflective skills if they receive expected, sincere, specific, supportive, and timely feedback.

In addition, self-assessment techniques may be particularly difficult for students who are in the process of becoming proficient in English or who are unaccustomed to the shifts in authority that are a part of evaluating one's own experiences. Further, brief exercises run the risk of trivializing opportunities for genuine reflection, reducing responses to sound bites of information. With this in mind, teachers may want to extend the time allotted for reflection or encourage students who would like more time or who would like to respond with a partner to use time outside of class to do so.

In addition to what we offer here, students may engage in self-assessment by comparing their work against rubrics and making self-adjustments (Walvoord and Anderson, 1998; Wiggins, 1999). Most of the methods we offer in this chapter are informal, reflective methods such as journals, post-writes, closure techniques, and the critical incident questionnaire. As you will see, the more elaborate forms of self- and collaborative assessment, that is, those that involve examining student work or videotaping and examining a lesson, are focused on the work of educators and contain clear guidelines and criteria for success based on the motivational framework.

Activity 1. Overview of Developing Journals

PURPOSE
To consider how journals can be used to learn from experiences and feelings associated with a learning experience. This activity is helpful both for teachers and for K–12 students who are co-creating their own journal writing process.

TIME
Thirty minutes.

FORMAT
Individuals and large group.

MATERIALS
Overhead transparencies or sheets of newsprint with prepared guidelines for students, handout (Using Journals: A Synopsis), and three-by-five-inch cards.

PROCESS

Step 1. Ask participants to read the following synopsis of the forms and functions of journals, and as they do so, to consider one way they can imagine using journals with students.

USING JOURNALS: A SYNOPSIS

Journals can take a number of forms. Consider, for example, a journal that is used in a science course to synthesize lab notes, address the quality of the work, examine the process(es) upon which work is based, and address emerging interests and concerns. Journals are an informative complement to more conventional forms of assessment.

With respect to sensitivity to cultural differences and encouraging critical awareness of the origins and meanings of subject-specific knowledge, journals can be used to address the following questions: From whose viewpoint are we seeing or reading or hearing? From what angle or perspective? How do we know what we know? What is the evidence and how reliable is it? Whose purposes are served by this information (Meier, 1995)?

Journals can also be used to address interests, ideas and issues related to course material and processes, work on recurring problems, think through responses to instructor-generated questions, develop responses to learner-generated questions, and note important connections that are being made. These connections may be learner observations in the classroom. But, optimally, connections are meanings that emerge as learners apply coursework to past, present, and future life experiences.

If we wish to promote this level of reflection, then we need to make the classroom a place where this can happen. Providing time in class for learners to respond in their journals to readings, discussions, and significant questions builds community around the journal process and sends yet another message that the classroom is a place in which the skills of writing, developing insights, and reflecting on personal meaning are valued.

Initially, it may be best for learners to pay less attention to mechanics, organization, and whether or not their writing makes sense and put more effort into simply getting their thoughts and feelings down on paper, where they can learn from them. Once it has sufficiently incubated, this material can be reorganized and summarized later.

Step 2. Ask participants to identify three to five journal guidelines or protocols that they believe are important to share with students. For example, if a teacher imagines using journals as a part of a writing course, she or he might want students to agree to the following items.

1. Your journal is your conversation with yourself. Trust your own voice.

2. If you cannot respond to a prompt for writing in your journal, try to explain why not.

3. From time to time I will ask you to submit a summary of your journal. You will

choose what you would like me to read from your journal or what you would like me to know about something that you have written.

4. Toward the end of the course, we will create a class anthology with at least one submission—or summary—from each person's journal. You will be asked to submit, along with your contribution, a brief preface telling why you selected the material you submitted.

5. In the back of your journal, keep a section for words you are learning—from menus, signs, books, newspapers, other people—that can help your writing to become abundant.

In addition, encourage educators to facilitate a discussion with students about the potential benefit of journals and to offer their own ideas about guidelines for journal entries and feedback.

Step 3. On one side of a three-by-five-inch card, ask participants to write how they might use a journal. On the other side, ask them to write the guidelines they would give to students. Ask for volunteers to share their ideas with the entire group. Seek a volunteer to collect the cards and transcribe everyone's ideas so that they can be distributed to the group.

Activity 2. Post-Writes

PURPOSE
To consider how post-writes can be used to reflect on experiences and feelings associated with a learning experience.

TIME
Thirty minutes.

FORMAT
Individuals and large group.

PROCESS
Explain to participants that post-writes are reflections that encourage learners to analyze a particular piece of work, considering how they created it and what it may mean to them (Allen and Roswell, 1989). For example, a teacher might say to students: "Now that you have finished your essay, please answer the following questions. There are no right or wrong answers. I am interested in your analysis of your experience with writing this essay." The questions might include the following.

1. What problems did you face in the writing of this essay?
2. What solutions did you find for these problems?

3. Imagine you had more time to write this essay. What would you do if you were to continue working on it?

4. Has your thinking changed in any way as a result of writing this essay? If so, briefly describe that change.

Also explain that it is easy to imagine ways in which this technique could be applied across disciplines. An educator might, for example, slightly redesign the previous questions to allow learners in math or science to identify and reflect on a problem that posed a particular challenge. Next ask participants to consider one way they can imagine using post-writes with students and to imagine ways they might redesign the sample questions. Teacher educators can revise the questions to reflect on something that they have facilitated with the group so that participants can practice the process on themselves. Examples of such questions follow:

1. What problems did you face in the activity?

2. What solutions did you find for these problems?

3. Imagine we had more time with the activity. What would you do if you were to continue working on it?

4. Has your thinking changed in any way as a result of the activity? If so, briefly describe the change.

Activity 3. Summarizing Questions

PURPOSE
Making meaning of an entire course or professional development program.

TIME
Twenty minutes.

FORMAT
Dyads and large group.

MATERIALS
List of questions on a handout or chart.

PROCESS
Point out that ongoing self-assessment instruments provide opportunities for students to engage in authentic assessment. One approach to self-assessment is the use of summarizing questions at the end of a course, semester, or year. For younger students, opportunities to respond to summarizing questions may occur at the end of a lesson or unit. Display a list of sample questions, such as the following (Elbow, 1986).

SAMPLE SUMMARIZING QUESTIONS

1. How do you feel now at the end? Why?

2. What are you proud of?

3. Compare your accomplishments with what you had hoped for and expected at the start.

4. Which kinds of things were difficult or frustrating? Which were easy?

5. What is the most important thing you did in this course?

6. Think of some important moments from this course: your best moments, typical moments, crises, or turning points. Describe five or six of these in a sentence or two for each.

7. What can you learn or did you learn from each of these moments?

8. Who is the person you studied that you cared the most about? Be that person and write the person's letter to you, telling you whatever it is they have to tell you.

9. What did you learn throughout the course? What were the skills and ideas? What was the most important thing? What idea or skill was hard to really "get"? What crucial idea or skill came naturally?

10. Describe this period of time as a journey. Where did this journey take you? What was the terrain like? Was it a complete trip or part of a longer one?

11. You learned something crucial that you won't discover for a while.
    Guess it now.

12. How could you have done a better job?

13. What advice would some friends in the class give you if they spoke with 100 percent honesty and caring?

14. What advice do you have for yourself?

Ask participants to select several questions that they might find particularly valuable to use with their students. Then ask them to discuss with a partner their rationale for selecting those items. In pairs and then in the large group, participants discuss how the selected questions might promote reflection and engender competence.

Activity 4. Student Self-Assessment Aligned with the Motivational Framework

PURPOSE

For K–12 students to reflect on personal accomplishments, challenges, and goals.

TIME

Twenty to thirty minutes.

FORMAT

Individual reflection.

MATERIALS

Handout (Student Self-Assessment).

PROCESS

Distribute the self-assessment handout, and ask students to respond to the questions. The questions are aligned with the Motivational Framework for Culturally Responsive Teaching.

STUDENT SELF-ASSESSMENT

Name:

Date:

Class:

1. What have I done to demonstrate respect for or provide support for other people in our class?

2. What kinds of decisions have I made throughout this period of time that have helped me to guide my own learning?

3. When have I felt so involved in learning that time seemed to fly?

4a. What are at least two things I can do to have this feeling more often?

4b. What are at least two things my teacher can do?

5a. What are some things I've been doing at school about which I feel academically successful?

5b. How are they important to other people or to society as well as to me?

6. What goals might I set for myself based on my responses to these questions?

Activity 5. Educator Self-Assessment

PURPOSE

For teachers or peer coaches to reflect on the motivational implications of a lesson plan or course design.

TIME

Variable.

FORMAT

Individual or peer reflection.

MATERIALS

Handout (Self- or Peer Review of a Lesson or Course).

PROCESS

Distribute a handout with the following questions that relate to the four conditions of the Motivational Framework for Culturally Responsive Teaching. The handout might allow space for answering each question and also have a place for additional review comments.

SELF- OR PEER REVIEW OF A LESSON OR COURSE: MOTIVATIONAL FRAMEWORK QUESTIONS

1. Establishing inclusion: How does the learning experience contribute to the development of participants as a community of learners who feel respected by and connected to one another and to the teacher?

2. Developing a positive attitude: How does the learning experience offer meaningful choices and promote personal relevance to contribute to participants' positive attitude?

3. Enhancing meaning: How does the learning experience engage participants in challenging learning that has social merit?

4. Engendering competence: How does the learning experience create participants' understanding that they are becoming more effective in authentic learning that they value?

5. Do you have any additional comments?

When using this activity during professional development courses or institutes, ask participants to use these questions to review a learning activity or a portion of the course, thus providing feedback to the facilitator. Participants might also discuss how they could use these questions for self-review, in relation to their own classroom teaching.

Activity 6. Using the Peer Coaching Rubric Based on the Motivational Framework

PURPOSE

For teachers and peer coaches to learn from classroom practice through analysis of a videotaped or real-time teaching experience.

TIME

One and one-half hours.

FORMAT

Interactive.

Materials

A videotaped lesson and a handout (Partnership Guide for Culturally Responsive Teaching).

Process

Step 1. Distribute a copy of the handout containing the Partnership Guide for Culturally Responsive Teaching (Exhibit 8.1) to participants who are going to practice using the Motivational Framework for Culturally Responsive Teaching for peer coaching (or for reviewing a videotaped lesson of their own). Explain that the partnership guide is a synthesis of the research on educational equity, opportunity, and intrinsically motivating teaching. It outlines what educators who are committed to highly motivating, culturally responsive teaching consider and, ideally, facilitate as they plan and implement learning experiences. Next, explain that you will show them a thirty-minute video of a lesson. Participants will use the partnership guide to help them identify the strengths of the lesson and any ways in which the lesson might be elaborated in order to enhance the four motivational conditions.

Step 2. After participants review the video, ask them to discuss their findings either with a partner or in small groups. In addition to noting strengths and ways in which the lesson might be motivationally enhanced, they should suggest ways in which they might communicate their findings to the teacher in the video.

Step 3. After fifteen to twenty minutes of discussion, reassemble participants in a large group and ask them to pretend that you are the teacher and colleague in the video. (Of course you may in fact be the teacher in the video, because one of the ways to practice what one preaches and to develop trust with the schools one serves is to facilitate demonstration lessons in actual classrooms and to videotape them for later examination with school-based educators.) The participants give you feedback about the videotaped performance, communicating their observations in ways that are respectful and encouraging. If comments are worded in ways that could impede trust or the teacher's ability to give serious consideration to the point made, simply say, "Ouch." The speaker then has an opportunity to rephrase the observation, and he or she may ask for assistance from others if he or she wishes. Finally, based on the feedback you have heard, model articulating and committing to one or two goals that would help you, as the teacher in the video, to enhance student motivation in future practice. Also model how you would garner support for these goals. For example, if one goal is to offer equally rigorous choices for learning from which collaborative student groups may select, support might be garnered by sharing the lesson plan with a skillful colleague or a focus group of students.

Step 4. Next, ask participants to set three goals for themselves. The first goal identifies one or two ways in which they might strengthen their own classroom practice, given what they may have learned about themselves from observing someone else. The second

Exhibit 8.1. Partnership Guide for Culturally Responsive Teaching.

Describe the lesson or unit, subject area(s), and goals:

Establishing Inclusion

How does the learning experience contribute to the development of students as a community of learners who feel respected by and connected to one another and to the teacher?
• Routines and rituals are visible and understood by all.
 __ Rituals are in place that help all students feel that they belong in the class.
 __ Students have opportunities to learn about each other.
 __ Students have opportunities to learn about each other's unique backgrounds.
 __ Class agreements or participation guidelines and consequences for violating agreements are negotiated.
 __ The system of personal and collective responsibility for agreements is understood by everyone and applied with fairness.
Describe the evidence:

• All students equitably and actively participate and interact.
 __ The teacher directs attention equitably.
 __ The teacher interacts respectfully with all students.
 __ The teacher demonstrates to all students that she or he cares about them.
 __ Students share ideas and perspectives with partners and small groups.
 __ Students respond to lessons by writing.
 __ Students know what to do, especially when making choices.
 __ Students help each other.
 __ Work is displayed (with students' permission).
Describe the evidence:

(Continued)

**Exhibit 8.1. Partnership Guide for
Culturally Responsive Teaching.** (*Continued*)

Developing a Positive Attitude

*How does the learning experience offer meaningful choices and promote personal
relevance to contribute to students' positive attitude?*
- The teacher works with students to personalize the relevance of
  course content.
    - __ Students' experiences, concerns, and interests are used to
      develop course content.
    - __ Students' experiences, concerns and interests are addressed in
      responses to questions.
    - __ Students' prior knowledge and their learning experiences are
      explicitly linked to course content and questions.
    - __ The teacher encourages students to understand, develop, and
      express different points of view.
    - __ The teacher encourages students to clarify their interests and
      set goals.
    - __ The teacher maintains flexibility in the pursuit of *teachable
      moments* and emerging interests.

Describe the evidence:
- The teacher encourages students to make real choices.
    - __ Students choose how to learn (multiple intelligences).
    - __ Students choose what to learn.
    - __ Students choose where to learn.
    - __ Students choose when a learning experience will be considered
      to be complete.
    - __ Students choose how learning will be assessed.
    - __ Students choose with whom to learn.
    - __ Students choose how to solve emerging problems.

Describe the evidence:

Enhancing Meaning

*How does this learning experience engage students in challenging learning that
has social merit?*
- The teacher encourages all students to learn, apply, create, and communicate knowledge.
    - __ The teacher helps students to activate prior knowledge and to
      use it as a guide to learning.

___ The teacher, in concert with students, creates opportunities for inquiry, investigation, and projects.

___ The teacher provides opportunities for students to actively participate in challenging ways when not involved in sedentary activities such as reflecting, reading, and writing.

___ The teacher asks higher-order questions of all students throughout a lesson.

___ The teacher elicits high-quality responses from all students.

___ The teacher uses multiple *safety nets* to ensure student success (for example, not grading all assignments, asking students to work with partners, designing cooperative learning experiences).

Describe the evidence:

Engendering Competence

How does the learning experience create students' understanding that they are becoming more effective in authentic learning that they value?

- There is information, consequence, or product that supports students in valuing and identifying learning.

    ___ The teacher clearly communicates the purpose of the lesson.

    ___ The teacher clearly communicates criteria for excellent final products.

    ___ The teacher provides opportunities for a diversity of competencies to be demonstrated in a variety of ways.

    ___ The teacher helps all students to concretely identify accomplishments.

    ___ The teacher assesses different students differently.

    ___ The teacher assesses progress continually in order to provide feedback on individual growth and progress.

    ___ The teacher creates opportunities for students to make explicit connections between new and prior learning.

    ___ The teacher creates opportunities for students to make explicit connections between their learning and the "real world."

    ___ The teacher provides opportunities for students to self-assess learning in order to reflect on their growth as learners.

    ___ The teacher provides opportunities for students to self-assess their personal responsibility for contributing to the classroom as a learning community.

Describe the evidence:

goal identifies one or two ways in which they will strengthen their potential as effective peer coaches. The third goal identifies when and how they will videotape a lesson of their own or invite a trusted colleague to their classroom to observe. Also ask participants to report out on ways to be an effective coach, so that their tips can be transcribed and distributed for everyone's future use.

Step 5. Finally, invite each participant to write his or her three goals on a three-by-five-inch card and a self-addressed postcard. The three-by-five-inch cards are collected for future reference, and the postcards are mailed to participants as a reminder. Encourage participants to have fun with their postcards, offering encouraging comments and uplifting thoughts to themselves.

Source: We are grateful to the U.S. Department of Defense education activity professional development and curriculum coordinators in the district offices of the Hessen and Heidelberg School Districts of Germany who assisted with the original design of this activity.

Activity 7. Enhancing the Motivational Influence of Professional Practice by Examining Student Work

PURPOSE
To engage educators in collegial examination of student work, to share and enhance understanding of ways in which student motivation and performance can be strengthened, to reinforce understanding of the Motivational Framework for Culturally Responsive Teaching, to expand approaches that professional learning teams can use to enhance instructional practice.

TIME
One hour.

FORMAT
Large group.

MATERIALS
Newsprint and markers.

PROCESS
Once educators have learned the Motivational Framework for Culturally Responsive Teaching, this exercise is a good performance-based approach to help them apply what they have learned. You may wish to write up the steps of the exercise as a handout, perhaps titling it "Protocol for Examining Student Work," so the participants will have a clear record of the process. We recommend focusing on the work of a low-performing student because it can provide a particularly rich context for sharing knowledge about teaching and learning. You may wish to ask some volunteers in advance to bring a sam-

ple of the work of a low-performing student, with the student's name removed. Explain the process of examining student work to potential volunteers so they can make an informed choice about whether they are willing to participate in a demonstration as well as about the sample of student work that might be most productive for the group to examine.

Step 1. Ask participants to form collegial teams, and invite a volunteer in each team to share a sample of the work of a historically low-performing student with the team members. Explain that the teacher should describe as much information related to the learning experience, criteria for success, the student, and any other information as she or he can to help the group understand the assignment, the approach to teaching, the context in which the student was learning, and the student's strengths and challenges.

Step 2. Ask team members to offer positive comments about the teaching activity and the student's work. They may also ask clarifying questions to strengthen their understanding of the teaching and learning experiences.

Step 3. The teacher responds to questions with clarifying information.

Step 4. A volunteer scribe on each team charts the ideas of the teacher's colleagues as they brainstorm pedagogical strategies that might enhance student motivation and lead to heightened academic accomplishment. The teacher agrees to remain silent during this step.

Ask participants to use the four conditions of the Motivational Framework for Culturally Responsive Teaching (see the lists in Chapter Four and Exhibit 8.1) to guide their thinking during the brainstorming and to ensure that they are offering ideas that promote all four motivational conditions. We suggest asking the teacher who presented the problem to remain silent so that the other participants can generate a broad range of ideas and not feel inhibited by, for example, the teacher's repeatedly remarking that she or he has already tried an idea. In addition, when a teacher feels particularly hopeless or frustrated, the uninterrupted brainstorming can disrupt the teacher's sense of despair or frustration as colleagues optimistically envision new ways to influence student performance.

Step 5. Without making a judgment, the teacher reviews the list of ideas that participants have offered. Collaboratively, the teacher and her or his colleagues ensure that ideas related to all four motivational conditions have been adequately represented.

Step 6. The teacher selects one or two ideas and sets personal goals to strengthen the likelihood of success for the student with upcoming learning experiences. The team also selects one or two ideas and sets personal goals on behalf of students—the idea being that what may be good for the few is often good for the many.

Step 7. Ask the team, including the teacher who provided student work, to reflect upon the process. The teacher is encouraged to communicate feelings, thoughts, or ideas that might help all team members feel respected and supported as they continue the process of collaboratively examining student work.

Step 8. In a large group setting, ask participants when, where, and how they might apply the process of examining student work.

Additional notes. Facilitators of school renewal might teach this process by meeting with different groups of teachers throughout the day during the teachers' planning time. Or the school might hire a team of substitutes to release four to five teachers per period over one to two days.

This process of examining student work can be extended to involve parents and students. To initiate this level of the process, the schoolwide instructional leadership cadre can do a demonstration for the rest of the faculty and for parents and students who are members of a professional learning team or study group.

Use Closure Activities

Closure activities are opportunities for learner synthesis—for learners to examine general or specific aspects of what they have learned, to identify emerging thoughts or feelings, to discern themes, to construct meaning, to relate learning to real-life experiences, and so forth. Activities can take the form of celebration, acknowledgment, or sharing. The basic idea is that something notable is coming to an end. At such times, positive closure enhances learner motivation because it affirms the entire process, verifies the value of the experience, directly or indirectly acknowledges learner competence, increases cohesiveness within the learning community, and encourages the surfacing of inspiration and other beneficial emotions within the learners themselves. For example, at the end of a professional development institute, we might ask participants to formulate a plan to apply what they have learned. This form of closure becomes a way of building coherence between the learning that has occurred and personal experience beyond the institute. A similar example of a closure exercise is asking participants to identify one particular obstacle they must still overcome to be more proficient with what they have learned. But positive closure can also take the form of a simple statement, such as a sincere thank-you to learners for their contributions, or of a more elaborate social event, such as an awards ceremony. Some specific activities for achieving positive closure follow.

Activity 8.   Closure Note-Taking Pairs

PURPOSE

To cooperatively reflect on a lesson, review major concepts and pertinent information, and illuminate unresolved issues or concerns.

TIME
Fifteen to thirty minutes.

FORMAT
Dyads.

MATERIALS
Notes from a lecture or other learning experience.

PROCESS
Step 1. Explain to participants that closure note-taking pairs are learners who pair with each other to cooperatively reflect on a lesson, review major concepts and pertinent information, and illuminate unresolved issues or concerns. Pairs then work together to review, add to, or modify their notes. Many learners, including but certainly not limited to students who speak English as a second language, benefit from summarizing their lecture notes with another person. You might request learners to ask each other questions such as: What have you got in your notes about this particular topic? What are the most important points made by the instructor? What is something that you are feeling uncertain about that we might clarify together?

To help educators practice the process, ask participants to turn to a person next to them and share their notes from, say, the minilecture on the Motivational Framework for Culturally Responsive Teaching (Activity 3 in Chapter Six). Ask participants to be sure that in addition to reviewing notes they ask each other, What is something you are feeling uncertain about that we might clarify together?

Step 2. Ask participants how they might use closure note-taking pairs in their own practice?

Note: This process is especially beneficial following a lecture. It may be used intermittently or as a culminating activity (Johnson, Johnson, and Smith, 1991).

Activity 9. Door Passes

PURPOSE
To reflect on experiences and feelings associated with a learning experience. This exercise is ideal for K–12 classrooms.

TIME
Five to ten minutes.

FORMAT
Individuals and large group.

MATERIALS

Three-by-five-inch cards.

PROCESS

This process is easy to practice with participants. Explain that *door passes* provide a quick way to check in with the opinions of any group of learners. Ask participants to respond to one question in writing on a three-by-five-inch card. Here are some sample questions:

DOOR PASS QUESTIONS

1. What is one thing that most surprised you in our work thus far?

2. What is one thing that you know you will tell someone else when you get home (or at work)?

3. When were you most confused, and what might have helped you at that time?

4. What is one thing you know that you will do differently because of our work together?

5. What is one thing you know you will do the same because of our work together?

6. What is a question you might have asked if we had more time?

7. What is a piece of advice, related to the topics we have been examining, that you can offer others?

Explain that participants will hand these cards to you personally when they leave the room. Point out that this ensures that the teacher makes contact with each student.

Activity 10. Seasonal Partners

PURPOSE

To reflect on experiences and feelings associated with a learning experience; to promote interaction among people who might not otherwise interact as learning partners. This exercise is ideal for K–12 classrooms.

TIME

Fifteen minutes.

FORMAT

Rotating dyads.

MATERIALS

Three-by-five-inch cards or notepaper and a chart with four questions.

PROCESS

Step 1. Post a chart with four questions, each one labeled with a season—fall, winter, spring, or summer. Distribute three-by-five-inch cards to participants, and ask them to list the seasons vertically down the card—fall, winter, spring, and summer. Explain that they will rotate around the room four times, finding a new partner for each season. With each rotation, partners greet one another and introduce themselves (if needed) and then write the name of the new partner on the index card alongside the appropriate season. In each season, partners discuss their reactions or responses to the question on the chart that corresponds with the season. These questions may be of any sort, depending on the topic at hand. But this procedure is particularly useful for reviewing prior learning. Here are some examples of questions that might be used for that purpose with educators.

> *Fall.* Discuss with your fall partner something you have learned from an in-service session, a course, a piece of literature, or an experience that enhances your understanding of student motivation.

> *Winter.* Discuss with your winter partner something you would like to learn more about given some of the issues we have examined.

> *Spring.* Discuss with your spring partner one recommendation for your school related to topics we have examined.

> *Summer.* Discuss with your summer partner something you learned today that you value and that you will definitely apply in your own work.

Step 2. In a large-group debriefing, ask participants to share some of the ideas that emerged in their discussions. Also ask educators how they might apply this activity to their own work.

Source: This activity was introduced to us by Bob Garmston and Bruce Wellman.

Activity 11. Head, Heart, Hand

PURPOSE

To make meaningful connections, especially at the end of a class period or day.

TIME

Fifteen minutes.

FORMAT

Individual reflection.

MATERIALS

Questions written on newsprint or overhead transparencies.

PROCESS

Ask participants to use the following prompts, which you have posted on sheets of newsprint or on overhead slides, as a guide for reflecting on a learning experience.

LEARNING EXPERIENCE REFLECTION PROMPTS

Head (thought). One thing that I will continue to *think* about as a consequence of participating in this learning experience is . . .

Heart (feelings). One thing that I am *feeling* now is . . .

Hand (action). One thing that I will *do* as a consequence of participating in this learning experience is . . .

Activity 12. Reflection Logs

PURPOSE

To reflect on learning.

TIME

Thirty minutes.

FORMAT

Individual reflection and large group.

MATERIALS

Handout (Reflection Log).

PROCESS

Distribute a handout with a reflection log, such as the one shown here, and ask participants to follow the instructions on the handout.

REFLECTION LOG

Please complete each of the following phrases in a sentence or two as you reflect on the learning experience in which you have just participated.

1. I learned . . .
2. I wonder . . .
3. I am surprised. . . .
4. I wish . . .
5. I think . . .
6. I suggest . . .

because . . .

Source: Beyer, 1995.

Activity 13. Reflection Trees for Group Projects

PURPOSE
To reflect on group learning experiences.

TIME
Thirty minutes.

FORMAT
Individuals and large group.

MATERIALS
Sticky notes; large, handmade trees of different types(an art teacher or the students themselves may agree to design the trees), and a handout or chart with the prompts.

PROCESS
Ask participants to complete each of the following statements about their group project on a sticky note (distribute the prompts as a handout or post them on a chart) and then post each note on the tree with which it is associated.

GROUP PROJECT PROMPTS

> *Linden tree:* What I liked best was . . .
>
> *Maple tree:* One thing I learned that I think is particularly important . . .
>
> *Cottonwood:* What surprised me most was . . .
>
> *Olive tree:* What I did best was . . .
>
> *Pine tree:* What the team did best was . . .
>
> *Flowering plum:* What I hope will happen as a consequence of our work is . . .
>
> *Fig tree:* What I am doing differently or more of now is . . .
>
> *Lotus tree:* The way I feel about what we accomplished is . . .

Examine Grading Practices

Grading is one of the mostly hotly contested issues in education. This renders most educators, not to mention students, vulnerable because it is perhaps the most idiosyncratic thing we do. Among school-based educators, there is little agreement on what should be included in a grade, whether the grade should be criteria or norm referenced, and whether grades should be used to motivate or communicate or both. Some teachers grade only according to a standard, others consider effort and individual progress, and many teachers factor in classroom behavior. Only 30 percent of U.S. school districts have grading policies, and it is difficult to know how many teachers in these districts actually follow the policies (*ASCD Education Update,* 1998). However, as we will examine in a later section in this chapter, precision of feedback ought to be a central concern of all assessment and grading processes. Accurate feedback makes it possible for *all* students to set realistic goals for themselves to improve their learning.

Activity 14. Examining Grading Practices

PURPOSE

For educators to reflect upon and refine personal approaches to grading for heightened student motivation and learning.

TIME

One and one-half hours.

FORMAT

Individuals and small groups.

MATERIALS

Sticky notes and handout (Grading Practices and Assessment Considerations).

PROCESS

You may wish to write up the steps of this exercise as an additional handout, perhaps titling it "Examining Grading Challenges: Learning from Each Other," so the participants will have a reference sheet for the process and a copy of the examples you give.

Step 1. Ask the group to read the handout on grading practices, shown at the end of this activity. Then invite participants to form groups of three. As it suggests at the top of the handout, tell participants they may want to place sticky notes next to those ideas they find most interesting or valuable for reference as they work with their group to problem solve personal grading challenges.

Step 2. Ask each person to identify three of his or her greatest challenges related to grading and assessment and write them on three separate sticky notes. Some examples of challenges are determining what to do when students do not turn in assignments, finding alternatives to averaging, and involving students in realistically assessing themselves.

Step 3. Ask participants, working in their groups of three, to place sticky notes on a Venn diagram to identify shared concerns and to prioritize the topics they can problem solve as a group (this is described in more detail in Activity 1 in Chapter Five). They should select no more than three topics to problem solve.

Step 4. Ask group members to share experiences, ideas, and resources related to their selected topics, noting information in the handout that they found interesting.

Step 5. For each topic, ask participants to complete this question, either individually or in their groups: What might happen if I (or we) . . . For example, a participant might ask: What might happen if I use students' median scores, instead of averaging, assuming the median score is a reasonable measure of what a student knows and can do? or, What might happen if I work with students to create methods of assessment and regularly assess personalized goals?

Step 6. Ask participants to use at least one of their questions to set one or two goals and to establish a process to put goals into action. For example, a participant might determine that one goal is to use students' median scores instead of averaging and that a second goal is to work with students to set and assess personalized goals related to success, and the participant might write out the process this way:

The process for the first goal is straightforward. With respect to the second goal, I will develop a "learning proposal" that asks a limited number of focused questions so that students will be thoughtful but not overwhelmed. Questions will ask students to identify personal goals, how they will achieve those goals, support that they might need, how they will know that they are progressing toward their goals, and how to assess the final product or performance. I will provide examples of good sample proposals and have students use the examples to establish criteria for their own proposals. Students will work with peers to fine-tune their proposals before they submit them, and I will conference with each student as well.

Step 7. Ask participants to write out at least three different ways that they can learn whether their goals are effective. For example, a participant might state the evidence this way:

To know whether my "learning proposal" goal is effective (1) I will observe how this approach affects two historically low-performing students and two historically high-performing students. (2) I will pay special attention to their commitment toward learning as evidenced by thoughtful proposal writing and enhanced follow-through and care directed toward learning activities. (I will regularly conference with all students to support their follow-through with or refinement of their proposal.) (3) At the conclusion of the project, I will ask the four students to serve as a focus group. I will ask them questions related to their proposal process, motivation, and learning. In addition, I will ask all students to complete a brief questionnaire about the learning proposal process.

Step 8. Ask participants to identify the ways they will garner support at their school for their ideas. For example, a participant might write out the following plan:

To garner support from my colleagues at school, I will interview two teachers whom I respect about my learning proposal process, and I will request ideas for anything else I might try. I will also ask them if they will help me learn from challenges as they arise.

GRADING PRACTICES AND ASSESSMENT CONSIDERATIONS

Following are some ideas provided by key theorists in the areas of assessment and evaluation. As you read, place sticky notes next to those ideas you find most interesting or valuable.

1. *Limit the attributes measured by grades to individual achievement.* Such things as effort, participation, or attitude should be reported separately, which may require an extended report card format. Do not make the mistake of using your assessment policy for things that ought to be addressed by your behavior or by discipline policy.

2. *Sample student performance.* Don't mark everything students do, and don't include all marks in the final grades. Provide feedback through formative assessments, and include only summative assessments in grade calculations.

3. *Grade in pencil.* Emphasize the most recent information when grading progress. For example, it makes little sense to average the marks of a student in the first week and the last week of a keyboarding class; the most recent marks offer the best assessment of the student's keyboarding skill. When possible, offer opportunities to improve the marks. This doesn't mean teachers have to offer unlimited chances to pass a test or improve a paper. Some teachers may require students who want to retake a test or to revise an assignment to demonstrate that they have done additional work that increases the likelihood that they will do better the second time around.

4. *Relate grading procedures to the intended learning goal.* The emphasis given to different topics or skills in a class should be reflected in the weight they have in determining the final grade. (A typical method that often *doesn't* stress particular topics or skills is to determine final grades by simply allotting 40 percent to tests and quizzes, 20 percent to homework, 20 percent to class participation, and so on.)

5. *Use care when crunching numbers.* One of teachers' biggest quandaries is what to do when a student gets a zero on an assignment. If scores on all assignments are simply averaged, a single zero in the batch can yield a grade that doesn't reflect the student's true performance. Teachers might consider using students' median score. Also, when a student earns a zero or a very low score on a major assignment, is there a chance he or she could revise the work? If not, could a future assignment demonstrate new learning and count for more credit?

6. *Use criterion-referenced standards to distribute grades.* Grading on a curve, in addition to its other problems, does not allow all students to see how close they are coming to high standards of performance. However, if there is a standard and all students reach that standard, it is okay for all students to reach the highest grade.

7. *Discuss assessment and grading with students at the beginning of instruction.* The criteria for quality work should not be a mystery to students. It is extremely help-

ful for students to see the grading schemes and rubrics that will be used to judge performance as well as a model of superior performance. It is even better if grading schemes and rubrics are co-created with students.

Here are some additional considerations:

- For each new area of study, work with students to compose a letter to parents or family that outlines what is being studied, the performance standards parents or family and students can expect, and the percentage of the grade related to each standard. For example, one standard might be that an effective oral presentation will be 10 percent of the final grade.
- Consider having agreed-upon districtwide or schoolwide rubrics that help students master, across content areas, literacy and learning skills such as learning vocabulary, constructing meaning from different kinds of text, and developing self-reflective processes. (Heidi Hayes Jacobs recommends schoolwide rubrics in writing so that every teacher shares responsibility for teaching reading, writing, speaking, and listening. She reminds us that vocabulary is the best predictor of overall success on any achievement measure and that speaking is the first way into a good job.)
- Be careful not to confuse standards with standardization. The idea that "all kids can learn" does not presume that all human beings can learn the same thing in the same way at the same time. Educators can avoid the trap of homogenizing curriculum, instruction, and assessment by teaching conceptually. For example, when the topic is the Civil War, the concept might be "conflict within a nation and within the minds of human beings." When the topic is planets, the concept might be systems; when the topic is equations, the topic might be balance (Tomlinson, 1999). In the case of conflict and the Civil War, a teacher might encourage students to research how it might have been possible for Abraham Lincoln to be "of two minds" about the issue of slavery. Using Abraham Lincoln as one of many possible examples, students could select or design their own methods to discover whether or not it is possible for an individual to be progressive and conservative at the same time.
- Bring in experts from the community to work with teachers and students to ensure that tasks and scoring systems are authentic. For example, an editor of a local paper might help create a scoring rubric based on what she or he looks for in a good article. Students might interview a panel of community experts to create criteria based on the range of the experts' opinions.
- Consider a dissertation and defense model, according to which students create inquiry-based projects with the support of a committee with teacher, peer, parent, and community representation.
- Hold quarterly demonstrations for students to display and engage in dialogue about work of their choice.

- Model for students and for the community your own interest in personal growth through learning. Educators at all levels can do this. Find ways to share things that you are learning that matter to you.

Source: This synopsis contains many ideas from *ASCD Education Update*, 1998.

Feedback

The ways that most people in a formal learning environment identify their competence is through feedback. *Informational* communication with students about their effectiveness has the best chance to cultivate their self-determination; such cultivation is an undergirding attribute of all of the activities in this book. According to the seminal work of Edward Deci and Richard Ryan (1991), when instructors tell learners about the quality of their work, these transactions can be either *informational* or *controlling*. Informational transactions tell learners something about their effectiveness and support their sense of self-determination in learning. Controlling transactions tend to undermine self-determination by making learner behavior appear to be dependent on implicit or explicit forces that demand, coerce, or seduce the learner's compliance. They encourage students to believe the reason for learning is some external condition outside themselves or the learning activity itself, such as a reward or teacher pressure. When verbally communicated, controlling messages often contain imperative locutions such as *should* and *must*. For example, an in-service facilitator might say to a teacher practicing an original lesson on a group of peers: "Your performance demonstrates that you are actively applying the four motivational conditions in ways that can powerfully enhance learning. Each condition works in a way that complements the other conditions, and your activities are likely to engage kids with a range of prior experiences. One hundred percent of the group on whom you practiced your lesson were consistently engaged." This is informational. In contrast, a facilitator might say: "Your performance was excellent. It is clear that you paid careful attention throughout the in-service training. You followed the outline step-by-step, and the end result is exactly as I had hoped." This is a controlling communication.

The difference between these two statements is important. The former encourages self-determination, and the latter gives much more of the credit for learning performance to the facilitator. An informational approach to feedback not only nurtures self-determination among people of all ages, it promotes self-direction and is more likely to increase intrinsic motivation.

Nonetheless, we have all encountered feedback that in an effort to be informational seemed strident. Consider, for example, the statement, "You've answered fifteen out of twenty spelling words correctly," or, with respect to professional development, "Twenty percent of your participants were fidgeting and restless." Although this factual orientation emphasizes making feedback clear and self-evident in order to encourage learners' self-assessment and self-direction, its minimalism can be alienating. It can also seem too individualistic to the many students who have collectivist orientations. For many students, how the message is delivered is inseparable from what the message means. Thus, the professional development example could easily be rephrased to make it less personal and applicable to a broader range of educators: "I noticed that 20 percent of your participants were fidgeting and restless. Disengagement is frustrating not only to learners but also to a dedicated facilitator. Let's discuss what can help in these kinds of situations."

Feedback is probably the most powerful process that teachers and other educators can regularly use to affect a learner's competence. The following activity gives educators an opportunity to apply the characteristics of effective feedback.

Activity 15. Effective Feedback

PURPOSE
For educators to apply the characteristics of effective feedback to personal practice.

TIME
One hour.

FORMAT
Individuals and small groups.

MATERIALS

Handout (Characteristics of Effective Feedback) and sticky notes.

PROCESS

Step 1. Distribute the handout on the characteristics of effective feedback shown at the end of this activity. Ask participants to review the information individually, placing a sticky note next to the points that they believe to be especially important.

    Step 2. Distribute a sample of student work, with the student's name removed, that contains teacher feedback. Explain as much as possible to participants about the student, the context, the assignment, and the criteria for success. (Alternatively, you may need to invent a piece of work as well as information about the student, the context, and so forth.) Ask participants to work with a partner to note (1) aspects of the sample that demonstrate characteristics of effective feedback, (2) ways in which the feedback may be ineffective, and (3) recommendations about the feedback based on the bulleted points in the handout.

    Step 3. Ask participants to develop an initial plan that delineates (1) with whom they will share this information, (2) how they will share it, and (3) two to three goals for themselves related to effective feedback.

CHARACTERISTICS OF EFFECTIVE FEEDBACK

Feedback is probably the most powerful process that teachers and other educators can regularly use to affect a learner's competence. As you review the characteristics of feedback, use sticky notes to indicate the most important points, from your perspective.

- *Effective feedback is informational rather than controlling.* It should emphasize a student's increasing effectiveness or creativity or capacity as a self-determined learner. For example, rather than making a controlling statement such as, "You are making progress and meeting the standards I have established for writing in this course," a teacher might say, "In your paper you have clearly identified three critical areas of concern; your writing was well organized and vivid; and I appreciate how well you have supported your rationale with facts and anecdotes."
- *Effective feedback provides evidence of the learner's effect relative to the learner's intent.* This most often is feedback that is based on *agreed-upon* standards, models, and criteria for success. The closer standards and criteria, including those represented by rubrics, come to students' own words, the better. In the case of models, students can compare their work against good and not-so-good examples of others' work. They are then in a position to determine what makes the good ones good and the bad ones bad. They determine standards and criteria for success, judge how well they have performed in terms of a specific target, and can explicitly indicate what needs to be

done for further effective learning. Self-assessment leads to self-adjustment. For example, in creating scrapbooks, students look at models of good examples and not-so-good ones to decide what makes them that way. They note what counts in quality work and articulate gradations of quality. Then they use this information, that is, this rubric, to reevaluate the models. Once they begin their own scrapbooks they compare them to the actual models, ranging from excellent to poor, and to their written agreements about quality. Students revise their work accordingly or request assistance from a peer or teacher.

- *Effective feedback is specific and constructive.* It is difficult for a person to improve performance when she or he can realize only in general terms how well she or he has done. Most people prefer specific information and realistic suggestions of how to improve, as are seen in this example: "I found your insights on government spending compelling. To emphasize your conclusion, you might consider restating your initial premise in your last paragraph." When you are giving guidance with feedback, it is important to keep in mind how much a student *wants to* or *ought to* decide on a course of action relative to the feedback. In general, the more the student can self-assess and self-adjust, the more self-determined he or she will be.

- *Effective feedback can be quantitative.* In some areas—athletics, for example—quantitative feedback has definite advantages. It is precise, and it can provide evidence of small improvements. Small improvements can have long-range effects. One way to understand learning is by *rate,* that is, an indication of how often something occurs over a fixed time. For example, students may be told they completed thirty laps during a one-hour swimming practice. Another way is to decide what percentage of learning performance is correct or appropriate. Percentages are calculated by dividing the number of times the learning performance occurs correctly by the total number of times the performance opportunity occurs, as in batting averages and field goal percentages. Another common form of quantitative feedback is *duration,* which is how long it takes a learning performance to be completed. For example, an environmental science student might receive feedback on how long it takes her to complete a practice analysis of a particular ecosystem, given that she will eventually perform the analysis under potentially adverse conditions. Whenever progress on learning a skill appears to be slow or difficult to ascertain, quantitative feedback may be an effective means to enhance learner motivation.

- *Effective feedback is prompt.* Promptness characterizes feedback that is given as the situation demands, which may not be immediately. Sometimes a moderate delay in feedback enhances learning because such a delay is culturally sensitive or polite. For example, some learners may experience discomfort with direct and specific performance judgments made very shortly after the occasion. Also, a short wait may allow learners to forget incorrect responses more easily and reduce their anxiety, as in the case of a public performance. In general, it is best to be quick with feedback but to pay careful attention to whether any delay might be beneficial.

- *Effective feedback is frequent.* Frequent feedback is probably most helpful when new learning is occurring. In general, we suggest providing feedback when improvement is most possible. Once errors have accumulated, learners may see improvements as more difficult to accomplish. Also, once multiple errors become established, the further learning encouraged through feedback may seem overwhelming and confusing to learners, making further progress seem even more remote.

- *Effective feedback is positive.* Positive feedback places emphasis on improvements and progress rather than on deficiencies and mistakes. It is an excellent form of feedback because it increases learners' intrinsic motivation, feelings of well-being, and sense of competence and helps students form a positive attitude toward the source of the information. Negative feedback, an emphasis on errors and deficiencies, can be discouraging. Even when students are prone to making mistakes, the instructor can point out any *decrease* in errors as positive feedback. Also, positive feedback can be given with constructive feedback. For example, a teacher might say to a student, "You've been able to solve most of this problem. Let's take a look at what's left and see if we can understand why you are getting stuck."

- *Effective feedback is related to impact criteria. Impact criteria* are the main reasons a person is learning something; they are the heart of the individual's learning goal (Wiggins, 1998). Often these criteria are unique to the individual or strongly related to a cultural perspective. One person may produce a speech or a piece of writing to inspire, arouse, or provoke. Another may wish to create a design or performance as a gift for family or friends. Assessment and feedback should support such goals and respectfully deal with what may be ineffable or accomplished only in a realm beyond mechanistic objectivity. This may require feedback that is more akin to dialogue or to what many artists do when they respond to another artist's work by describing how it affects them rather than by evaluating it.

- *Effective feedback is personal and differential.* Differential feedback is self-comparison. It focuses on the ways in which personal improvement has occurred since a learning activity was last performed. In skill or procedural learning, for such things as writing, operating a machine, or learning a particular sport, emphasizing small steps of progress can be very encouraging to learner motivation. The amount of time that lapses before a teacher gives such differential feedback can be quite important. For example, students are able to see larger gains and feel a greater sense of accomplishment when improvement is considered on a daily or weekly schedule rather than after each performance.

In addition to paying attention to the specific characteristics of feedback just listed, making some refinements in the composition and delivery of feedback may be helpful. For many skills, *graphing* or *charting* feedback can be encouraging to student motivation because it can make progress more concrete and show a record of increasing improvement. Asking students what they would like feedback on is a strategy that should be considered. Their perspectives may be different from ours as teachers, and the knowledge gained from such discussion can make feedback more relevant and motivating. Student *readiness to receive feedback* is also important. If people are resistant to feedback, they are not likely to learn or self-adjust. This may mean holding off on feedback until a personal conference can be arranged or until students are more comfortable with the learning situation. There are times when *checking to make sure your feedback was understood* can be important. This is certainly true for complex feedback or situations in which students are developing proficiency in English.

Everything that has been said about feedback thus far also applies to *group feedback*. Whether the group is a team, a collaborative group, or an entire class, feedback on total performance can influence each individual, and because group feedback consolidates members' mutual identification and sense of connection, it helps enhance group cohesiveness and morale.

As a final point, consider that sometimes the best form of feedback is simply to encourage students to move forward to the next, more challenging learning opportunity. Too much comment can emphasize a teacher's authority and diminish her or his role as a co-learner. This is true in class discussion as well. When K–12 teachers or adult educators respond to each and every student comment, it can imply that a perspective is incomplete if it does not include the instructor's view. In addition to suggesting arrogance, a continual commentary by a teacher can silence others, disrupting opportunities for students to consider and validate each other's perspectives. In the absence of other student-generated comments, a simple acknowledgment in the form of a sincere thank-you for a person's participation is often appreciated. This is especially true when working with adults, many of whom have uncomfortable histories of encounters with teachers who believe that the opinions of learners need to be confirmed or elaborated on by someone supposed to have a superior knowledge base. Although there are times when additional information from teachers or facilitators is necessary, we urge moderation. There is a disturbing contradiction in claiming to respect diverse opinions and ways of knowing and simultaneously positioning oneself as the ultimate authority.

Overall, Carol Kasworm and Catherine Marienau (1997) remind us, learners of all ages become more competent, feel more confident, and look forward to assessment when these procedures are

1. Related to goals they understand, find relevant, and want to accomplish

2. Reflective of growth in learning

3. Indicative of clear ways to improve learning without penalty

4. Expected

5. Returned promptly

6. Permeated with instructor or peer comments that are informative and supportive

7. Used to encourage new challenges in learning

Source: Adapted from Wlodkowski, 1999, p. 274.

Feedback for Educators

Whether educators are teaching courses, facilitating professional development inservices, or advising students, feedback is essential to heightened responsiveness to student needs and perspectives. We offer the following exercises as additions to the ongoing process of self-reflection and professional growth.

Activity 16. Class Evaluation from the Perspective of K–12 Students

PURPOSE
To introduce educators to a way to receive student feedback on their instructional practice.

TIME
Ten minutes.

FORMAT
Individual reflection.

MATERIALS
Handout (Evaluation Form).

PROCESS
Distribute a handout similar to the one in Exhibit 8.2, and ask participants to gain familiarity with it by providing feedback to you, as the facilitator, about their learning experiences thus far. Next, ask participants how and when they might use such a form in their own classrooms.

Exhibit 8.2. Evaluation Form.

Please circle how you felt about the class today. Four is high and means "very true," one is low and means "not true at all", NA means "not applicable."

1. What I learned is useful.	4	3	2	1	NA
2. What we did was interesting.	4	3	2	1	NA
3. I had some choices.	4	3	2	1	NA
4. What we did was challenging.	4	3	2	1	NA
5. What we did was involving.	4	3	2	1	NA
6. It made me really think.	4	3	2	1	NA
7. It was too hard.	4	3	2	1	NA
8. It was too easy.	4	3	2	1	NA
9. It was boring.	4	3	2	1	NA
10. I felt respected by my teacher.	4	3	2	1	NA
11. I didn't feel listened to by my teacher.	4	3	2	1	NA
12. As a class we tried to support each other.	4	3	2	1	NA
13. I sank or swam alone.	4	3	2	1	NA
14. I felt respected by my classmates.	4	3	2	1	NA
15. I did not feel respected by my classmates.	4	3	2	1	NA
16. I learned some things that are important to me.	4	3	2	1	NA
17. I learned some things that could be important to my community.	4	3	2	1	NA
18. I felt successful.	4	3	2	1	NA
19. I'm getting better at things I value.	4	3	2	1	NA
20. The work related to life outside of the classroom.	4	3	2	1	NA
21. We could learn from our mistakes.	4	3	2	1	NA
22. I felt unsuccessful.	4	3	2	1	NA
23. I need more time to do well.	4	3	2	1	NA
24. The way we were graded was fair.	4	3	2	1	NA
25. I didn't have a chance to show what I learned.	4	3	2	1	NA

Activity 17. Institute Evaluation from the Perspective of K–12 Educators

PURPOSE

To provide feedback on instructional practice to a professional development institute facilitator; to help adult learners be reflective about their most significant experiences.

TIME

Twenty minutes.

FORMAT

Individual reflection.

MATERIALS

Handout (Critical Incident Questionnaire).

PROCESS

The handout for this exercise is a critical incident questionnaire of five items, each of which asks learners to write details about important events that took place while they were learning. For longer institutes or courses it can be used at the end of each week. For intensive workshops and seminars, it has value at the end of each session (four hours or longer). Type the following questions on a handout with space beneath each question for participants to respond. If necessary, change *institute* to whatever term is appropriate.

CRITICAL INCIDENT QUESTIONNAIRE

1. At what moment in this institute did you feel most engaged with what was happening?

2. At what moment in this institute did you feel most distanced from what was happening?

3. What action that anyone (facilitator or learner) took in the institute did you find most affirming and helpful.

4. What action that anyone (instructor or learner) took in the institute did you find most puzzling or confusing?

5. What about the institute surprised you the most? (This might be something about your own reactions to a topic or event, something that someone did, or anything else that occurs to you.)

Step 1. Ask participants to complete the questionnaire anonymously. Then photocopy the responses so that each person can retain a copy of what he or she has written.

Step 2. After collecting the papers, explore them for themes, patterns, and concerns that need adjustment or that warrant responses. We also look for the part of our learning and teaching that has been affirmed. This exploration suggests areas to probe or strengthen. Our experience has been that this questionnaire provides a sensitive reading of the emotional reactions of learners and those areas that may create controversy or conflict. However, we also realize that some students may find that writing answers inhibits their responses, and we acknowledge this shortcoming of the process.

Source: Adapted from Brookfield, 1995, p. 115.

Activity 18. Evaluating the Motivational Conditions of an Institute

PURPOSE
To provide feedback on how well a professional development institute or course is fulfilling the four conditions of the motivational framework.

TIME
Five minutes.

FORMAT
Individual reflection.

MATERIALS
Handout (Motivational Conditions Evaluation).

PROCESS
Give participants handouts with the motivational conditions evaluation shown in Exhibit 8.3, and ask them to complete it. If necessary, change *institute* to whatever term is appropriate.

Authentic Assessment

Authentic assessment makes it possible for K–12 students and adult learners to know that they can proficiently apply what they are learning to their real lives. Although it is outside the scope of this book to address this topic in detail, we would like to underscore what key theorists have been writing for years (Freire, 1970; Knowles, 1980). That is, the closer assessment processes come to allowing learners to demonstrate what they know in an environment where they will eventually use that learning, the greater will be the student's motivation to do well and the more able the student will become in understanding his or her competence and the meaning it has to others.

Exhibit 8.3. Motivational Conditions Evaluation.

Please circle the number from one to four that represents how you feel about this professional development institute. Four means "strongly agree," and one means "strongly disagree." Each statement is followed by the motivational condition that it represents.

1. The institute climate is friendly and respectful. (Establishing Inclusion)   4   3   2   1

2. This institute is relevant to my life. (Developing a Positive Attitude)   4   3   2   1

3. This institute is challenging me to think. (Enhancing Meaning)   4   3   2   1

4. This institute is helping me to be effective at what I value. (Engendering Competence)   4   3   2   1

5. The facilitator respects learners' opinions and ideas. (Establishing Inclusion)   4   3   2   1

6. In this institute I can use my experiences and ways of knowing to support my learning. (Developing a Positive Attitude)   4   3   2   1

7. Most of the time during this institute I feel engaged in what's going on. (Enhancing Meaning)   4   3   2   1

8. I actually will use the information or skills I am learning in this institute. (Engendering Competence)   4   3   2   1

Giving learners an opportunity to complete an authentic task is one of the best ways to conclude a learning activity because it promotes transfer of learning, enhances motivation for related work, and clarifies learner competence. According to Wiggins (1989, 1998) a task, problem, or project is authentic if it

1. *Is realistic.* The task replicates the ways people's knowledge and capacities are tested in their real world.
2. *Requires judgment and innovation.* People use knowledge wisely to solve unstructured problems—as carpenters do, for example, when they remodel part of a house and must adapt to the situation at hand rather than follow a routine procedure.

3. *Asks learners to "do" the subject.* Rather than recite or demonstrate what they have been taught or what is already known, learners explore and work within the discipline—for example, to demonstrate their competence for a history course, learners might write history from the perspective of particular people who lived in the time they are studying.

4. *Replicates or simulates the contexts that students find in their work-places, communities, or personal lives.* These contexts involve specific situations and their demands: for example, students learning peer mediation skills apply them to what happens on the school playground with consideration of the actual personalities and responsibilities involved.

5. *Assesses learners' ability to effectively use an integration of knowledge and skill to negotiate a complex task.* Learners blend their knowledge and skills to address real-life challenges. This is analogous to taking real shots in a real basketball game or writing a real proposal to change a law, as opposed to taking a few shots in a warm-up drill or writing a paper on that law.

6. *Allows appropriate opportunities to rehearse, practice, consult resources for, and get feedback on and refine performances and products.* This is so important. Learning and, consequently, assessment are not one-shot enterprises! Almost all learning is formative, whether it addresses how to repair plumbing, write a publishable article, or create a lesson that elicits the motivation of *all* students. We put out our first attempt and see how it looks, sounds, or tastes. We repeatedly move through the cycle of *perform, get feedback, revise, perform.* That is how most high-quality products and performances are attained—especially in real life. *We must use assessment procedures that contribute to the improvement of people's performance and learning over time.* This means that much of the time learning ought to be separated from grading processes to assure learners that their mistakes are not counted against them but are a legitimate part of the learning process.

When instructors make assessments partners to exciting learning and continuing motivation for K–12 students and adults, rather than only audits to assign grades or scores, assessments become important learning activities in and of themselves, worthy of everyone's time and effort. Nonetheless (we know you are thinking), time will still be a challenge. Realizing this, we offer next some worthwhile assessment possibilities that can complement authentic tasks or be transformed into authentic tasks.

Assessment Options Based on Gardner's Multiple Intelligences

Each of us has a different profile of intelligences (see the descriptions of the eight intelligences in Chapter Six). When students have the opportunity to select an assessment process that reflects their particular intellectual strengths, it encourages their participation and enthusiasm for demonstrating competence. The following menu of options is categorized by intelligence (adapted from Campbell, Campbell, and Dickson, 1992).

1. Logical-Mathematical

Complete a cost-benefit analysis of . . .

Write a computer program for . . .

Design and conduct an experiment to . . .

Create story problems for . . .

Induce or deduce a set of principles on . . .

Create a time line for . . .

2. Verbal-Linguistic

Tell or write a short story to explain . . .

Keep a journal to illustrate . . .

Write a poem, myth, play, editorial about . . .

Create a debate to discuss . . .

Create an advertising campaign to depict . . .

Create a talk show about . . .

3. Visual-Spatial

Create a piece of art that demonstrates . . .

Create a poster to . . .

Create a videotape, collage, or photo album of . . .

Chart, map, or graph . . .

Design a flag or logo to express . . .

Create a scale model of . . .

4. Musical

Create a song that explains or expresses . . .

Revise lyrics of a song to . . .

Collect and present music and songs to . . .

Create a musical piece to . . .

Create a music video to illustrate . . .

Use music to . . .

5. Bodily-Kinesthetic

Perform a play on . . .

Build or construct a . . .

Role play or simulate . . .

Use puppets to explore . . .

Create a sequence of movements to explain . . .

Create a scavenger hunt to . . .

6. Interpersonal

Participate in a service project that will . . .

Offer multiple perspectives of . . .

Contribute to resolving a local problem by . . .

Teach a group to . . .

Use what you've learned to change or influence . . .

Conduct a discussion to . . .

7. Intrapersonal

Create a personal philosophy about . . .

Discern what is essential in . . .

Explain your intuitive hunches about . . .

Explain your emotions about . . .

Explain your assumptions in a critical incident . . .

Use a journal to . . .

8. Naturalist

Discover and describe the patterns in . . .

Create a typology for . . .

Relate and describe the interdependence of . . .

Create a flow chart for . . .

Use a field trip to analyze . . .

Observe and describe . . .

This menu offers a range of higher-order performance verbs, such as design, teach, discern, explain, analyze, and write, that can be used to create assessments. For example, a student in a science course might *design* an experiment to analyze the chemicals in the local water supply and *write* an editorial based on the results for the local paper. Such assessment tasks provide opportunities for imaginative experiences that allow students to use their unique capabilities and strengths. Furthermore, with these assessments students of all ages can develop deeper relationships between new learning and their cultural backgrounds and values.

Activity 19. Using Multiple Intelligences for Assessment

PURPOSE

For educators to apply and examine different intelligences through reteaching the motivational framework.

TIME

One and one-half hours.

FORMAT

Small groups.

MATERIALS

Handout listing the multiple intelligences, newsprint, and marker.

PROCESS

Step 1. Create eight groups of no more than six people each, and assign a different intelligence to each group. Try to get each participant into a group that represents one of his or her strongest intelligences.

Step 2. Invite each group to create a presentation on the motivational framework, using primarily the intelligence to which they have been assigned. You may wish to have the following directions posted on a piece of newsprint and then read them aloud at this point. Ask each group to (1) share their notes about the Motivational Framework for Culturally Responsive Teaching (see Activity 3 in Chapter Six); (2) determine a focus, that is, aspects of the motivational framework they would like others to remember; and (3) create a five- to seven-minute teaching segment that demonstrates the intelligence with which they are working through reteaching to others something about the motivational framework. The group representing visual-spatial intelligence might draw a series of shapes and ask participants which shape best represents the characteristics of intrinsic motivation and why? The logical-mathematical group might outline a math lesson that teaches a particular skill and includes all four motivational conditions. And the verbal-linguistic group might develop other words for the four conditions of the motivational framework. For example, Lester Middle School in Okinawa, Japan, created a new framework that staff and students call SOBA. *S* stands for *success* (engendering competence), *O* stands for *ownership* (developing a positive attitude), *B* stands for *belonging* (establishing inclusion), and *A* stands for *active learning* (enhancing meaning).

Before the groups begin their work, ask participants to consider what success will look like. In other words, each group should have some criteria for success. Owing to the time constraints, we suggest asking each group to name just three criteria. For example, a group might decide that success means everybody in the group assists in the presentation, the presentation holds the attention of the audience, and the presentation makes clear connections between the Motivational Framework for Culturally Responsive Teaching and the use of a particular intelligence. Also tell participants that at the end of each presentation, the other participants, the audience, will provide brief feedback. They will be asked to raise three fingers if all three criteria were reasonably well met or two fingers if two out of three criteria were met. Because it is unimaginable that a group of talented people would meet only one of the criteria, we suggest you forgo a rating of one.

Step 3. After the presentations and audience feedback, reassemble participants in a large group and ask them to express anything that occurs to them as a consequence of participating in this activity. Ask them how they currently create opportunities for students to learn in ways that allow those students to build on their strengths.

Step 4. Finally, ask participants to think through, with a partner, one or two goals for integrating the multiple intelligences into the teaching and learning process. After participants write their goals on three-by-five-inch cards, they share them with others by posting the cards on a reading wall.

Rubrics

A rubric is a scoring tool that lists criteria, or *what counts*. For example, purpose, organization, details, voice, and mechanics are often what count in a piece of writing. A rubric also articulates gradations of quality for each criterion, from excellent to poor (Goodrich, 1997). There is currently a cottage industry in books about how to write rubrics. Although we are strong advocates of clear criteria for success, at this time we find many rubrics overly linear and rigid.

The challenge to creating and using rubrics is to ensure that they are fair and valid, that they assess the essential features of performance, and that they are sufficiently clear so learners can accurately self-assess. Rubrics are where the rubber meets the road. That's because rubrics often mean more than assessment; they mean evaluation. Assessment describes or compares, but evaluation makes a value judgment. In evaluation we fix passing scores or criteria that determine how acceptable or unacceptable a given performance is. Grades or scores are often assigned and recorded according to a rubric. Combined, these judgments determine a great deal about how students see themselves as learners and the choices they will have as their schooling progresses.

Essentially, a rubric is a set of scoring guidelines for evaluating student work. It strongly *controls* learning because, as Wiggins (1998, p. 154) points out, a rubric is used by many instructors to answer the following questions:

- By what criteria should performance be judged?
- Where should we look and what should we look for to judge performance success?
- What does the range in quality of performance look like?
- How do we determine validly, reliably, and fairly what score should be given and what that score should mean?
- How should the different levels of quality be described and distinguished from one another?

We have been cautiously using rubrics for several years, and although they can be powerful tools for teaching and assessment, they can also be deceptive in ways not obvious at first glance. In some ways they are like a large wall seen from a distance. The cracks are visible only when you get closer. Baseball averages afford a good example of the complexity and elusiveness of rubrics. Rubrics contain a scale of possible points along a continuum of quality. Batting averages are calculated by a rubric that tells us to evaluate how good batters are by their percentage of hits for times at bat. The higher the average, the better the player. But is a .300 hitter a good hitter? Well, that depends: How many times has the player been to bat? Does she get extra base hits? How does she hit when players are on base? At night? With two strikes? When the team is behind? Against left-hand pitching? As many team managers know, you don't use batting average alone to evaluate a player—not even to judge only her hitting. And that is how it is with rubrics. They may seem concrete, specific, and telling, but life's contexts and complexities can make the simplest performance a defying puzzle (Wlodkowski, 1999).

Yet rubrics do provide the answer to that important, if controversial, question, What are you going to use to judge my work? If rubrics are fair, clear, reliable, and valid, if they get at the essentials of performance, and if learners can self-assess with them to improve before performance is evaluated, they enhance motivation because they significantly increase the probability of becoming competent. However, rubrics need to be accompanied by models and indicators that make each level of quality concretely understandable. And they need to be created and revised often with input from students and their families to be meaningful and culturally sensitive. We recently reviewed a rubric for public presentations that included criteria, worded in children's language, such as "How did I look?" The gradations of this particular criterion ranged from "hair combed, clean clothes, smiled, looked happy" to "lazy look" to "just-got-out-of-bed look." As useful as these indicators may seem at first, they may also be interpreted as containing and perpetuating ideas about physical appearance that are *loaded* with cultural assumptions. The term *lazy*, for example, has historically been a stereotype applied to certain groups of people, and this stereotype has been perpetuated by the popular media through messages about *alertness* and *enthusiasm.*

Excellent rubrics are valuable but flawed assistants in making judgments about learning because language at best renders experience. It never duplicates experience. Let's look at one straightforward rubric for judging the clear expression of a main idea in an essay (Exhibit 8.4). (In actual use, the rubric would of course have to be extended to evaluate other dimensions of performance such as critical thinking or writing mechanics.)

This sample rubric can help us to better understand some of Wiggins's (1998, p. 154) guidelines for creating effective rubrics. Thus, if we were using this rubric (and had a model for the descriptor of each level of performance) to evaluate twenty essays *only for the main idea,* we should be able to

1. Use this rubric to accurately discriminate among the essays by assessing the essential features of performance. This makes the rubric valid.
2. Rely on the rubric's descriptive language (what quality or its absence looks like), as opposed to merely evaluative language such as "excellent product," to make the discrimination.
3. Use this rubric to consistently make fine discriminations across the four levels of performance. When a rubric can be repeat-

Exhibit 8.4. A Rubric for Expressing an Idea Clearly.

Rating	Descriptor with Indicators
Exemplary = 4	Clearly communicates the main idea or theme, and provides support that contains rich, vivid, and powerful detail.
Competent = 3	Clearly communicates the main idea or theme, and provides suitable support and detail.
Acceptable with flaws = 2	Clearly communicates the main idea or theme, but support is sketchy or vague.
Needs revision = 1	The main idea or theme is not discernible.

edly used to make the same discriminations with the same sample of performances, it is reliable. To maintain reliability rubrics seldom have more than six levels of performance.

4. Make sure learners can use this same rubric and its descriptors (and models) of each level of performance to accurately self-assess and self-correct their work.

5. Make sure this rubric is parallel. Each descriptor generally matches the others in terms of criteria language used.

6. Make sure this rubric is coherent. The rubric focuses on the same criteria throughout.

7. Make sure this rubric is continuous. The degree of difference between each descriptor (level of performance) tends to be equal.

Activity 20. Rubric Roundtables

PURPOSE

To share knowledge among educators about rubrics; to share rubrics that teachers believe have best supported student success.

TIME

One hour.

FORMAT

Triads.

MATERIALS

Handout (Rubric Discussion Questions)

PROCESS

Ask participants to bring samples of rubrics with which they have experienced the most success. Samples can be part of an off-the-shelf curriculum or homegrown. Ask participants to form groups of three and use a roundtable dialogue format to discuss their rubrics. Distribute a handout with the following questions, which participants can use as a discussion guide.

RUBRIC DISCUSSION QUESTIONS

1. Did you develop the rubric, and if so, what was the process?

2. In using the rubric, what do you do to clarify what each portion describes?

3. How do you ascertain whether all students understand the rubric before they begin a learning experience?

4. Do you believe that all aspects of the rubric are equally important, and if not, what do you do about that?

5. In what ways do you find the number of performance levels to be just right?

6. What do you do about student work that seems to fall between performance levels on the rubric?

7. Are there any ways in which you could make your rubric more culturally sensitive?

Annual Demonstrations of Schoolwide Accomplishment

The next activity helps schools prepare for an annual end-of-the-year event that is both celebratory and informative. It brings schools and people together across a district to learn about the process of school renewal, as depicted through the eyes of key facilitators and participants. Typically, each display offers a complimentary one-page description of the display to visitors. Often these descriptions, along with photographs and other representations of the occasion and of other significant accomplishments throughout the year, are collated into a school or district portfolio.

Activity 21. Poster Conferences

PURPOSE
To imaginatively create and learn from displays that illuminate aspects of a school-based or districtwide renewal initiative based on highly motivating teaching and learning for *all* students.

TIME
Two and one-half hours.

FORMAT
Interactive.

MATERIALS
Handouts (Planning a Poster Conference and Schools of Significance).

PROCESS
Step 1. This is an opportunity for educators to collaboratively plan a poster conference to represent yearlong actions, learning, and accomplishments. Ask participants to review the handout that follows.

PLANNING A POSTER CONFERENCE

1. *What is it?* A poster conference is an efficient and interactive method for sharing exhibitions, ideas, and questions related to a central topic or theme, in this case school renewal. Participants create posters that represent the design and evolution of their initiatives, sample courses or lessons based on the motivational framework, culturally responsive teaching strategies, and other applications of learning. School renewal initiative participants and guests engage in dialogue about display topics, elaborating upon aspects of what they are learning and most value.

2. *Who might attend?* People who might attend include, but are not limited to, poster conference presenters, other educators, district personnel, students, parents and family members, and other community members.

3. *How might people interact?* The process can be informal with 50 percent of the presenters and other initiative participants selecting displays to visit and spontaneously engaging in dialogue with display presenters. After a given time, the other 50 percent of the presenters visit displays. Presenters are asked to provide a one-page summary of their display topic for guests who visit their display. Dialogue or feedback sheets are distributed in a *welcome packet* so presenters can receive explicit feedback from display visitors. Visitors might be asked, for example, to submit a written responses to display presenters on such topics as something of particular value learned from a display, ways to achieve enhanced effectiveness with a strategy presented, or ways a display might influence participation or personal practice among students, parents, educators, or community members.

Step 2. Give participants copies of Figure 8.1, a sample handout from a poster conference exhibition. Explain that it charts the initial year of professional development for a school renewal initiative in a district in Northern California. This particular district has chosen not only to focus on culturally responsive pedagogy and organizational culture but to directly address as well the ways in which race and racism influence people's lives and organizations.

The poster illustrates the work of cadres from six schools plus the regional superintendent, curriculum and instruction, and state and federal program cadres. A minimum of one intersession meeting follows each work session, and the topics and activities are indicated. For example, the poster shows that coaching occurs and that one intersession meeting is reserved to visit demonstration classrooms.

Step 3. Once participants have looked at the handouts, explain that the group will begin planning by brainstorming ideas for its poster conference, using the carousel graffiti process outlined in Activity 1 of Chapter Six. Here are some questions we recommend for brainstorming:

Figure 8.1. Schools of Significance.

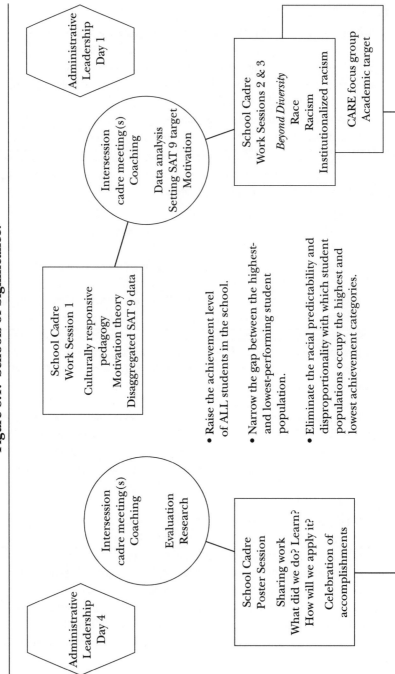

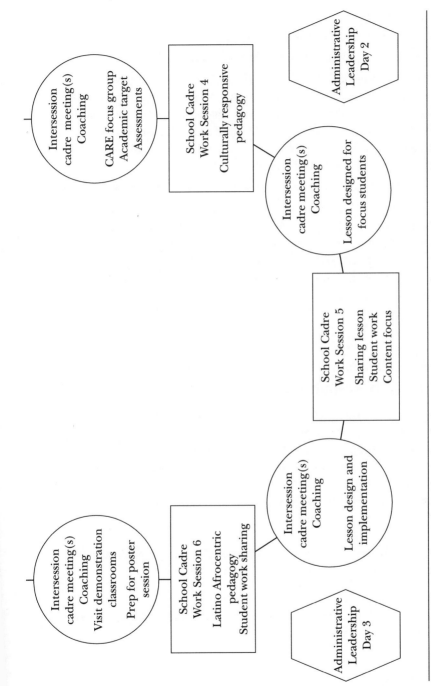

Intersession cadre meeting(s)
Coaching
CARE focus group
Academic target
Assessments

School Cadre
Work Session 4
Culturally responsive
pedagogy

Administrative
Leadership
Day 2

Intersession cadre meeting(s)
Coaching
Lesson designed for focus students

School Cadre
Work Session 5
Sharing lesson
Student work
Content focus

Intersession cadre meeting(s)
Coaching
Visit demonstration classrooms
Prep for poster session

School Cadre
Work Session 6
Latino Afrocentric pedagogy
Student work sharing

Intersession cadre meeting(s)
Coaching
Lesson design and implementation

Administrative
Leadership
Day 3

Source: We thank Pamala Noli and Margaret McCreary of the Bay Area School Leadership Center, Glen Singleton of the Pacific Educational Group, and Joan Davies of the Bay Region IV School Support Center for their central role in creating this schemata.

Brainstorming Questions

1. What might be the goals of this poster conference?

2. What topics might be presented through different poster conference displays?

3. What might a display look like? (For example, it might outline an approach, display pictures and photographs showing an idea in action, show excerpts from interviews with students about their learning experiences, demonstrate how the school found time for job-embedded learning and other forms of adult collaboration, present a scrapbook, and so forth. Going beyond posters, a display might present a video of a teacher showing the motivational framework in action.)

4. How might a poster conference be a stepping-stone to other forms of professional development learning?

5. What kinds of logistics should be considered? (For example, the conference might need a coordinating team and action plans from each subteam of the coordinating team, and an outline of what posters might look like. The coordinating team might have to plan for publicity before and after, room for a district-level display, a one-page written summary for visitors about each display, photography, food, a portfolio based on the conference, and so forth.)

Designing Lessons Using the Motivational Framework for Culturally Responsive Teaching

Although this topic is central to the school renewal initiatives we have developed, we are discussing it at the end of the book because lesson design integrates everything that participants in professional development have learned. Throughout professional development institutes, however, we pause and ask participants to identify how professional development has, thus far, demonstrated the motivational framework in action.

Activity 22. Designing Lessons Using the Motivational Framework for Culturally Responsive Teaching

Purpose

For educators to apply their learning about the motivational framework to customized lesson design.

Time

One and one-half hours.

FORMAT
Dyads or small groups.

MATERIALS
Handouts (a blank and a completed conceptual map of the motivational framework).

PROCESS
Step 1. Review the four motivational conditions with participants and provide a list of the activities that they have examined over the course of the professional development institute. (Activity lists are located at the backs of Chapters Five through Eight.) Ask participants to locate the Partnership Guide for Culturally Responsive Teaching (Exhibit 8.1) for additional reference.

Step 2. Distribute copies of a blank version of Figure 8.2 for participants to complete. On the blank framework, ask participants to join you in mapping their learning as it occurred over the course of at least one of the days you worked together, noting in which motivational condition quadrant the participants might locate the different strategies that they learned. Alternatively, you might wish to map a portion of a day, assuming all four motivational conditions were adequately met by the material taught in that day. Participants will see that several strategies fit more than one condition. Encourage them to select the condition that seems most appropriate. Ultimately, the goal is to ensure that all four conditions have been addressed and that they cohesively support learning goals. What should be avoided is using the framework to transform the motivational conditions into a contrived and fragmented set of activities.

Step 3. Next, you may wish to show participants—in storytelling fashion—how you would map a single lesson you created for a K–12 classroom. It is often interesting, and sometimes amusing, to do this with a demonstration lesson you may have taught. Participants typically enjoy the successes and challenges of a facilitator who is trying to practice what she preaches. The handout that follows contains a sample. It chronicles a block schedule lesson for a culturally and ethnically diverse eleventh-grade social science class at a large urban high school. This example uses a linear approach to outlining a lesson using the motivational framework; Figure 8.2 shows the conceptual map (for the same lesson) that may also be used.

A MOTIVATIONAL FRAMEWORK FOR CULTURALLY RESPONSIVE TEACHING LESSON PLAN
Topic: The Blame Cycle
Goals: (1) To help students understand the concept of "blame," how it works, and what we can do to control the tendency to blame; (2) to develop "higher-order thinking skills" through a reframing exercise that helps people look at something that is a problem for them in a new and more positive way; and (3) to diminish the tendency to blame.

Establishing Inclusion
How does the learning experience contribute to the development of participants as a community of learners who feel respected by and connected to one another and to the teacher?

Explain who I am and why I am here, do (Activity 2, Chapter Five) two wishes and a truth exercise (model for the class three things about myself and ask students to guess which one is the truth), then facilitate personal introductions (ask each person to introduce himself or herself and to simultaneously mention "one thing about this school that people wouldn't know just by looking in").

Developing a Positive Attitude
How does the learning experience offer meaningful choices and promote personal relevance to contribute to participants' positive attitude?

Provide an agenda to assure students that they will have a sense of choice in what we do. Provide an overview of blame, to develop relevance by helping students see that throughout the world all people tend to attribute bad things that happen to forces outside themselves: for example, on one end of the spectrum we say things like, "It was a *bad* day," or, "It wasn't in the stars." On the other end of the spectrum we say things like, "It's her fault," or, "He's a . . ." (fill in the blank with a common label). Ask students, in pairs, to think about why blame comes in so handy (for example, it lets us off the hook, gives us a sense of control, provides a solution to complex problems). Ask students, in pairs, to think of reasons why blame is a problem, demonstrate a map of the blame cycle using a personal experience, and ask students to map personal blame cycles.

Enhancing Meaning
How does the learning experience engage participants in challenging learning that has social merit?

Explain that we are going to use a volunteer's "blame cycle map" to interrupt the tendency to blame, through a process called "reframing." (Ask for a volunteer who doesn't mind coming to the front of the room and sharing her or his blame map). Demonstrate reframing, asking the entire class to think of all the *positive* reasons that the "antagonist" might have had for his or her actions. Chart the responses. Then ask the volunteer to select *one* of the class's positive "reframes" to work with. (It needs to be something the volunteer can honestly believe about the other person.) Next, ask the class to brainstorm all of the things that the volunteer could do, knowing about this more positive way to understand the antagonist's behavior. Ask the volunteer to select a course of action from the options the class has provided.

Engendering Competence
How does the learning experience create participants' understanding that they are becoming more effective in authentic learning that they value?

Ask students to work with a partner to repeat the process, using either partner's blame cycle.

Closure: Ask students to suggest "blame metaphors" (for example: Blame is like a . . . because . . .).

Closing question: How might you use the blame cycle outside of this classroom?

Undergirding every strategy in this chapter is a belief that assessment ought to figuratively and literally include *sitting beside* students so teachers and students understand together what students know and can do because of what they have learned and so teachers can inspire the emergence of new ideas.

Conclusion

As we close this chapter, we would like to once more talk about the process of change. Whether we are trying new learning activities, designing lessons from a cultural and motivational perspective, or rethinking the meaning of cultural responsiveness throughout an entire school, none of us can ever know beforehand, with certainty, what all the consequences of our actions will be. Culturally responsive, highly motivating schools depend on imagination and faith as well as on planning and prediction.

Risking cliché, there simply are no quick fixes to enhancing the vitality of an entire system. Educators need sustained opportunities to learn with and from each other. Even then, there will be fears and hesitations, shifts in sentiment, and other human foibles—our own as well as those of others. Increasing the opportunities for students from *all* backgrounds to experience success as human beings, students, and civic participants requires us to embrace hopeful, if uncertain, human bonds as we change. Ultimately, that may be the point.

The following checklist can serve as a guide for teachers and other facilitators of learning as they work to create the conditions in which authenticity and effectiveness contribute to engendering competence.

Engendering Competence

How does the learning experience create students' understanding that they are becoming more effective in authentic learning that they value?

There is information, consequence, or product that supports students in valuing and identifying learning.

__ The teacher clearly communicates the purpose of the lesson.

__ The teacher clearly communicates criteria for excellent final products.

__ The teacher provides opportunities for a diversity of competencies to be demonstrated in a variety of ways.

__ The teacher helps all students to concretely identify accomplishments.

__ The teacher assesses different students differently.

__ The teacher assesses progress continually in order to provide feedback on individual growth and progress.

__ The teacher creates opportunities for students to make explicit connections between new and prior learning.

__ The teacher creates opportunities for students to make explicit connections between their learning and the "real world."

__ The teacher provides opportunities for students to self-assess learning in order to reflect on their growth as learners.

__ The teacher provides opportunities for students to self-assess their personal responsibility for contributing to the classroom as a learning community.

Describe the evidence:

Activity Guide for Engendering Competence

Engendering Competence: Classroom Activities for Students

Post-Writes (Activity 2)

Summarizing Questions (Activity 3)

Student Self-Assessment Aligned with the Motivational Framework (Activity 4)

Closure Note-Taking Pairs (Activity 8)

Door Passes (Activity 9)

Seasonal Partners (Activity 10)

Head, Heart, Hand (Activity 11)

Reflection Logs (Activity 12)

Reflection Trees for Group Projects (Activity 13)

Class Evaluation from the Perspective of K–12 Students (Activity 16)

Engendering Competence: Professional Development Activities for Educators

Overview of Developing Journals (Activity 1)

Summarizing Questions (Activity 3)

Educator Self-Assessment (Activity 5)

Using the Peer Coaching Rubric Based on the Motivational Framework (Activity 6)

Enhancing the Motivational Influence of Professional Practice by Examining Student Work (Activity 7)

Closure Note-Taking Pairs (Activity 8)

Door Passes (Activity 9)

Seasonal Partners (Activity 10)

Head, Heart, Hand (Activity 11)

Reflection Logs (Activity 12)

Reflection Trees for Group Projects (Activity 13)

Examining Grading Practices (Activity 14)

Effective Feedback (Activity 15)

Feedback for Educators (Activity 16)

Evaluating the Motivational Conditions of an Institute (Activity 18)

Using Multiple Intelligences for Assessment (Activity 19)

Rubric Roundtables (Activity 20)

Poster Conferences (Activity 21)

Designing Lessons Using the Motivational Framework for Culturally Responsive Teaching (Activity 22)

Chapter Nine

Organizing a Districtwide Initiative

This chapter describes how to organize a districtwide initiative for culturally responsive teaching. It presents criteria for success and provides an overview of the components of an initiative, such as schoolwide instructional leadership cadres and school institutes that are cofacilitated by the cadre and a staff developer. Most of the information is presented in an idealized form. All school improvement initiatives take place amid challenges and, at times, outrageous acts of sabotage. Nonetheless, to face organizational realities imaginatively and productively, it is helpful to have a vision of the attributes of a successful initiative. The illumination of idealized attributes makes it possible to experience challenge as informative rather than adversarial. It also permits an understanding of what might be missing from an effort and paves the way for informed improvisation.

Components for Success

First, we look at eight components commonly found in successful initiatives for culturally responsive teaching.

- Supportive district-level administrative leadership
- An external consultant or staff developer with expertise in the motivational framework and a commitment to principles of adult learning
- A district liaison for coordination and support

- Supportive, school-based administrative leadership
- Schoolwide instructional leadership cadres that reflect the diversity of the broader community and that include, when possible, two members of each grade-level, discipline-specific, or interdisciplinary planning team
- A willingness at all levels to creatively manage time constraints and maximize opportunities for faculty learning and planning
- A willingness at all levels to make culturally responsive teaching the focus of the school improvement plan
- Parent, family, student, and community encouragement and involvement

Supportive District-Level Administrative Leadership

Strong district-level leadership support is very important. The superintendent ought to be fully supportive of the principles and practices of culturally responsive teaching, ongoing professional development, and the participation of district-level liaisons. Ideally, she or he communicates and demonstrates unequivocal support for the initiative. In doing so, the superintendent should

- Meet on a regular basis with school-based leadership and leadership teams.
- Model continuous support for collaboration and shared decision making.
- Encourage the formation of a district-level team whose members serve as liaisons, advocates, and coaches and consultants to initiative schools.
- Lead visits of a district-level team to schools to observe classroom practice and speak with teachers and other members of the school community about school strengths and challenges.
- Carry a message about continuous school improvement as a process (as opposed to an event) that is ambitious, culturally responsive, instructionally focused, and schoolwide.
- Encourage ongoing, job-embedded professional development and be willing to provide additional professional development days for staff to attend awareness institutes and do planning and decision making.

- Recognize and illuminate the accomplishments of schools that are engaging in and achieving courageous visions of success for all students.
- Forge community forums and partnerships focused on improving support for student learning and achievement.
- Be willing to face, with candor and empathy, the harsh realities of the district's or community's own contributions to disparities in the academic achievement of different student groups; be prepared to make authentic statements in the face of disapproval; and emphasize a vision of unity.

External Consultant or Staff Developer with Expertise in the Motivational Framework for Culturally Responsive Teaching

A knowledgeable and flexible consultant is indispensable. The consultant must be able to

- Co-conceptualize the design for the districtwide initiative with district-level, school-based, and community representatives.
- Unite the initiative with a process of strong continuous school improvement.
- Facilitate regularly scheduled institutes for cadres to help cadre members develop and take action as school-based leaders who are highly motivating, culturally responsive teachers and visionary schoolwide planners for improvement.
- Facilitate regularly scheduled principals' institutes to encourage instructional leadership and professional goal setting with teachers that is linked to highly motivating instruction for *all* students.
- Establish a system of regular communication with the district liaison(s).
- Engage in ongoing role clarification, planning, and problem solving with district representatives and team members.
- Provide resource support.
- Co-create an evaluation design.
- Interact with existing districtwide communication structures such as forums for parents and community members (for example, PTA meetings) and meetings of local chapters of national educational and civic organizations.

- Recognize and illuminate school-based accomplishment.
- Share the *ownership of knowing* and respectfully understand and work with local perspectives, knowledge bases, and interests and needs.

District Liaison for Coordination and Support

Success for the initiative depends on having at least one district-level staff member who is committed to and can devote at least half time to the principles and practices of culturally responsive teaching and to the challenges of implementing this initiative. The district liaison should

- Co-conceptualize the design for the districtwide initiative with the consultant or staff developer and with other district-level, school-based, and community representatives.
- Unite the individuals and teams in the initiative with a process of strong, continuous school improvement.
- Carry a message about continuous school improvement as a process (as opposed to an event) that is ambitious, culturally responsive, instructionally focused, and schoolwide.
- Meet regularly with school-based leadership and with leadership teams.
- Model continuous support for collaboration and shared decision making.
- Encourage the formation of a district-level team whose members serve as liaisons, advocates, and coaches and consultants to initiative schools.
- Encourage ongoing, job-embedded professional development and be willing to advocate for resources and additional professional development days for staff to attend awareness institutes and do planning and decision making.
- Cofacilitate regularly scheduled institutes for cadres to help cadre members develop and take action as school-based leaders who are highly motivating, culturally responsive teachers and visionary schoolwide planners for improvement.
- Participate in regularly scheduled principals' institutes and meetings to encourage instructional leadership and

professional goal setting with teachers that is linked to highly motivating instruction for *all* students.

- Design, in collaboration with cadres and the external consultant or staff developer, awareness institute agendas for the respective schools of the cadres.
- Cofacilitate, in collaboration with cadres and the external consultant or staff developer, awareness institutes for the respective schools of the cadres.
- Establish a system of regular communication with cadres, which includes school visits. (Ideally, this responsibility is shared with other members of the district-level team.)
- Engage in ongoing role clarification, planning, and problem solving with district representatives and cadres.
- Provide resource support.
- Co-create an evaluation design.
- Interact with existing districtwide communication structures such as district newsletters, advisory councils, forums for parents and community members (for example, PTA meetings), and meetings of local chapters of national educational and civic organizations.
- Recognize and illuminate school-based accomplishments.
- Share the *ownership of knowing* and respectfully understand and work with community and school-based perspectives, knowledge bases, and interests and needs.

Supportive School-Based Administrative Leadership

Ideally, school-based administrators are respectful of cultural diversity and supportive of ambitious and ongoing school renewal. Although many school-based administrators have not had the opportunity to examine issues related to culturally responsive teaching in depth, a successful initiative requires their active participation in learning. School-based administrators must be willing to

- Establish in concert with other stakeholders a strong and positive academic learning climate in which informed experimentation and a passion for teaching and learning among the whole school community are actively supported.

- Regularly visit classrooms to support and encourage teaching practices and goal setting that incorporate culturally responsive teaching.
- Regularly hold dialogue sessions to identify the school's perceived strengths and challenges and explore potential reasons for differences in opinion.
- Model continuous support for collaboration and shared decision making.
- Actively encourage parent, community, and when practical, student participation.
- Establish along with teachers and staff a *no-excuses* orientation to problem solving so that in spite of societal influences on student success the school is consistently willing to challenge its limits.
- Ensure that schoolwide policies and organizational procedures are consistent with the school's beliefs and vision and are intentionally designed to maximize the learning of *all* students.
- Carry a message about continuous school improvement as a process (as opposed to an event) that is ambitious, culturally responsive, instructionally focused, and schoolwide.
- Ensure that the use and allocation of resources are aligned with the school's goals and initiatives.
- Meet on a regular basis with or participate as a member of the leadership cadre, and when the cadre and the school improvement team are different entities, build bridges between their work.
- Provide support for ongoing, job-embedded professional development and be willing to advocate for resources and additional professional development days for staff to attend awareness institutes and do planning or decision making.
- Participate in regularly scheduled institutes for cadres to help cadre members develop and take action as school-based leaders who are highly motivating, culturally responsive teachers and visionary schoolwide planners.
- Participate in regularly scheduled principals' institutes and meetings to encourage instructional leadership and professional goal setting with teachers that is linked to highly motivating instruction for *all* students.

- Participate in the design of awareness institute agendas for the respective schools of the cadres.
- Participate, in collaboration with cadre members, the district liaison, and the external consultant or staff developer, in awareness institutes for the respective schools of the cadres.
- Establish a regular system of communication with cadres (unless the principal is already a member of the team).
- Establish a regular system of communication with the district liaison so the liaison is informed of important school accomplishments and events.
- Engage in ongoing planning and problem solving with district representatives and cadres.
- Assist with the collection and analysis of school-specific data related to teacher performance and student achievement within and across student groups.
- Use communication structures such as the school newsletter, advisory councils, forums for parents and community members (for example, PTA meetings), and meetings of local chapters of national educational and civic organizations to inform others of important goals and accomplishments related to culturally responsive teaching.
- Share the *ownership of knowing* and respectfully understand and work with district-level, community, and school-based perspectives, knowledge bases, and interests and needs.

Schoolwide Instructional Leadership Cadres

Schoolwide instructional leadership cadres, or more simply, leadership cadres, are the core of the initiative. Ideally, cadre membership includes two teachers from each content area, grade level, or conference-period planning team, as well as representatives from the arts and federally funded programs such as bilingual education. Cadre membership should also include parent and community representatives. In middle and high schools, it is advisable to recruit department chairs and, at all levels, we recommend representation from the school governance team. A key objective is to support them in developing their capacity and leadership in ways that keep the initiative focused at the school level. In essence, these cadres provide a means for schools to integrate the expertise of an external consultant or staff developer yet avoid unnecessary dependence on this individual. Members of each cadre assist their school in planning, implementing, and sustaining culturally responsive teaching practices by offering leadership as expert learners, site-based staff developers, mentors of instructional improvement, and advocates of meaningful, continuous school improvement. In concert with the district-level team, which comprises the district superintendent's staff, each cadre uses capacity-building institutes, quarterly work sessions, monthly self-directed study groups, school-based institutes, peer coaching, and an end-of-the-year poster conference to develop and share with its school community

- Awareness and commitment to instructionally focused, continuous school improvement as a vehicle for supporting the success of *all* students in a school, especially as success relates to addressing the disparities in student performance indicated by district data.
- Understanding of the relationship between culture and motivation to learn.
- Insights on the role of the overall school environment, curriculum, and instructional practice in creating a culturally responsive school.
- A Motivational Framework for Culturally Responsive Teaching, with each component delineated and supported through practical teaching and learning strategies.
- Highly motivating and culturally responsive case studies and demonstration lessons.
- Systematic approaches to collaborative, job-embedded learning, planning, and peer coaching.
- Features of successful schoolwide and districtwide school improvement initiatives that really matter and go beyond quick fixes.
- Methods to document accomplishment in ways that are useful to teachers (for example, process folios that can be shared with others to reflect on growth over time) and trustworthy (that is, supported by reliable data).
- Resources.

Typically, the school principal or the school improvement team designates one administrator, a minimum of four to five instructional staff, two to three parents, possibly one other key staff member (such as an ESL teacher), and when appropriate, at least one student to the cadre. The size of the team is influenced by the number of schools that are participating in the initiative. For example, if the initiative is focused on three middle schools, it is desirable for each school to have a large cadre, with two faculty from each grade-level planning team. This facilitates the likelihood that new learning in the cadre will be more effectively shared with the regular school-based planning teams. When there is only one grade-level planning team representative per cadre, the ideas this representative shares may not be as well heard. The superintendent also designates one educator on the cadre to serve on the district-level team. One parent on the cadre should also serve on the district team. The cadre has primary responsibility for supporting the school community in

- Understanding opportunities related to highly motivating, culturally responsive teaching and learning and continuous school improvement.
- Making decisions about a *coherent* schoolwide approach to instruction that consistently supports the motivation of *all* students.
- Making decisions about policies and practices that contribute to the learning and satisfaction of students (for example, meaningful parent, family, and community involvement; counseling programs that support high expectations for all students and provide scaffolding that helps students achieve goals; governance and decision-making agreements; and effective schoolwide discipline).
- Facilitating school-based actions that lead to the implementation of a highly motivating and culturally responsive system of teaching and learning.
- Building a professional learning team so that all school staff can experience enhanced learning and communication structures, a rich diversity of relationships, and shared leadership as they all work together for continuous, instructionally focused school improvement.

- Collecting evidence of the ways in which the principles and practices of culturally responsive teaching are becoming internalized.

The cadre elects a leader or employs a shared leadership model, plans regular meetings, systematically communicates and coordinates with the school improvement team, participates in district-sponsored capacity-building institutes, and codesigns and cofacilitates, with the consultant or staff developer, a school-based professional development institute. In addition, it communicates regularly with the district liaison and with the school community as a whole. A sample format for communicating with the district liaison is provided at the end of this chapter.

Willingness at All Levels to Manage Time Constraints Creatively and Maximize Opportunities for Faculty Learning and Planning

An initiative this comprehensive requires time for learning, dialogue, and planning. Culturally responsive teaching is not a lockstep approach to improving instructional practice schoolwide. Because such teaching is essentially *practice based,* it is the evolving convergence of classroom teaching, learning theory, and context that supports and maintains faculty commitment. This interaction, that is, this marriage of the science and art of education, defies simplistic school improvement formulas.

In order for initiative participants to respect and manage the complexity of the issues that influence learning within and across cultures and within and across a school, they must have adequate opportunities for learning, for reflection and dialogue, for working things out emotionally, and for planning. The goal is to create structures that permit informed improvisation related to highly motivating teaching and learning for *all* students and to eliminate the easy beauty that is undergirded by shortcuts. The superintendent's staff, school-based administrators, teachers, parents, and community members must understand and support professional development time to address this goal and its inherent challenges. This support is most likely to arise when the stakeholders are clear about what students have to gain from professional development time for adult members of the school community.

Willingness at All Levels to Make Culturally Responsive Teaching the Focus of the School Improvement Plan

At some point in the process, culturally responsive teaching has to become an integral part of the school improvement plan if it is to be the fundamental focus for schoolwide practice. This step, of course, is not meaningful if school improvement is a cursory process that has little to do with a community's genuine dreams. Nor is it meaningful if the decision is forced. As learning about culturally responsive teaching deepens, as it is examined alongside of learning about school improvement that matters, and as commitment to culturally responsive teaching and strong school improvement planning increases, leadership cadres and their schools will be more inclined to focus on culturally responsive teaching in their plan for continuous improvement. This may happen at different times in different schools in the process of continuous school improvement—because all plans, like all schools, are works in progress.

To ensure that culturally responsive teaching actively resides in the school improvement plan, all institutes should include dialogue and some initial decision making that positively influences an instructional focus for school improvement planning. As a part of this process, schools need to reclaim the school improvement process as something other than a political mandate. Certain practices tend to reinforce superficiality, even when they are pursued by some in earnest. For example, when members of the school community divide themselves into benchmark committees, that is, committees that strategize about ways to meet district standards, they tend to create random checklists of abstract ideas. But when they come together to examine data that illuminate how students are performing across ethnic and cultural groups, and when they then apply their observations to a shared vision of an ideal school for working in, sending one's own children to, and supporting the success of all students, school improvement ideas generally become more concrete, innovative, and promising. Attaching benchmarks to human dreams tends to create greater sincerity and depth than attaching ideas to benchmarks.

In addition, this approach eliminates redundancy because sincere ideas frequently contribute to several different benchmarks or standards. For example, reconfiguring the school day and using a motivational instructional plan to inspire active and deep learning throughout extended blocks of time might help to meet math standards, reading standards, and equity standards, three different benchmark goals.

Parent, Family, Student, and Community Encouragement and Involvement

Community encouragement and involvement springs from parents, community members, and students who are supportive of opportunities for *all* students to achieve academic success. Sometimes communities have articulated a need for school improvement action because of community members' specific concerns or complaints. Community encouragement, however, is not always rooted in conflict or explicit concern. It can also stem from a clear desire to strengthen the instructional program for *all* students. In the long run, parents, family members, and student leaders are really the conscience of any strong initiative. Perhaps this why they are so often feared and kept at a "respectful" distance when it comes to real decision making.

Although we find that it is neither feasible nor desirable for students to attend cadre meetings regularly, there are many important roles for students. In one school, for example, a math class learned about statistics by disaggregating and analyzing school data on student performance within and between groups. Further, students helped to create approaches to charting schoolwide change by designing ways to analyze school and student performance over time. This included a process known as Data in a Day, developed at the Northwest Regional Educational Laboratory. Teams of students, parents, and teachers visited classrooms to look for the ways in which the school was moving toward the motivational ideals to which it aspired. After observing, in several classrooms over the course of a day, the teams provided feedback to the entire school community. In another school, students developed a coffeehouse to encourage parents and students to participate in an evening literacy program. In many schools, students serve as focus groups, providing input to teachers on lesson designs and outcomes, and often historically low-performing students are recruited to help teachers design and implement demonstration lessons.

Key Elements

The key elements of an initiative for culturally responsive teaching are structures designed for convening various school community members in order for them to work and learn together. These structures are

- Inter- or intradistrict work sessions for central office liaisons
- Institutes for schoolwide instructional leadership cadres
- Interteam work sessions (meetings involving two or more teams)
- Intrateam work sessions (meetings of a single team)
- Institutes for the whole school
- Professional learning teams for the whole school
- Annual poster conferences
- District-level team meetings
- Interschool visits

Inter- or Intradistrict Work Sessions for Central Office Liaisons

At the district level, there needs to be clear agreement on who will serve in a leadership capacity as the district liaison to the external consultant or staff developer and who will serve as a liaison to participating schools. District staff who might participate in this initiative include, but are not limited to, school improvement specialists, staff development specialists, curriculum specialists, and federal programs coordinators. The district liaison to the external consultant serves as a coordinator of the initiative, a coordinator of resources, a coplanner with cadres, a facilitator, and a learner. Once a district liaison is appointed, the district-level team can begin to plan with the external consultant or staff developer and to clarify team members' roles as advocates of students, schools, and instructionally focused school improvement.

Institutes for Schoolwide Instructional Leadership Cadres

An initial professional development institute, conducted by the external consultant or staff developer, allows cadres and district-level staff, including the superintendent, to begin to develop a knowledge base for culturally responsive teaching and learning. It is also an opportunity for them to catalyze team goal setting and planning that is or will be customized to the school improvement plans and the characteristics of each school. Finally, the initial institute creates a districtwide community of learners committed to ongoing study and practice in the area of highly motivating, culturally responsive teaching. A three-day initial institute is desirable. A sample agenda for this institute is provided in the next chapter. As the agenda indicates, it is important to give participants the opportunity to substantively *experience* highly motivating adult learning, examine key issues related to motivation and cultural diversity, apply these issues to the school context, and begin planning an inquiry-based project that encourages their ongoing learning in an area of their choice.

An example of an inquiry-based project is the exploration conducted by one cadre into whether or not the children's literature that is most frequently read by individual teachers reflects the multiculturalism of the United States and of each teacher's school. In collaboration with the faculty of their school, they designed an approach to sensitively investigate and report findings related to the equitable and fair representation of all students in children's literature. As a consequence of this investigation, school staff became more aware of the ways in which historically underrepresented groups have been traditionally marginalized or misrepresented in curriculum materials. They could also see how the heroes and holidays focus they had been employing had been an inadequate approach to affirming cultural pluralism. As a next step the faculty agreed to examine ways to teach the same inquiry-based process to students, to critically reflect on a regular basis with students about print materials and other media used in everyday learning and to locate and use additional resources for broader and more accurate representation of diverse groups. The cadre that chose to examine curriculum materials for equity was responding to the second condition in the Motivational Framework for Culturally Responsive Teaching, develop a positive attitude toward learning, and was addressing the importance of personal and cultural relevance in what students learn and how they learn.

An initial three-day institute also provides an opportunity for district-level staff and school-based cadre members to examine the value of the motivational framework for diminishing the fragmentation that results from random application of "a little bit of this and a little bit of that," for unifying best practices, and for expanding and deepening best practices in order to consistently support the motivation of *all* students. By valuing participants' prior learning and providing a nonthreatening environment in which individuals can pose hard questions, institutes allow cadre members to take a hard look at ways to strengthen the instructional focus of their schools' improvement plans and to see themselves as the locus of control for professional development and continuous schoolwide planning.

Interteam Work Sessions (Meetings Involving Two or More Teams)

In addition to institutes that assist cadre members in developing their knowledge base, there is a need for dialogue across cadres. Periodic dialogue between different teams builds a districtwide community of learners. The advantages for team members include coming to see issues as broader than one's own school, broadening one's perspectives by sharing insights and ideas with others, and heightening one's level of commitment by sharing plans and accomplishments. Quarterly interteam meetings are advisable.

Intrateam Work Sessions (Meetings of a Single Team)

Systematic dialogue within a cadre ensures that members regularly identify challenges and opportunities at the school site and continue the process of implementing school renewal goals. As a part of or in addition to its regularly scheduled team meetings, each cadre ought to plan with the district liaison. This provides an opportunity to coordinate resources, refine plans, and learn from the liaison's experiences with other teams. A minimum of once a month is advised for cadre meetings, although many schools prefer weekly meetings. (These meetings are typically referred to as *intercession meetings* because they often occur in between the work sessions that are facilitated by an external consultant or staff developer.) A minimum of one quarterly meeting with the district liaison is advised. Activities with the liaison can include reporting on the progress on the team's inquiry-based project or action plan, conducting a dialogue on schoolwide successes and challenges, problem solving, and making requests for human and material resources.

Institutes for the Whole School

One of the strongest transition points for a school that is becoming a community of learners committed to well-aligned instructional practices that support motivation and achievement among all groups of learners is the cofacilitation process. With the assistance of the external consultant and district staff, the members of the schoolwide instructional leadership cadre create original agendas based on aspects of their learning they believe to be most relevant to their school's interests. Professional development institutes are predicated upon the notion that for educators to trust instructional ideas that others deem valuable and to apply those ideas in their own classrooms, they need to experience them as a part of their own learning. Institutes are therefore designed so that adults can consistently experience the motivational framework for culturally responsive teaching.

We have been conducting these institutes for the last five years, and responses on questionnaires distributed to cadre members about the cofacilitation process have been consistently positive. They reflect individuals' beliefs that they have experienced personal accomplishments, team accomplishments, and school improvement accomplishments. We have frequently seen comments like these: "I feel more connected to the whole notion of cultural diversity and can see how the school improvement process should include multiculturalism," and, "Cofacilitation built ownership in the school improvement process and created a new framework for school improvement."

When professional development institutes are designed for the entire school, they have four goals. The first goal is to create awareness among all school staff of the Motivational Framework for Culturally Responsive Teaching and of the options and related strategies for supporting the academic success of *all* students. The second goal is to further develop the capacity of the cadres by providing the experience of cooperatively planning an agenda and cofacilitating the school institute with the external consultant. This gives each cadre the opportunity to deepen its understanding of the motivational framework and of school improvement issues related to cultural diversity and to identify its own emerging competence. As a consequence, the third goal is accomplished: the cadre enhances the quality of its teamwork and planning processes and its members begin to see themselves as well as to be seen by peers as school-based leaders. And, finally, the fourth goal is achieved as the teacher participants make classroom applications and begin planning in grade- or department-level teams.

Although the planning for the institute focuses on the Motivational Framework for Culturally Responsive Teaching, as earlier stated, it also strengthens the process of continuous school improvement. A sample agenda for planning the school-based institute with members of the cadre is included in the next chapter along with a sample agenda for the school-based institute itself.

Professional Learning Teams for the Whole School

Although whole school institutes provide a strong overview of theory and practice and offer faculty the time to do some preliminary planning, there is no substitute for adult learning that is a regular part of school life. In almost all schools, adults find time to engage in dialogue with other adults. But this dialogue is frequently focused on personal anecdotes and does not necessarily provide systematic opportunities for reflection and action related to instructional practice. Similarly, in almost all schools, the forces of change maintain a constant presence. But change is not the same thing as improvement—especially improvement that has a strong instructional focus. The most successful schools nationwide use collaborative learning, or *professional learning teams* to ensure a focus on and passion for learning related to instructional practice. This learning can be brought about in many different ways. Consistently, however, the goal is to be thoughtful and systematic about collaborative adult learning.

Our approach is to encourage teachers to plan and reflect on lessons collaboratively, using the motivational framework as a guide. This is also how shared learning time can become a key to collaboratively finding ways to use the framework. In one school, for example, the schoolwide leadership cadre provided faculty with articles on different approaches to effectively using shared learning time. After significant dialogue, faculty agreed that they would meet in grade-level interdisciplinary teams from 2:30 P.M. to 4:00 P.M. the first Wednesday of every month in order to plan a collaborative lesson. This, they believed, would allow them to deepen their skill at motivational planning and teaching. The second Wednesday of the month they would use shared learning time to reflect on the implementation of the jointly planned lesson. The third Wednesday they would collectively examine a piece of student work for insights into how to better support the motivation of a low-performing student. Their intention was to learn how to enrich instructional practice for *all* students by learning how to best assist students who have historically not been successful. The last Wednesday of the month they would reflect on and document key learning and summarize it in two to three sentences on the school's intranet for schoolwide reflection. In addition, once a month an interdisciplinary team, on a rotating basis, would synthesize the team reports as they appeared on the intranet and identify how the school as a whole—through learning communities and instructional practice—had been contributing to school improvement goals.

The school found time for this adult learning by adding half an hour to every Wednesday school day. School was dismissed at 2:15 P.M., and typically teachers stayed until at least 3:30 P.M. Because they were staying until 4:00 P.M. on Wednesdays, thereby extending the workday into personal time, faculty and administration agreed that teachers could select another day of the week to leave school a half hour earlier than they ordinarily would. In this way, teachers had more time for shared learning and felt adequately compensated. (Of course in some ways the flexibility offered by the school was symbolic, because, as a matter of choice and necessity, teachers typically donate hours that far exceed contractual requirements.) For ideas on the ways that schools across the country are finding more time for shared learning, please see Activity 12 in Chapter Six.

Another important way that faculty have been learning together is through peer observations of classroom practice and subsequent partnership dialogue. This strategy is also referred to as *peer coaching*. If educators are going to be highly effective at something new, they need some form of support. Although the idea of inviting a trusted colleague to provide feedback on self-identified instructional priorities is exciting to many, it is threatening to others. In some schools, cadre members who are classroom teachers have created receptivity to peer coaching or partnership dialogue by using their own experiences to generate schoolwide interest. In fact, in one school, a cadre created an inquiry-based project to examine the process.

They agreed that for two months each team member would make biweekly visits to the classroom of a partner for a minimum of thirty minutes during the visitor's independent planning period. Each pair of partners alternated visits to one another's classrooms. Visits were preceded by approximately fifteen minutes of dialogue and followed by a minimum of fifteen minutes of dialogue so partners could share insights. To start, team members noted only the strengths that they observed. Over time, they began to identify challenges about which they would appreciate collegial dialogue. Eventually, they reflected upon the extent to which they had been applying all four motivational conditions with consistency and depth. The rubric for culturally responsive teaching that many have found helpful for this process is called the Partnership Guide for Culturally Responsive Teaching (Exhibit 8.1). Activity 6 in Chapter Eight offers additional information on peer coaching.

Annual Poster Conference

As indicated in Activity 21, Chapter Eight, a poster conference is an interactive method for sharing exhibitions, ideas, and questions. It provides an opportunity for cadre members to engage in dia-

logue with each other, central office staff, school board members, and key members of the community about creatively displayed topics. Each team prepares a poster, a display, or a demonstration that represents its focus and accomplishments. Poster conference exhibitions have included sample lesson designs using the motivational framework, with photographs of the learning process labeled with the four motivational conditions; creative displays of student work that illustrate how the four conditions supported student success; descriptions of strategies that correspond to the framework, with visual aids to demonstrate how they work; and computer simulations, time lines, and cognitive maps that show how the initiative for culturally responsive teaching evolved and was integrated into their school improvement plan. A reflection sheet for each exhibit can be filled out by observers, providing evidence of ways the observers increased their knowledge of how to create highly motivating classroom instruction, design school inquiry-based projects, provide school improvement processes that matter, create strong collaborative teams focused on improving student learning, examine student work in order to transform historically low-achieving students into intellectual leaders, and develop faculty institutes that invite an ongoing dialogue about cultural diversity and student achievement. When each exhibit hands out a one-page summary, visitors have something to help them recall their learning and the school has contributions to a process folio that includes insights and best practices from the initiative.

District Team Meetings

The purpose of the district-level team, sometimes referred to as a school support team, is threefold. First, the team serves as the link between the community and the district superintendent and his or her staff. Second, it provides ongoing representation for and support to the school-based teams. Third, by using a shared leadership model and generating its own understanding of cultural responsiveness, the district team can emulate the district's high expectations for building learning communities throughout district schools. An essential ingredient for a successful district team is an appropriate structure. The district team comprises the superintendent, the assistant superintendent, school-based cadre representatives (a parent and an educator from each cadre), and other community representatives, including students, when possible. Regular meetings with collaboratively planned agendas, based on negotiated priorities, provide opportunities for capacity building as well as opportunities to make recommendations on district needs and issues. One district team, for example, identified three initial priorities: districtwide conflict negotiation, ongoing community education about the initiative, and a comprehensive initiative evaluation. A sample district team work session agenda is included in the next chapter.

Interschool Visits

Interschool visits provide a two-way opportunity for collegial dialogue and support. By visiting other schools, teams garner ideas for their own schools. In addition, these visits can become a rich source of knowledge about the ways other schools have developed highly motivating classrooms and school renewal processes. These school visits provide an opportunity for practitioners to dialogue about pragmatic topics ranging from the reduction of pullout classes to job-embedded professional development.

Many school visits are quite informal. Often a member of the cadre, on behalf of the team, negotiates an agenda before the visit. This creates a shared purpose and gives members of both teams a sense of how their time together will unfold. Generally, a cadre begins by sitting down with the team whose school it is visiting to learn about that school's strengths and to discuss a topic of shared interest. It is wise to begin by identifying and talking about strengths. Not only does this facilitate trust but it contributes to the foundation of hope on which all continuous school improvement relies.

Next, the visiting cadre typically tours the building with a personal guide, optimally a student. The cadre has an opportunity to experience the way the school looks and feels and to observe classes. If time permits, many cadres appreciate the opportunity to informally shadow a student for a period of time. Students are selected who represent a cross-section of the student body, and no particular protocol is used. Simply getting to know about a student's experience at the school is the goal. At some point both teams may wish to sit down together again to review the host school's improvement plan and vision statement and talk about the ways in which the school tour has provided evidence of stated aspirations. *If the topic is initiated by the host school,* the teams may wish to share insights about perceived challenges. Typically, cadres are empathic to each other, but generally it is a good idea for the visiting team to begin any dialogue about its perceptions of the host school's challenges with carefully worded clarifying questions. For example, using the word *why* at the beginning of a sentence can be off-putting, whatever the degree of trust. Alternatives are phrases like, "How do you understand . . . ?" or "Can you tell me more about . . . ?" or "Have you had a chance to think about . . . ?" Cadres may want to review *Educators Supporting Educators* (Ginsberg, Johnson, and Moffett, 1997) for additional suggestions for successful school visits.

Before the visit is complete, it is important to make its meaning concrete. For example, the visiting cadre might write its school's emerging priorities for continuous improvement on a piece of newsprint and share its strategies and possible next steps that were stimulated by the visit to the host school. The teams may want to discuss ways they might provide support for one another over time. A brief closure activity, such as asking members of each team to mention something that they are thinking about personally as a consequence of the visit, might illuminate new learning.

Consistently, our experience is that teams enjoy visiting each other's schools. As vulnerable as some schools may feel in opening their doors to others, it is a way to recall how the sharing of stories can become a manifesto of solidarity and a wellspring of new ideas.

Sample Process Design for Year One

Year one focuses on cadre development so that cadre members understand, apply, and develop leadership in creating highly motivating classrooms and schoolwide initiatives for all students.

1. *Organization: five schools and five cadres.* Cadres consist of the principal and six to eight teachers—each of whom chooses a peer *learning partner* to share learning with as part of an *each one teach one* approach to growing the initiative for culturally responsive teaching in the school. In addition, cadre members

share information with others in grade-level or discipline-specific planning teams

2. *Highly motivating teaching and learning and schoolwide change: six work sessions.*

3. *Implementation: six intercession meetings led by principals and coaches.* A minimum of one intercession meeting follows each work session. A minimum of one intercession meeting is reserved to visit demonstration classrooms in specific content areas. Intercession meetings also provide opportunities to engage in inquiry on culturally responsive teaching, to experiment with peer coaching, to begin study groups, and to consider a school *signature*, a theme that focuses the school as a place of significance for *all* students.

4. *Teaching demonstrations.* Teaching demonstrations provide an opportunity for schoolwide facilitators to model the motivational framework and related strategies by working directly with students. Sessions can be videotaped for later examination and critique.

5. *On-site support.* On-site support involves opportunities to identify evolving needs and interests, share resources, facilitate problem solving, visit classrooms, and shadow students.

6. *Administrative leadership: half-day sessions for principals.* Sessions for principals include problem posing on issues specific to administrative challenges. In addition, they address ways to provide support for faculty in bringing forth student motivation: for example, by setting professional goals, using the Partnership Guide for Culturally Responsive Teaching, designing lessons, and so forth. Ideally, administrators will design and videotape a demonstration lesson.

7. *Community forum for parents and community members.* Community forums are an opportunity to engage parents and community members in a dialogue on motivation.

8. *Demonstration: annual poster conference.* A poster conference allows individuals and cadre members to share their accomplishments in applying the Motivational Framework for Culturally Responsive Teaching to lesson design, professional learning teams, coaching, and systemic challenges. The poster session also serves as a celebration of learning.

9. *Evaluation and research.* With support, each site develops a customized plan for evaluation and research, in the initial stages of the initiative. This plan is systematically implemented and provides data about teaching, student performance, and other indicators of schoolwide accomplishment. Data are used for continuous improvement and are often the basis for faculty presentations at local, state, and national conferences.

Process Design for Year Two

Year two focuses on the whole school implementation cycle.

1. *Whole school institute: cofacilitated by cadre members and schoolwide facilitator(s).*
2. *Whole school professional learning teams: with one to two cadre members on each professional learning team.* Professional learning teams collaborate to design, implement, and reflect upon lessons using the motivational framework, engage in collegial coaching, examine student work, and reflect upon shared readings.
3. *Whole school examination and adoption of a signature.* A school-specific signature helps the school to evolve its identity and focus and strengthen its significance. Signatures can be themes such as literacy across the curriculum, integrating the arts, or service learning.
4. *Demonstration: annual poster conference.* This conference provides an opportunity for cadre members and professional learning teams to share their accomplishments related to applying the motivational framework to lesson design, professional learning teams, coaching, and systemic challenges. The poster conference also serves as a celebration of learning.
5. *Evaluation and research.* With support, the school continues to evolve and implement the customized plan for evaluation and research developed in the initial stages of the initiative. It provides data about teaching, student performance, and other indicators of schoolwide accomplishment. Data are used for continuous improvement as well as faculty presentations at local, state, and national conferences in concert with the schoolwide leadership cadre.

Chapter Ten

Designing Training Institutes and Work Sessions

Emerging knowledge about the nature and purposes of learning has caused us to think carefully about the kind of professional development needed to develop capacity. We have directly applied this leadership knowledge to the development of schoolwide instructional leadership cadres. The Motivational Framework for Culturally Responsive Teaching supports learning for adults as well as students and provides an effective model for designing professional development. All institutes and meetings are constructed so that, ideally, participants simultaneously experience the four motivational conditions of establishing inclusion, developing a positive attitude, enhancing meaning, and engendering competence, as defined in Chapter Four.

Professional Development Topics

We outline in the first part of this chapter professional development topics and their related goals and activities, so that staff developers and educators can select strategies to match their purposes. The chapter concludes with sample agendas for professional development.

Goals and Activities Related to Developing a Successful Initiative

We suggest a few preliminary goals and activities that address fundamental aspects of an initiative for culturally responsive teaching.

We recommend that facilitators include them in introductory professional development institutes.

1. Create a Clear Sense of Purpose

Exercise. Activity 13, Chapter Six, Creating a Statement of Purpose.

Rationale. It is important for learners to know why they are doing what they are doing. Like a compass, a clear sense of purpose allows us to end up where we intend, without restricting our inventiveness by being overly prescriptive. When we understand the purpose for doing something, we can be more confident, creative, and effective in aligning our actions and goals. Clarity of purpose for the culturally responsive teaching initiative includes understanding how the initiative addresses the goals of a district's strategic plan or equity plan, the school improvement plan in general, and districtwide standards. Clarity of purpose is also valuable because it reduces confusion about other team-based initiatives. Perhaps the most important statement to be made up front, however, is that a key to the ongoing effectiveness of any organization is its ability to renew itself. All schools ought to be engaged in renewal—all the time. The goal is to enhance the vitality of the school, which in no way diminishes the work and caring that has always been a part of the school. It is an opportunity to blend continuity with change, in ways that are research supported but that ultimately emanate from the hearts and minds and wills of teachers.

2. Distinguish the School as the Locus of Control for Decision Making

Rationale. Some educators are cautious about school improvement initiatives because they may see them as a process of compliance with local and state politics, experiences in which an outside expert underestimates the expertise and imagination of educators and community members. It is critical that schools feel competent and supported in making decisions that address their strengths and needs. Establishing a reliable communication process between the external consultant and cadre representatives as well as between the external consultant and the district liaison is key. Also, many external consultants travel quite a bit, and it is important to keep schools abreast of travel schedules and the best ways to be in contact. The trust that is an inherent part of school renewal relationships needs to be safeguarded to the extent possible.

3. Examine the Potential of Teams to Influence School Change

Exercise. Activity 1, Chapter Six, Carousel Graffiti.

Rationale. Although the idea of collaboration is certainly not new, many educators have not had an opportunity to consider the significance of teaming for *ongoing* school renewal. Capacity-building exercises, in which cadre members explore the potential of a team approach to assisting change, undergird the cadre's ability to believe in, articulate, and work toward exemplary collaborative practices. Team members need to develop an understanding, through reflection and imagination, of the reasons the team process can benefit themselves and others. (An excellent resource on topics related to collaboration and new ways of designing professional development is the entire Summer 1999 issue of the *Journal of Staff Development,* titled *Powerful Designs: New Approaches Ignite Professional Learning.*)

Goals and Activities Related to the Concept of Culture

1. Personalize the Concept of Culture in a Community of Learners

Exercise. Activity 1, Chapter Five, Venn Diagram Sharing.

Rationale. It is important for institute participants from all backgrounds to see themselves as an integral part of the dialogue on cultural diversity. Opportunities that assist educators in personalizing the concept of culture are fundamental to their appreciating and supporting the broad range of diversity in schools today.

2. Assist Adults to Experience Activities and Reflect on Their Potential in Ways That Help Them Build Strategies for Implementing the Four Motivational Conditions

Experiencing, modifying, and implementing instructional strategies that support the intrinsic motivation of all students is the primary focus of the initiative. The exercises in Chapters Five through Eight apply to developing culturally responsive classrooms. The Partnership Guide (Exhibit 8.1) provides a holistic overview of culturally responsive teaching and is useful for peer coaching. When the facilitator reviews this guide (usually as part of the introduction to the motivational framework), it is a good idea to ask participants to note those aspects of the guide that they believe are most important to educational practice that supports the success of all students. It is also worthwhile to ask participants to identify the attributes of culturally responsive teaching in the guide that they feel are reasonably strong in their practice and the attributes they would like in particular to learn more about. To elicit this information, a think-pair-share approach that respects participants' confidence works well. Only volunteers are asked to share aloud with the whole group what they talked about with their partner.

Rationale. How courses are taught and organized on a daily basis is one of the primary influences on academic success. This is why the focus of the initiative is on classroom teaching and learning.

3. Identify and Review Options Related to Curriculum Development and Usage

Although the focus of this book is teaching methods, content that is relevant as well as challenging is essential. This topic is addressed in Chapter Three.

Rationale. It is important to ensure that all students are able to see themselves represented in course content. Equally important are opportunities for educators and students to examine subject matter from culturally diverse perspectives. This promotes personal relevance and meaning as well as reflectiveness in the areas of social and civic justice.

4. Review Options and Opportunities for the Total School Environment

See the Resource titled "Evaluating the School Environment for Ethnic and Cultural Pluralism."

Rationale. Although what happens in each and every classroom throughout a school is of primary importance, the school environment, as a whole, sends powerful messages about what a school genuinely values. The environment can support or erode motivation. It should extend beyond a fix-the-child orientation. Many participants in school renewal initiatives are new to the study of culturally responsive teaching as it relates to student motivation. When they think of the school as a whole, they may think that respect for cultural pluralism has to do with such things as periodic celebrations of heroes and holidays. Institute participants generally appreciate an opportunity to become more aware of the broad range of considerations that contribute to a total school environment that supports *all* students. This opportunity might include, for example, examining entryways and hallways for implicit messages about whom the school represents and examining policies for attracting and retaining faculty from a variety of backgrounds.

Goals and Activities Related to the Processes of School Renewal and the Effectiveness of Change Agents

1. Understand the Change Process

Exercise. Activity 15, Chapter Six, Roundtable Dialogue on Change.

Rationale. The ultimate goal of cadres is to serve as catalysts for meaningful school improvement. As stated earlier, a key to the ongoing effectiveness of any organization is its ability to renew itself. However, as educators at all levels know, innovation does not occur in a vacuum. Habits, attitudes, and assumptions can rigidify into inviolable routines for individual teachers, entire schools, or a bureaucracy. Although remarkable changes are occurring in many schools and districts, cadre members need a chance to think about the complexity of change. The authors have found it useful to ask small groups to discuss some of the following statements (first, discussing what the statement means; next, relating the statement to their own experiences; and then, thinking about what can be done to meet the challenge): (1) what works in one setting may not necessarily apply in another; (2) change is rarely, if ever, a linear process; (3) conflict and resistance are predictable and inevitable when attempting a school improvement process; (4) problems are also an inevitable part of change and can be helpful when they are reframed as opportunities for creative thinking; (5) organizations do not change until the individuals in them change; and (6) a repertoire of strategies is needed to deal with the complexity of moving a school from where it is to where it wants to be (Fullan and Miles, 1992).

2. Construct Effective Teams

Exercise. Activity 14, Chapter Six, Establishing Norms for Teamwork.

Rationale. Members of the cadres and the district team appreciate an opportunity to examine principles of effective teams and prioritize ways in which to facilitate their teaming processes. This creates a clear understanding about how to contribute as a team member to a school renewal process that is rooted in respect and invention rather than in resentment and compliance.

3. Plan in Thoughtful Ways

Rationale. Planning guides help members of the cadre and district team organize and sustain involvement. Most guides encourage teams to engage in focused dialogue, delineate ideas, establish communication processes, clarify roles, and think through scheduling challenges. Although the guides offered in an institute vary according to their function—for example, some are for individual lesson design, some are for meetings, some are for goal setting at the end of institutes—they have helped teams deliberate issues, decrease ambiguity, and heighten their likelihood of success. (See Chapter Eight and the Resource for various planning guides).

Goals and Activities That Build Commitment Among Schoolwide Leadership Cadres and District Teams

1. Find Time

Exercise. Activity 12, Chapter Six, Creating Time for Collaboration.

   Rationale. One thing that invariably wears people down is not having enough time to learn together; share knowledge, resources, and experiences; think ideas through; plan; and provide encouragement.

2. Make Meaningful Connections

Exercises. Activity 5: Chapter Six, Identifying the Emotions and Conditions of Being Intrinsically Motivated; Activity 2, Chapter Six, Scaffolding for Success, or, The 360-Degree Turnaround.

   Rationale. Learning and motivational theory teaches us that new ideas need to be connected to prior learning for enhanced meaning. Such connection contributes to high-level synthesis of concepts and substantive applications for teaching and schoolwide planning. The normal condition of the mind is that thoughts randomly chase one another instead of lining up in causal sequences. Unless a person has the opportunity and encouragement to link together some sort of "mental motion picture" (Csikszentmihalyi,

1997, p. 26) that connects past and present experiences, she or he will have fragments of learning and half-hearted commitments. Of course, when learners find personalized ways to understand and apply new ideas, it heightens not only the cognitive aspects of making meaning but relevance, which is essential to commitment. As educators we need to see that individuals' deepest values and prized experiences can be used to enhance the vitality of a system. The activities provided in this book contain, as a fundamental aspect, opportunities for students and initiative participants to make connections to prior experiences and learning.

With this in mind, the way in which Activity 12 in Chapter Six introduces the motivational framework is especially noteworthy. It is important for people—from the very start—to be able to recall their own feelings of intrinsic motivation and to recognize the significance of intrinsic sources of motivation for themselves as well as for others. In addition to the exercise of examining the emotions and conditions of feeling intrinsically motivated, the exercise of the 360-degree turnaround is a compelling activity—especially when it follows the introduction of the motivational framework. It provides an opportunity for educators to see that they already apply the four conditions of the motivational framework when they facilitate their own best practices. When educators make this connection, it typically heightens their interest in finding ways to consistently hit on all four.

3. Identify Schoolwide Accomplishments

Exercise. Activity 11, Chapter Six, Metaphorical Ecosystems; also review "Evaluating the Initiative" in the Resource, so that participants can see some of the ways that the changes can be identified over time.

Rationale. We know that adults as well as children require confidence and optimism to achieve a goal. Although some of our most worthy actions have important abstract consequences, concrete evidence of small and large successes is also needed in the process of school renewal. The challenge is to balance optimism and realism.

Undoubtedly, setbacks are going to occur. Some people will use them to confirm their notions about "school reform failure" and see them as proof of hopelessness. But others will see them as a reason to strengthen resolve. These are the people who most need to sustain their energy. Their optimism can ultimately influence one of the largest groups of people in many organizations, the fence-sitters—those who try not to shake things up either way and who generally accept things as they are. Schools committed to enhancing their vitality benefit from multiple processes and indicators to identify success. Evidence of success can help sustain a positive attitude, offer documentation of forward movement over time, and muster the energy and courage that engages those who doubt or do not currently see the value of school improvement as an ongoing process.

The metaphorical ecosystems activity helps cadres comprehensively identify prior accomplishments on which to build. The results of this activity can send a powerful message that team members are working together to build on strengths (as opposed to deficits). The indicators in the section entitled "Evaluating the Initiative" can help participants to see that there are many ways to anticipate and identify success.

Agendas for Building Capacity

The rest of this chapter contains four sections that describe how to contribute to districtwide capacity building and that present institute and work session agendas.

The first section, "How to Prepare and Support Cadres," focuses on developing the capacity of cadres through institutes and work sessions. *Institutes* provide foundational information and activities related to creating motivating classrooms and schoolwide programs for *all* students. *Work sessions* provide opportunities for cadres to examine and develop experiences related to *intercession meeting* activities, that is, the implementation of new ideas in the time in between institutes or work sessions. Intercession activities include, for example, peer coaching, action research, visits to other schools, meetings of professional learning teams and study groups, examinations of student work, and demonstration lessons. Work sessions help participants refine and develop ways to facilitate instructionally focused school renewal.

Essentially, institutes and work sessions allow cadre members to develop knowledge and skills and to design schoolwide approaches to job-embedded professional development. The teams receive customized support, that is, support that responds to the strengths and challenges of each team's school, in applying their emerging understanding to school improvement goals and to their schools' overall efforts to support the motivation and success of *all* students.

A minimum of one intercession meeting follows each work session. This intercession meeting is lead by the principal, district cadre coach, or some form of shared facilitation. To the fullest degree possible, all cadre members attend intercession meetings. Each teacher brings one teacher partner who teaches in the same department or at the same level with common planning time. This facilitates the each one teach one approach, which builds support for new ideas a layer at a time. A minimum of one intercession meeting is reserved for visiting demonstration classrooms. Intercession meetings also include support for activities that have been agreed to at work sessions.

For example, it is not uncommon for a cadre member to be asked to partner with a colleague during the intercession to create, implement, and critique a model lesson based on the four motivational conditions. As part of the design for this lesson, student feedback is elicited as an indicator of effectiveness. After a work session in which cadres examine and practice a peer coaching simulation, they may be asked to begin a peer coaching demonstration project at their schools. As the initiative progresses, cadres also use intercessions to work with small teams of colleagues (the professional learning teams or study groups) to share processes such as examining student work or to plan interdisciplinary lessons with the motivational framework as a guide. We always encourage cadre members to use intercession time to independently try new strategies with their students and to share these experiences at intercession meetings.

The second section, "How to Prepare and Support School Faculties," describes how an external consultant or staff developer can plan and cofacilitate a two-day school-based institute with the leadership cadre. This requires a one-day planning session with each cadre so that its schoolwide institute effectively links new understandings and ideas from prior cadre work with the school's instructional challenges and school improvement plans.

The third section, "How to Prepare and Support a District Instructional Leadership Team," presents a sample agenda delineating suggestions for developing and working with the district-level team. A district team plays a critical role in fostering school-based commitment to highly motivating teaching and learning.

Finally, the last section, "How to Prepare and Support Administrative Leaders," describes administrative work sessions that give administrators opportunities to reflect and learn in a safe setting. This section includes sample agenda topics from administrative work sessions we have facilitated.

How to Prepare and Support Cadres

In this section we provide agendas based on our experience in preparing cadre members to serve on their teams. These agendas incorporate experiential learning activities, cooperative and collaborative learning activities, structured opportunities for participants to share expertise, and designated time for reflection and for constructing personal meaning about new ideas. The first agenda is a sample three-day cadre institute agenda that is facilitated by the external consultant. The agenda includes activities that demonstrate the motivational framework and are also immediately applicable to classrooms and to designing a customized school-based institute. This is important because cadres will eventually cofacilitate a similar institute for their colleagues at their individual school sites. The agenda can be modified for two days if time for a third day is simply not available.

An important goal, whether preparing cadres or working directly with schools, is to model, support, and encourage teaching (and learning) that is intrinsically motivating. That is why we periodically ask participants to reflect on the way these institutes have been designed and implemented and to identify the ways in which the four conditions of the motivational framework have been modeled, or could be strengthened. We also ask participants after each activity how they might adapt a particular strategy to their own classrooms or area of work.

We have found it helpful to post a large sheet of newsprint in a visible location throughout all institutes. We list on this sheet the exercises used and key ideas learned. This posting serves as a visible reminder of ideas participants may wish to adapt to their classroom practice or share with their colleagues. The list also has the additional benefit of symbolically making participants' accomplishments concrete.

The consistent application of the four motivational conditions for culturally responsive teaching assists educators at all levels in creating the conditions for learning that engages participants. The framework is detailed in Chapter Four, and a blank framework for planning professional development experiences as well as K–12 lesson designs is located at the end of Chapter Eight.

Sample Agenda for the First Leadership Cadre Capacity-Building Institute (Three Days)

Title: Designing Lessons That Support the Motivation of All Students

Institute participants: A schoolwide instructional leadership cadre, the district liaison

Goals: To examine the purpose and potential of a schoolwide leadership cadre, to learn and apply the Motivational Framework for Culturally Responsive Teaching to lesson design, and to develop awareness about some of the reasons for academic disparity among student groups and about what can be done schoolwide to support the motivation of all students

Day 1

Note: Distribute three colored three-by-five-inch cards to each participant, and as participants seat themselves, introduce yourself as the facilitator and ask each person to prepare response cards, as described in Activity 10, Chapter Five. Also place a stack of white three-by-five-inch cards on each table. At an appropriate time, indicate that these cards are for anonymous questions that can be placed in a box by the door and that will be addressed at the following intervals: after morning break, after lunch, and prior to closure each day.

8:30–8:45	WELCOME, GOALS, OVERVIEW
8:45–9:00	BUILDING COMMUNITY (GETTING ACQUAINTED)
	*Round-Robin: Please introduce yourself and respond to the following question: What is one

thing an outsider might not know about your school at first glance?

9:00–9:30	INTRODUCTION TO THE CONCEPT OF CULTURE *Venn Diagram Sharing.
9:30–10:15	INTRODUCTION TO THE MOTIVATIONAL FRAMEWORK FOR CULTURALLY RESPONSIVE TEACHING *Scaffolding Minilecture with Human Highlighters. *Note:* Periodically use response cards to check the response of the large group to a statement or example.
10:15–10:30	BREAK
10:30–11:00	REFLECTION ON MINILECTURE Share notes and dialogue with a partner to identify two or three of the most important points. Comments and questions.
11:00–11:45	APPLYING THE MOTIVATIONAL FRAMEWORK TO PERSONAL EXPERIENCE AND INSTRUCTION *Scaffolding for Success, or the 360-Degree Turnaround.
11:45–12:00	REVIEW OF THE MORNING, PREVIEW OF THE AFTERNOON *Door Passes: Use this question: Given our work together this morning, what is something that most surprises you?
12:00–1:15	LUNCH

1:15–2:00	INCLUSION
	*Select two or three of the following strategies to examine and practice.
	    Class Agreements
	    Note Cues
	    Response Cards (with which participants will have already practiced)
	    Fist-to-Five
	    Dialogue journals
	    Review exercises (Class Historian)
	*Think-pair-share: Select a strategy and tell a partner how you will use it and how you will gauge its effectiveness.

| 2:00–2:15 | BREAK |
| 2:15–3:00 | DEVELOPING A POSITIVE ATTITUDE |

*Select one of the following strategies to examine or practice.

> Carousel Graffiti
>
> Multiple intelligences theory

Free-writing: Write about how you will adapt the strategy to classroom use; post your idea on the designated reading wall for gallery-style review.

| 3:00–3:30 | REVIEW OF THE DAY, PREVIEW OF DAY 2, CLOSING COMMENTS |

Day 2

| 8:30–8:45 | WELCOME, OVERVIEW, REVIEW |
| 8:45–9:15 | BUILDING COMMUNITY |

*Two Wishes and a Truth

| 9:15–10:15 | ENHANCING MEANING |

*Framed Summaries for Cooperative Jigsaw (using the article "Canary in the Mine," Singham, 1998)

| 10:15–10:30 | BREAK |
| 10:30–11:15 | ENHANCING MEANING (continued) |

*Problem-based learning in small groups: One person presents a problem she or he is working on. Group members check for clarity. Once the problem is well understood, a round of suggestions follows, with each suggestion posed as a question: What might happen if . . . ? The person sharing the question selects a course of action and creates an implementation plan.

| 11:15–11:45 | REVIEW OF THE MORNING, PREVIEW OF THE AFTERNOON |

*Head, Heart, Hand

| 11:45–1:00 | LUNCH |
| 1:00–2:00 | ENGENDERING COMPETENCE |

*Examining grading policies and practices: Minilecture, individual review of perspectives from key theorists, small-group reflection.

2:00–2:15	BREAK
2:15–3:15	ENGENDERING COMPETENCE (continued) *Enhancing the Motivational Influence of Professional Practice by Examining Student Work.
3:15–3:45	THE ROLE OF SCHOOLWIDE INSTRUCTIONAL LEADERSHIP CADRES, THE CHANGE PROCESS *Statement of Purpose for Leadership Cadres: review and personalize statement. Change quotes, small-group reflection, original bumper stickers (to summarize).
3:45–4:00	REVIEW OF THE DAY, PREVIEW OF DAY 3, CLOSING COMMENTS

Day 3

8:30–8:45	WELCOME, OVERVIEW, REVIEW
8:45–9:15	BUILDING COMMUNITY *Multicultural Inventory.
9:15–10:15	USING THE MOTIVATIONAL FRAMEWORK FOR LESSON DESIGN *Demonstration with planning guide; subject-specific design teams have the option to create individual lessons. *Note:* Between this institute and the next work session, participants will design and implement two lessons—one of which may be the lesson that was collaboratively designed at the institute using the motivational framework. For the second design, participants are encouraged to continue to collaborate with a partner— either when preparing the lesson or to fine-tune it.
10:00–10:15	BREAK
10:15–10:30	EXAMPLES OF LESSON DESIGNS
10:30–11:30	TEACHING THE MOTIVATIONAL FRAMEWORK TO A TRUSTED COLLEAGUE Demonstration simulation to model a sample approach to teaching the motivational framework to someone else; then, in dyads, participants review their materials and notes and develop their own approach to *each one teach one.*

11:30–11:45	REVIEW OF THE MORNING, PREVIEW OF THE AFTERNOON
11:45–1:00	LUNCH
1:00–1:45	EXAMINING THE BIG PICTURE *Metaphorical ecosystems.
1:45–2:00	BREAK
2:00–3:00	CREATING A VISION OF SUCCESS FOR THE SCHOOLWIDE INSTRUCTIONAL LEADERSHIP TEAM *Blue Skies.
3:00–3:30	REVIEW OF THE DAY, FUTURE DIRECTIONS Round-robin closing comments.

Note: * Designates activities and discussions that can be found in the previous chapters of this book and located in the Index.

Sample Agenda for a Work Session for Cadres (One Day)

Title: Implementing the Motivational Framework

Work session participants: Cadre members and the district liaison

Goals: To strengthen understanding of the Motivational Framework for Culturally Responsive Teaching, to practice a peer coaching process using the partnership guide, and to design a peer coaching demonstration project

8:30–8:45	WELCOME, INTRODUCTIONS, OVERVIEW
8:45–9:15	BUILDING COMMUNITY *Decades and Diversity
9:15–9:30	REFLECTION ON THE THREE-DAY INSTITUTE Ask participants to discuss this question, in triads: What aspects of this first institute are particularly meaningful to you now?
9:30–10:15	REVIEW OF MOTIVATIONAL FRAMEWORK *Minilecture and Modified Cooperative Jigsaw: Divide participants into four groups. Prior to the minilecture, ask each group to pay special attention to the condition assigned to it and to be prepared to reteach that condition at the conclusion of the lecture. Following cooperative reteaching, ask for a volunteer to reteach the framework at the next work session.

10:15–10:30   BREAK

10:30–11:30   THE PARTNERSHIP OBSERVATION PROCESS AS A WAY TO
                SUPPORT MOTIVATING TEACHING
                *Partnership Guide for Culturally Responsive
                Teaching: Apply the partnership guide to a
                videotaped teaching segment. After viewing the
                video, (1) in small groups, participants identify
                the lesson's strengths, (2) they also discuss ways
                they might sensitively interact with the teacher
                to help her improve her teaching based on the
                motivational framework, (3) the large group
                comes back together and interacts with the facil-
                itator as if she were the teacher on the video-
                tape, (4) the facilitator responds as she imagines
                an actual teacher might who is receiving helpful
                feedback, and (5) the group creates a set of
                guidelines for a peer coaching demonstration
                project using the motivational framework.

Note: For the intercession, cadre members choose partners and
agree upon a schedule according to which they will alternate
weekly visits to each other's classroom for one class period, applying the set of partner observation guidelines from the work session.

Note: When the facilitator is the teacher in the video, it strengthens
his or her role as a co-learner as well as a facilitator and builds trust.

11:30–12:00   REFLECTING ON PERSONAL EXPERIENCE
                Self-reflection and discussion with a partner: In
                dyads, partners discuss one of the two lessons
                that each cadre member designed and imple-
                mented during the previous intercession with
                the motivational framework as a guide. They
                share what they did as well as successes and chal-
                lenges. Partners work together to think through
                challenges that may have occurred.

12:00–12:15   REFLECTION ON THE MORNING, PREVIEW OF THE
                AFTERNOON
                *Door Passes: Participants respond to two ques-
                tions—one on each side of a three-by-five-inch

card: (1) Given our work together this morning, what is something you will do to strengthen your own practice? (2) What is something, related to our work, about which you are curious or would like more information?

12:15–1:30   LUNCH

1:30–2:30   AN APPROACH TO SAFELY RAISING SCHOOLWIDE ISSUES
*Dot Graphing: Select three or four of the following questions. Post each question across the top of a separate piece of newsprint with a Likert scale from one to seven at the bottom. One is low, seven is high. Give participants one dot for each question and ask them to position a dot above a point along each of the scales as a response to the question at the top of the newsprint.

To what extent does our school have a shared vision for teaching and learning?

To what extent do staff feel ownership in decision making related to school renewal?

To what extent is classroom learning highly motivating and relevant to students?

To what extent do we systematically engage in collaborative adult learning?

To what extent does our school encourage diverse parents and community members to participate in meaningful ways?

To what extent do we have an effective way to negotiate conflict among ourselves?

Ask participants to share any observations or questions for further inquiry that they may have as they reflect on the possible meanings of the patterns of the Likert scale responses. After all responses have been posted, the whole group discusses them.

Ask participants how they might use this exercise—and when—at their own school sites.

2:30–3:00   REVIEW OF THE DAY, REVIEW OF INTERCESSION ACTIVI-
               TIES, FUTURE DIRECTIONS
               Closure: (1) Group members review vision state-
               ments from the first institute; (2) each person
               identifies two or three things thus far learned
               that can help move him or her closer to the
               cadre's vision; (2) each person writes a message
               he or she would like to deliver to the group or
               an individual.

Note: * Designates activities and discussions that can be found in
the previous chapters of this book and located in the Index.

How to Prepare and Support School Faculties

The following agendas illustrate a process through which cadre
members design and cofacilitate an institute with the district liaison and external consultant. This process can be frightening to
some cadre members. That is why no one is asked to do anything
she or he does not wish to do. Some team members, for example,
might provide extra support for developing materials or working
with small groups. Others might enjoy facilitating, as long as they
do so with another person.

Nonetheless, the cofacilitation opens many doors. It symbolically establishes cadre members as educators of adults as well as of
children and youth, and as expert learners in motivating instructional practice. In addition, it sends a message that the work of the
school is guided by people from within the school. Further, systematic, job-embedded learning through such methods as professional learning teams and peer coaching is an essential feature of
school renewal. The opportunity for an entire school to develop
awareness together about motivating and culturally responsive
teaching provides the foundation for a shared language and philosophy to support continual staff development. Finally, cadre
members consistently report that cofacilitating deepens their own
learning, contributes to team cohesiveness, and provides perspectives on adult learning that are invaluable for facilitators of school
renewal.

Generally, the first whole school institute focuses primarily on the motivational framework and related strategies that educators can immediately use. This kind of pragmatism contributes to deepening trust and positive attitudes so that staff can eventually grapple with the often controversial issues that accompany change.

Sample Agenda for a Planning Session to Co-Create and Collaboratively Facilitate a School-Based Institute

Title: Cadre Planning Session for Two-Day School-Based Institute

Planning session participants: Schoolwide instructional leadership cadre members and liaisons from the district team

Goals: To strengthen understanding of the motivational framework, to plan a school-based institute that reflects the school's strengths and challenges as they relate to student motivation and schoolwide success, and to enhance the leadership capacity of the cadre

8:30–8:45	WELCOME, INTRODUCTIONS, GOALS
8:45–9:00	BUILDING COMMUNITY *Metaphors for facilitating adult learning.
9:00–9:15	INFORMAL DIALOGUE Catch up and touch base on the team's school improvement plan and discuss how the two-day institute can strengthen school improvement goals.
9:15–10:15	REVIEW OF TOPICS AND TEACHING STRATEGIES FROM THE INITIAL INSTITUTE Ask participants to review their agenda and notes from the foundational three-day institute, think about their school improvement plan, and suggest issues and ideas that are most relevant to their school.
10:15–10:30	BREAK
10:30–11:30	AGENDA DESIGN On an overhead or large piece of newsprint, use suggestions and ideas from the previous activity to outline a two-day agenda. Be very specific. For example, start with the time period 8:30–9:00, and so on. Ask people not

to worry about who will do what. No one will
be asked to do anything that he or she would
prefer not to do. Also, the external facilitator
will provide the theoretical underpinnings.
The cadre members, as individuals or in small
groups, will facilitate different activities.

| 11:30–12:30 | LUNCH |
| 12:30–1:30 | INDIVIDUAL AND COLLECTIVE COMMITMENTS |

Who will do what. This is a good time to
review how activities were originally facilitated.

MATERIAL RESOURCES FOR THE INSTITUTE

What supplies and materials are needed? Who
will organize or create them? Who will type up
the agenda?

| 1:30–1:45 | BREAK |
| 1:45–3:00 | PRACTICE AND PREPARATION |

Ask participants to outline their approach and
to identify materials they will need and how
they will find or create them. They then share
their approach with the rest of the cadre.

| 3:00–3:15 | SUGGESTIONS AND REMINDERS |

During the institute, keep a list of what has
been accomplished on a posted sheet of
newsprint for everyone to see.
At the conclusion of an activity, always remember to ask: How could you adapt this activity
to your own grade level or content area?
If someone would like to add to or clarify
what the facilitator of an activity is saying, she
or he joins the facilitator wherever he or she is
positioned (as opposed to calling out from
somewhere in the room).
The anticipated time allotted for each activity
is just a good guess. It is best to distribute an
agenda to participants in the school-based
institute that specifies exact times only for
breaks and lunch.

| 3:15–3:30 | CLOSURE |

Round-robin: How will we know if we have been successful? List the responses.
Closing quotation: "The road was new to me, as roads always are, going back."—Sarah Orne Jewett

Note: * Designates activities and discussions that can be found in the previous chapters of this book and located in the Index.

Sample Agenda for the Whole School Capacity-Building Institute Cofacilitated by the Cadre, District Liaison, and External Consultant (Two Days)

Title: A Schoolwide Approach to Supporting the Motivation of All Students

Institute participants: School staff, parent and community representatives, the leadership cadre, liaisons from the district team and the external consultant.

Goals: To create schoolwide understanding of the motivational framework, to develop awareness about some of the reasons for academic disparity among student groups and what can be done schoolwide to support the motivation of all students, to examine sustainable approaches to collaborative adult learning, and to clarify the purpose and potential of a leadership cadre

Day 1

Note: Distribute three colored three-by-five-inch cards to each participant, and as participants seat themselves, introduce yourself as the facilitator and ask each person to prepare response cards, as described in Activity 10, Chapter Five. Also place a stack of white three-by-five-inch cards on each table. At an appropriate time, indicate that these cards are for anonymous questions that can be placed in a box by the door and that will be addressed at the following intervals: after morning break, after lunch, and prior to closure each day.

- Welcome, introductions, goals, overview
- Foundation for the motivational framework

Research and literature base

Macrocultural orientation

Social, emotional, and cognitive significance of intrinsic motivation

Other considerations (overall environment, curriculum content)

*Seasonal Partners debriefing.

- Building community
  *"ASK ME ABOUT . . ." POSTERS: PARTICIPANTS CREATE A POSTER THAT SYMBOLIZES SOMETHING THAT IS HAPPENING IN THEIR CLASSROOM OR SCHOOL THAT IS INTERESTING OR EXCITING.

- Introduction to the framework
  *IDENTIFYING THE EMOTIONS AND CONDITIONS OF BEING INTRINSICALLY MOTIVATED.
  *MINILECTURE FOLLOWED BY MODIFIED COOPERATIVE JIGSAW.

- First condition: establishing inclusion
  *CAROUSEL GRAFFITI FOCUSED ON SCHOOLWIDE SUCCESS.

- Reflection on the morning; preview of the afternoon
  *DOOR PASSES

- Lunch

- Second condition: developing a positive attitude
  *STORY POSTERS, *PROFESSIONAL AGREEMENTS.

- Reflection on the day, preview of tomorrow
  *HEAD, HEART, HAND.

Day 2

- Welcome, goals, overview

- Review
  ANALOGIES FOR INTRINSIC MOTIVATION.

- Building community
  *TWO WISHES AND A TRUTH.

- Video review
  *BUMPER STICKERS DEBRIEFING.

- Third condition: enhancing meaning
  *SCAFFOLDING FOR SUCCESS, OR THE 360-DEGREE TURNAROUND,

TO APPLY THE MOTIVATIONAL FRAMEWORK TO PERSONAL TEACHING
EXPERIENCE; * ENHANCING THE MOTIVATIONAL INFLUENCE OF PRO-
FESSIONAL PRACTICE BY EXAMINING STUDENT WORK.

- Reflection on morning, preview of afternoon
- Lunch
- Fourth condition: engendering competence
  *EXAMINING GRADING PRACTICES.
  *DESIGNING LESSONS USING THE MOTIVATIONAL FRAMEWORK FOR
  CULTURALLY RESPONSIVE TEACHING.
  WRITE A NOTE TO A COLLEAGUE SETTING PERSONAL GOALS AND
  MAKING A WISH FOR THE SCHOOL AS A WHOLE: FOR EXAMPLE, NOTES
  MIGHT ADDRESS NEW UNDERSTANDINGS, IDEAS FOR PERSONAL USE,
  RECOMMENDATIONS FOR THE CADRE, RECOMMENDATIONS FOR THE
  SCHOOL.
- Future directions, closure

Note: * Designates activities and discussions that can be found in
the previous chapters of this book and located in the Index.

How to Prepare and Support a District Instructional Leadership Team

This section provides ideas and agendas for preparing district team
members to assist district staff in implementing the initiative. The
topics district team members should initially understand are

- The components of the initiative
- The Motivational Framework for Culturally Responsive Teaching
- District team members' roles in advising and supporting the
  district superintendent and staff

One of the primary purposes of district team support is to give
school-based teams contacts and liaisons at the district level to assist
with garnering resources, providing support for ideas, and representing emerging school-based issues at district team meetings. To
offer this support, district teams try to commit to regular meetings
with clearly delineated agendas and, generally, rotate their leadership.

A Sample Agenda for Planning District Team Work Sessions Facilitated by the District Liaison and External Consultant

Title: A Districtwide Approach to Culturally Responsive Teaching and Learning (Initial District Team Work Session)

Planning session participants: The superintendent, assistant superintendent, federal programs coordinator, staff development coordinator, curriculum coordinators, coordinator of bilingual and ESL education, representative of community organizations, parent and family involvement leaders, school-based administrative representatives, school-based faculty representatives

Goals: To develop norms for shared governance, to build community among team members, to inform members about the progress of the initiative, to identify issues of concern to district team members, and to develop work committees at the district level to address key areas of concern (for example, conflict resolution, community outreach to inform the broader community about the initiative, and input into an evaluation design)

8:30–8:45	WELCOME, INTRODUCTIONS, GOALS
8:45–9:00	BUILDING COMMUNITY
	Each participant introduces himself or herself to someone he or she hasn't met, and together they identify one or two things that they believe need to happen for meaningful school renewal to occur.
9:00–9:30	OVERVIEW
	This overview includes discussion of district-sponsored institutes and examples of activities in which the schoolwide leadership cadres are involved. Participants appreciate a brief narrative description of the initiative, sample agendas, photographs of the cadres learning together, and so forth.
9:30–9:45	BREAK
9:45–10:45	ROUNDTABLE DIALOGUE WITH DIALOGUE GUIDE
	Participants prioritize questions provided in a

dialogue guide. They divide into subgroups according to the topic in which they are interested: for example, How can we regularly provide support to cadres given our number of other commitments? What can we provide for schools that they might not be able to provide for themselves? How can we respect school-based decision making, especially as it relates to educational equity and opportunity, and maintain a strong clear district agenda? What do we know about helping schools successfully negotiate conflict at the school level, before it becomes a districtwide issue? How can we help schools collect and analyze data related to the initiative so that it is useful and understandable to all constituencies? What programs exist for parents and community members to have more significant kinds of involvement in schools? What agreements do we recommend for our meetings about such things as shared governance, cofacilitation, record keeping, and attendance that is consistent as well as inclusive? What ought to be a regular part of every district team meeting?

10:45–11:15	DIALOGUE SUMMARIES AND RECOMMENDATIONS
11:15–11:45	AGREEMENT ON DISTRICT-LEVEL GOALS AND ACTIVITIES
11:45–12:00	REFLECTION ON THE MORNING, FUTURE DIRECTIONS

How to Prepare and Support Administrative Leadership

Principals foster more powerful faculty and student learning when they have opportunities to focus on their own learning. As difficult as it may be for administrative leaders to pull away from their usual work, they typically appreciate an opportunity to build their capacity in instructional leadership and to share ideas for student success. In our experience, ongoing work sessions with small groups of administrators have greatly contributed to initiative goals. For example, one team of assistant high school principals, as champions of highly motivating instruction, used work sessions to design model lessons. They then agreed to do videotaped teaching demonstrations for schoolwide study groups to analyze. In addition to contributing to schoolwide learning, this encouraged staff members to create their own videos from which to learn.

Administrative sessions also provide time for leaders to examine the process of school renewal, explore ways that they can help teachers set professional goals linked to the initiative, become more effective during classroom visits, and problem pose on issues specific to administrative challenges. School renewal is about people renewal—at all levels. Principals who examine their practices and actively work on their own processes of transformation are more capable of facilitating renewal at their schools. Following are examples of agenda topics from several administrative work sessions.

Sample Agenda Topics

- REVIEW OF THE MOTIVATIONAL FRAMEWORK
  Participants engage in a group dialogue on what a classroom would look like if all four motivational conditions were happening simultaneously.

- CREATING A DEMONSTRATION LESSON
  Participants design individual lessons using the motivational framework as a guide.
  Note: Because so many administrators are removed from their original areas of study, lesson designs have included anything in which administrators currently engage—personally or professionally: for example, how to help others solve a conflict, how to deal with dissonance, how to prune a tree.

- SETTING PROFESSIONAL GOALS AND DEVELOPING PERSONALIZED PROFESSIONAL DEVELOPMENT PLANS WITH TEACHERS—IN WAYS THAT REALLY MATTER

- HOLDING A DIALOGUE ON WHAT SUCCESSFUL SCHOOLS DO TO DEVELOP AS LABORATORIES FOR ADULT LEARNING
  Here are some examples of what successful schools do.

Develop professional learning teams and peer coaching focused on student motivation (teams examine student work, review videotaped demonstrations, co-create lessons, and so forth)

Use the motivational framework for lesson design

Develop a team of faculty as in-house staff developers who each coach and consult with five other teachers, with release time or additional pay

Use faculty meetings and team meetings to analyze videotaped teaching demonstrations

Ask highly motivating teachers (*resident teachers*) to adopt an open-door policy that allows for spontaneous ongoing observation; ask resident teachers to mentor others

Ask faculty to examine student performance weekly and set weekly goals about supporting the motivation of all students: What am I going to do? How will I do it? How will I know when I get there?

Begin a project that pulls everyone together—like literacy across the curriculum, quarterly student and teacher demonstrations, service learning

Begin a collaborative action research project that includes getting to know two low-performing students well and designing lessons with them in mind; monitor their performance as well as the performance of a high-performing student

- FOCUSING REFLECTION ON TOPICS IDENTIFIED IN COLLABORATION WITH ADMINISTRATORS

  These topics might take the form of questions such as: What are our fears or concerns around culturally responsive teaching, and what can we do about them? How do I, as a leader, include all voices in the discourse on school renewal and at the same time have a strong, clear agenda of my own?

- CREATING AN ANTHOLOGY

  This is an opportunity for administrators to act as schoolwide editors as they encourage staff to search for works of literature that connect with agreed-upon themes that match staff interests. Poems, essays, and short works of fiction are accepted along with research articles and other scholarly publications.

The anthology contains a title page, a table of contents, a preface that talks about why certain works were chosen, and a bibliography. It is distributed for schoolwide learning (often certain pieces in the anthology are designated for professional learning teams to discuss).

All the activities mentioned in this chapter have been used successfully in professional development sessions in a variety of settings. They have helped educators to create shared understanding and plan specific applications of motivating instruction and school renewal. In addition, they have helped us to scrutinize our own beliefs and teaching—learning from the range and style of discourse that this work evokes. Although we have created far more agendas than would be useful to share, we have never found scripts or formulas that allowed us to overlook the intricacies of human behavior. Even when working from a very thoughtful plan, there simply is no substitute for imagination.

A Final Note About Learning with and Listening to Teachers

As we conclude this book, we would like to discuss a few things we have learned in working with teachers. Perhaps the most important is that all the ideas we offer in this book about teaching K–12 students relate as well to working with teachers. Fundamental to these ideas is the belief that all people need to feel genuinely respected. Although this may mean different things to different people, it has been our experience that there is general agreement among teachers that respect includes listening to and thoughtfully considering different perspectives. We have found that when teachers' opinions are an integral part of their learning and working together, relationships based on shared goals can be forged and sustained.

We have all experienced "road shows," in which the presentation approximates a highly scripted and impersonal routine, sometimes designed around a trend rather than a cohesive philosophy. Our goal has been to maintain a sense of intimacy with participants, incorporating their stories, interests, and concerns into everything we do. We try to picture teachers wearing neon signs that say, "Don't waste my time!" Teaching about culture and motivation and school renewal in a responsive and substantive manner and through activities *that can be applied in K–12 classrooms* is greatly appreciated. This teaching includes personalized ways to reflect and plan.

We have also learned that teachers usually need time to let an idea *incubate* prior to taking action. Further, it is not enough for people to learn about something once or twice. New ideas and activities seem to develop roots when teachers have an opportunity to experiment with them and to reteach them in different ways to their colleagues and students. This is how their commitment often begins to develop. Sometimes, in our eagerness to facilitate change, we have made the mistake of simply moving too fast. The challenge with which we will undoubtedly always grapple is how to balance our sense of urgency with respect for the complexity of any learning process—and for the hard work so many teachers are already doing.

And finally, there is no substitute for authenticity. Most teachers with whom we work are not impressed with expensive clothing, evangelistic monologues, or résumés the size of Texas. They seem to most appreciate those adult educators who try to practice what they preach. This includes having a sincere interest in kids, the ability to use personal experience to demonstrate ideas, and a sense of humor. For all of us, the sharing of mistakes and the ways we have learned from them—once we have scraped our egos off the ground—can inspire.

Whether we call it school renewal, school change, school restructuring, school reculturing, or systemic school reform, it is plain hard work. Perhaps the most exhausting aspect is knowing that we are asking teachers to do things for which all of society should be responsible. Although we have remarkable examples of what human beings and schools have accomplished, we should realize the kind of rigor this requires—often amid a backdrop of shifting or superficial political agendas. Try as we may to dignify the work of school renewal with statistics and bar charts, it is in relationships that we help each other reach and act upon personal significance. The quality of a school does not depend upon success alone, but on what we do to experience it.

Evaluation Tools and Strategies for School and District Initiatives

This resource offers evaluations and guides: a guide, or comprehensive plan, for evaluating a school's initiative for culturally responsive teaching; a planning and communication guide for schoolwide instructional leadership cadre meetings; a guide for a cadre to use in its initial planning; a guide for cadre members to examine their individual actions and insights; a planning guide for lesson design according to the motivational framework; and a means of evaluating ethnic and cultural pluralism in the school environment.

Evaluating the Initiative

We find a comprehensive plan to evaluate the progress and success of culturally responsive teaching initiatives to be an invaluable tool. The plan offered here is largely based on the steps for developing an innovation configuration as described in Tools for Change Workshops, by Robby Champion (1993). Any assessment of this sort should be accomplished using a variety of qualitative and quantitative data.

We recommend an evaluation team composed of at least one teacher, administrator, parent, and district staff member. This team plans the evaluation process and assists in its implementation. Input from all stakeholders will increase everyone's commitment and support of the team's efforts.

Step 1. Identify the Components of the Initiative

The evaluation team should identify the initiative components. As an example, one district we worked with identified four components, expecting that the following growth and improvement should occur.

- Increased knowledge about culturally responsive teaching practices
- Increased use of culturally responsive instructional strategies, skills, and behaviors in classrooms
- Improved attitudes of teachers, students, and parents in terms of respect for and acceptance of diverse cultures
- Improved learning of students across cultures

Step 2. Describe Ideal Future Results for Each Goal

An evaluation team should recommend the expected results for each component. For example, it may be expected that by the end of the second year of implementation, all teachers in a random sample will be able to describe the four conditions that encourage the motivation of all students (increased knowledge) and that all teachers in a random sample will be able to describe a lesson they teach that incorporates these four conditions as part of its plan or design (increased use of instructional strategies).

Step 3. Describe What Exists Today for Each Goal

Baseline data should be collected either prior to the implementation or during the first year and used to determine the current status of each component. In some cases, one assessment tool can provide data about progress in more than one area. Here are some examples of assessment processes and the data that can be collected.

Data Collection to Support Increased Knowledge About Culturally Responsive Teaching Practices

Annual Poster Conference. A poster conference is an interactive method for sharing exhibitions, ideas, and questions. Participants engage in dialogue about creatively displayed topics. For this initiative, the topics might include

School inquiry-based projects

A lesson design based on the Motivational Framework for Culturally Responsive Teaching

Sample lessons that highlight the four conditions of the framework and that are illustrated with photographs and descriptions of strategies

The ways the initiative is related to the school improvement or schoolwide planning process

The ways faculty institutes and other professional development opportunities have been implemented

Participants in the initiative, usually teams, have an opportunity to exhibit and discuss their goals, projects, and successes in culturally responsive teaching. The displays may include photographs and collages, video segments, diagrams, handouts, and so forth. A presenter may be stationed at each display to give an overview and answer questions. In addition, each team usually provides a one-page summary of its exhibition to visitors. For additional ideas for planning a poster conference, please see Activity 21 in Chapter Eight.

Sample Lesson Plans. Sample lesson plans from different grade levels can be collected and analyzed for evidence of the four conditions of the motivational framework. One method for collecting them is to ask each cadre to solicit plans from teachers on a voluntary basis. (We have found that commitment often develops over time and that the request ought to invite rather than require staff to share work.) A second method is to request that teachers new to the school submit a sample lesson plan prior to their participation in the schoolwide institute. These plans can then be compared later to lesson designs they create following involvement in the initiative. The evaluation team should assist in developing this assessment process.

Classroom Observations. The evaluation team assists in developing protocols for this classroom assessment process. Classroom observations are conducted by teams of observers who understand the motivational framework well. A good preliminary exercise for observers is to view several video clips of classroom teaching and to compare and contrast their analysis, focusing on motivating teaching and learning for all students. The observation process may involve the use of written narratives or selected priority items from the partnership guide (Exhibit 8.1) that staff have examined and agreed to implement. One of the goals of the observations is to collect evidence of classroom activities and interactions that contribute to the four motivational conditions. This formative assessment can help faculty to understand, collectively, where they are particularly strong and to identify areas of challenge for collaborative study and implementation.

Data Collection to Support Increased Use of Culturally Responsive Instructional Strategies, Skills, and Behaviors in Classrooms

- Annual poster conference: see previous description.
- Sample lesson plans: see previous description.
- Classroom observations: see previous description.
- Review of school improvement plans: Review existing and emerging programs that support and enhance culturally responsive teaching practices. Examine the extent to which ideas are conceptualized and integrated in ways that have a strong likelihood of contributing to substantive change. This can indicate that schools are becoming knowledgeable about innovations in ways that transcend an unfortunate feature of many school improvement plans—lists of superficial activities that although addressing district accountability categories (such as academic achievement, curricular and instructional strategies, professional development, and parent and community involvement) lack faithfulness to an exciting, shared schoolwide philosophy and vision. Reviewers may wish to compare school improvement plans over time for indications of how the school is evolving in its understanding and commitment to the challenges related to creating highly motivating teaching and learning for all students.

Data Collection to Support Improved Attitudes Among Teachers, Students, and Parents

- Climate surveys: District-made or commercially prepared climate surveys may be administered, but they ought to be examined by the evaluation team for values and beliefs that are relevant to the school. Focus groups are another valuable way to ascertain attitudes of parents, teachers, and students. The dot graphing exercise in Chapter Seven can also be an efficient means of collecting attitudinal data.

- Student attendance and discipline referral data are another means to assess school climate. Data should be collected in a way that is not intrusive. It is informative to be able to disaggregate data by gender, ethnicity, income level (for example, whether a student receives free or reduced-price lunch), and grade level. (This can be achieved if students put their student identification numbers on the climate surveys.) These data can then be compared annually to detect whether improvement in attendance and a decrease in discipline referrals are occurring.

Data to Support Improved Learning of Students Across All Cultures

- Student data on grades: Even though these data are not generally known to be reliable for most purposes because of the variation in grading policies and practices, it can be informative to look for patterns that may exist among student groups with respect to high, middle, and low grades. For example, one school was able to see that across student groups, recent patterns showed significantly fewer F's than the older patterns. This change might be interpreted in a number of ways. However, the dialogue that ensued from noticing this pattern was of real value.
- Standardized test scores.
- Retention rates.
- Student enrollment in advanced and remedial courses.
- A systemwide writing assessment.

These sources of data, when disaggregated by gender, ethnicity, income, and grade level and compared annually, can serve as indications of change in student performance.

Step 4. Describe Interim Steps for Each Goal

The evaluation team should determine the intermediate steps to be accomplished. The steps may be modified based on the review of data collected annually.

Step 5. Identify and Graphically Represent Unacceptable States or Targets for Each Goal

The evaluation team, in concert with state and district policy, should clarify unacceptable states.

Step 6. Identify and Graphically Represent Ideal States or Targets for Each Goal

The task force should determine these ideal states.

Cadre Planning and Communication Guide

The Cadre Planning and Communication Guide can be used to record outcomes of schoolwide instructional leadership cadre meetings. It is intended as a record both for the cadre and for others in the school and district who might learn from the cadre's accomplishments. It asks the record keeper to record these items.

Today's date:

Meeting facilitator:

Participants:

Topics discussed:

Decisions:

Activities between today's meeting and the next meeting:

Date for next meeting:

Agenda for next meeting:

Please forward completed form to:

Initial Guide to Planning: Schoolwide Leadership Cadre

The Initial Guide to Planning contributes to basic agreements among cadre members to find time to plan, prioritize goals, work effectively as a team, and communicate well with others. The guide asks the team to answer these questions.

School:

Date:

Contact person:

1. How will our cadre find uninterrupted time to meet?
2. Given our work together, what are some of our current priorities related to creating highly motivating teaching and learning for all students?
3. What kind of an approach and approximate time line can help our school to experiment with and routinize new approaches to teaching, to collaborative adult learning, and to assessing and strengthening of its accomplishments?
4. What roles might cadre members accept to implement cadre ideas? (Roles should correspond to features of the time line as well as to general needs. The team will have to answer questions such as these: What two people will serve as team leaders and what will their functions be? Who will prepare agendas for meetings? Who will facilitate meetings? Who will oversee communication with the school community?)
5. How will our cadre solicit input from the school community in order to develop new ideas and commitment among staff for helping all students experience motivating learning and academic success?
6. How and when will our cadre keep members of the school community informed as planning progresses?
7. What resources might facilitate our meaningful planning?
8. How will our school ensure that decisions directly influence teaching and learning?

Actions and Insights

The Actions and Insights guide provides a way for cadres to reflect on their role, knowledge, and priorities once they are more invested in the initiative. It can also serve as a formative assessment to take stock of emerging ideas and challenges. The individual considers these items.

Name:

Position:

Cadre:

1. Please describe how you and your cadre could:

   Help others relearn the motivational framework

Help others learn strategies related to the four motivational conditions

Work with a school to create teachers' agreement to use the motivational framework in lesson planning

Work with a school to find time and use time for such things as examining student work

Achieve anything else that it believes may be of benefit to a school's vision of high-quality teaching and learning for *all* students

2. What insights have you gained on how to create openness throughout a school to thinking motivationally on behalf of all students?

3. What insights in general have you gained about schoolwide planning or about highly motivating, culturally responsive teaching?

4. Please list two or three goals for yourself in applying what you have learned thus far. Also, please identify what you hope to learn more about.

Planning Guide for Lesson Design

Answering each of the following questions reveals how well a lesson meets the four motivational conditions. An example of a completed guide is shown in Exhibit 22, Chapter Eight.

Description of lesson (or unit), including goals:

Establishing Inclusion

How does the learning experience contribute to the development of participants as a community of learners who feel respected by and connected to one another and to the teacher?

Developing a Positive Attitude

How does the learning experience offer meaningful choices and promote personal relevance to contribute to participants' positive attitude?

Enhancing Meaning

How does the learning experience engage participants in challenging learning that has social merit?

Engendering Competence

How does the learning experience create participants' understanding that they are becoming more effective in authentic learning that they value?

Evaluating the School Environment for Ethnic and Cultural Pluralism

The questionnaire in Exhibit R.1 provides an overview of the issues found in the literature on cultural pluralism and education. The essential ambiguity of each question allows respondents to bring forth their own definitions and meanings for key terms in the questions.

Exhibit R.1. A Rating Form for Evaluation of the School Environment for Ethnic and Cultural Pluralism.

Briefly consider each item according to your experience with schools **in general**, and rate it as **no evidence (1), minimal evidence (2), or clear evidence (3)**. In addition, please use the opportunity for reflection at the end of each section to identify one or two of the section items that from your perspective are most important or critical.

School Environment

1. Do school professional libraries include   1   2   3   NA
   books, magazines, videos, music, and so forth
   about different ethnic and cultural groups
   and ways to teach new information?

1a. If so, have these materials been evaluated   1   2   3   NA
    for bias?

2. Are there pictures of members of different   1   2   3   NA
   groups of people in the classrooms and halls
   of schools (this includes pictures that
   challenge stereotypes)?

Source: Banks, J. A. *Teaching Strategies for Ethnic Studies.* (6th ed.) ©1997 by Allyn & Bacon. Adapted by permission.

Exhibit R.1. A Rating Form for Evaluation of the School Environment for Ethnic and Cultural Pluralism. (*Continued*)

3. Do calendars in the schools include information about ethnic holidays and outstanding people of diverse ethnic and cultural origin?	1	2	3	NA
4. Do foods served for snacks and meals reflect the ethnic and cultural diversity of the United States?	1	2	3	NA
5. Do school assemblies and plays reflect the ethnic and cultural diversity of the United States?	1	2	3	NA
6. Do school holidays and celebrations reflect the ethnic and cultural diversity of the United States?	1	2	3	NA
7. Do bulletin boards and other displays reflect the ethnic and cultural diversity of the United States? (If so, in what ways?)	1	2	3	NA
8. Do schools try to encourage students from ethnic minority and other distinct cultural communities to attend?	1	2	3	NA
9. Is participation in class and community decision making balanced for gender equity, ethnic representation, and so forth (for example, on the student council, in athletics, in parent and school decision making)?	1	2	3	NA
10. Are there advocacy-oriented and personalized approaches to advising students and conferencing with students and parents?	1	2	3	NA

Reflection: Please identify one or two of the school environment items that from your perspective are most important or critical.

Curriculum and Instruction

11. Do schools systematically disaggregate data to examine student outcomes for disproportionality in achievement among different groups of learners?	1	2	3	NA

11a. If disparity exists, have schools assessed their   1   2   3   NA
goals, methods, and materials for ways to
better support the motivation of all learners
(for example, stronger linkages to personal
experience, broader use of multiple
intelligences, creating with learners
meaningful levels of challenge)?

12. To what extent do all courses and learning   1   2   3   NA
experiences offer information about
ethnically and culturally diverse groups?

13. Does the curriculum enable students to view   1   2   3   NA
concepts, issues, events, and themes from
the perspectives of diverse ethnic and
cultural groups?

14. Does the curriculum support values, attitudes,   1   2   3   NA
and behaviors that support ethnic and
cultural pluralism (for example, teaching
about equality and social justice)?

15. Do schools support language diversity   1   2   3   NA
(that is, do they support bilingual students
in the development of their first language
and encourage monolingual students to
become proficient in a second language)?

16. Do staff have an awareness of systematic   1   2   3   NA
inequalities (that is, subtle, everyday acts of
discrimination that can influence the amount
of teacher attention or the quality of feedback
that all students receive)?

17. Is there evidence of respect for personal   1   2   3   NA
safety issues in self-disclosure or other ways
staff might inadvertently embarrass learners
(for example, exercises that inhibit
participation because they are too personal,
praise that embarrasses, competition among
peers, and so forth)?

18. Are staff aware of effective approaches for   1   2   3   NA
responding to offensive comments (for
example, distancing students from comments
and transforming controversial questions into
analytical questions)?

Reflection: Please identify one or two of the curriculum and instruction
items that from your perspective are most important or critical.

(Continued)

Exhibit R.1. A Rating Form for Evaluation of the School Environment for Ethnic and Cultural Pluralism. (*Continued*)

Professional Support

19. Have schools developed and implemented a policy to attract and retain staff members from ethnically and culturally diverse backgrounds?	1	2	3	NA
20. Do teachers and administrators have high-quality professional development opportunities aligned with clear and purposeful multicultural goals?	1	2	3	NA
21. Is there a procedure for helping staff evaluate the treatment of underrepresented groups in textbooks and other sources of required reading?	1	2	3	NA
21a. If so, to what extent is it effective?				
22. Do schools have a curriculum committee created to identify community resources that can provide additional support for improving the curriculum for ethnic and cultural plurality?	1	2	3	NA
23. Are individuals from various ethnic and cultural community organizations invited to speak and participate in substantive ways?	1	2	3	NA
24. Are parents from various ethnic and cultural backgrounds encouraged to participate in classroom and schoolwide processes in meaningful ways?	1	2	3	NA

Reflection: Please identify one or two of the professional support items that from your perspective are most important or critical.

References

Adams, M. "Cultural Inclusion in the American College Classroom." In L.L.B. Border and N. Van Note Chism (eds.), *Teaching for Diversity.* New Directions for Teaching and Learning, no. 49. San Francisco: Jossey-Bass, 1992.

Allen, M. S., and Roswell, B. S. "Self-Evaluation as Holistic Assessment." Paper presented at the annual meeting of the Conference on College Composition and Communication, Mar. 1989. (ED 303 809)

Association for Supervision and Curriculum Development. "Effective Teaching Redux." *ASCD Update,* 1990, *32*(6), 5.

Association for Supervision and Curriculum Development. *Educating Everybody's Children: Diverse Teaching Strategies for Diverse Learners.* Alexandria, Va.: Association for Supervision and Curriculum Development, 1995.

ASCD Education Update, 1998, *40*(entire issue 8).

Banks, J. A. *Teaching Strategies for Ethnic Studies.* (6th ed.) Needham Heights, Mass.: Allyn & Bacon, 1997.

Bean, J. C. *Engaging Ideas: The Professor's Guide to Integrating Writing, Critical Thinking, and Active Learning in the Classroom.* San Francisco: Jossey-Bass, 1996.

Bempechat, J., Graham, S., and Jimenez, N. "The Socialization of Achievement in Poor and Minority Students: A Comparative Study." *Journal of Cross-Cultural Psychology,* 1999, *30*(2), 139–158.

Beyer, B. K. *Practical Strategies for the Teaching of Thinking.* Needham Heights, Mass.: Allyn & Bacon, 1987.

Beyer, B. K. *How to Conduct a Formative Evaluation.* Alexandria, Va.: Association for Supervision and Curriculum Development, 1995.

Boyer, E. L. *The Basic School: A Community for Learning.* Princeton, N.J.: Carnegie Foundation for the Advancement of Teaching, 1995.

Brookfield, S. D. *Becoming a Critically Reflective Teacher.* San Francisco: Jossey-Bass, 1995.

Butler, J. E. "Transforming the Curriculum: Teaching About Women of Color." In J. A. Banks and C.A.M. Banks (eds.), *Multicultural Education: Issues and Perspectives.* (2nd ed.) Needham Heights, Mass.: Allyn & Bacon, 1993.

Butler, J. E., and Walter, J. C. (eds.). *Transforming the Curriculum: Ethnic*

Studies and Women's Studies. Albany: State University of New York Press, 1991.

Caine, R. N., and Caine, G. *Making Connections: Teaching and the Human Brain.* Alexandria, Va.: Association for Supervision and Curriculum Development, 1991.

Campbell, B., Campbell, L., and Dickinson, D. *Teaching and Learning Through Multiple Intelligences.* Seattle: New Horizons for Learning, 1992.

Center on Learning, Assessment, and School Structure, Rochester, N.Y., 1991.

Champion, R. H. *Tools for Change Workshops.* Ellicot City, Md.: National Staff Development Council, 1993.

Checkley, K. "The First Seven . . . and the Eighth: A Conversation with Howard Gardner." *Educational Leadership,* 1997, *55*(1), 8–13.

Children's Defense Fund. *The State of America's Children, 1992.* Washington, D.C.: The Children's Defense Fund, 1992.

Christensen, L. "Where I'm From." *Rethinking Schools,* 1997, *12*(2), 22–23.

Clifford, J. "Introduction: Partial Truths." In J. Clifford and G. E. Marcus (eds.), *Writing Culture: The Poetics and Politics of Ethnography.* Berkeley: University of California Press, 1986.

Cochran-Smith, M. "Color Blindness and Basket Making Are Not the Answers: Confronting the Dilemmas of Race, Culture, and Language Diversity in Teacher Education." *American Educational Research Journal,* 1995, *32,* 493–522.

Cole, J. (ed.). *All American Women: Lines That Divide, Ties That Bind.* New York: Free Press, 1986.

Comer, J. "Creating Learning Communities: The Comer Process." Experimental session of the annual conference of the Association for Supervision and Curriculum Development, Washington, D.C., 1993.

Conley, D. T. *Roadmap to Restructuring: Policies, Practices and the Emerging Values of Schooling.* Eugene, Oreg.: ERIC Clearinghouse on Educational Management, 1993.

Conyers, M. "Teaching with Memory in Mind." Presentation at Spring Branch High School, Nov. 1, 1998.

Council on Interracial Books for Children. *Ten Quick Ways to Analyze Children's Book for Racism and Sexism.* New York: Council on Interracial Books for Children, 1980.

Crandall, D. "The Teacher's Role in School Improvement." *Educational Leadership,* 1983, *41*(3), 6–9.

Csikszentmihalyi, M. *Finding Flow: The Psychology of Engagement with Everyday Life.* New York: Cambridge University Press, 1997.

Csikszentmihalyi, M., and Csikszentmihalyi, I. S. *Optimal Experience: Psychological Studies of Flow in Consciousness.* New York: Cambridge University Press, 1988.

Cunningham, P. M. "Making a More Significant Impact on Society." In B. A. Quigley (ed.), *Fulfilling the Promise of Adult and Continuing Edu-*

cation. New Directions for Continuing Education, no. 44. San Francisco: Jossey-Bass, 1989.

Darling-Hammond, L. "Reframing the School Reform Agenda: Developing Capacity for School Transformation." *Phi Delta Kappan,* 1993, *74*(10), 753–761.

Deci, E. L., and Ryan, R. M. "A Motivational Approach to Self: Integration in Personality." In R. Dienstbier (ed.), *Nebraska Symposium on Motivation.* Vol. 38: *Perspectives on Motivation.* Lincoln: University of Nebraska Press, 1991.

Delpit, L. D. "The Silenced Dialogue: Power and Pedagogy in Educating Other People's Children." *Harvard Educational Review,* 1998, *58*(3), 280–298.

Dewey, J. *How We Think.* (Rev. ed.) Lexington, Mass.: Heath, 1933.

Dillon, J. T. *Questioning and Teaching: A Manual of Practice.* New York: Teachers College Press, 1988.

Elbow, P. *Embracing Contraries: Explorations in Learning and Teaching.* New York: Oxford University Press, 1986.

Eldridge, D. B. *Teacher Talk: Multicultural Lesson Plans for the Elementary Classroom.* Needham Heights, Mass.: Allyn & Bacon, 1998.

Fordham, S., and Ogbu, J. A. "Black Students and School Success: Coping with the Burden of Acting White." *Urban Review,* 1986, *18*, 176–206.

Francis, S., Hirsh, S., and Rowland, E. "Improving School Culture Through Study Groups." *Journal of Staff Development,* 1994, *15*(2), 12–15.

Freire, P. *Pedagogy of the Oppressed.* New York: Seabury Press, 1970.

Fullan, M. G. *The New Meaning of Educational Change.* (2nd ed.) New York: Teachers College Press, 1991.

Fullan, M. G. *Change Forces.* London: Falmer Press, 1993.

Fullan, M. G., and Miles, M. B. "Getting Reform Right: What Works and What Doesn't." *Phi Delta Kappan,* 1992, *73*(10), 745–752.

Gardner, H. *Multiple Intelligence: The Theory in Practice.* New York: Basic Books, 1993.

Gardner, H., and Hatch, T. "Multiple Intelligences Go to School." *Education Researcher,* 1989, *1*(8), 4–10.

Garfield, C. *Peak Performers.* New York: Morrow, 1986.

Garmston, R., and Wellman, B. "Humility: Attitude Readies the Adult Mind for Learning in Public." *Journal of Staff Development,* 1999, *20*(3), 71–73.

Gay, G. "A Multicultural School Curriculum." In C. A. Grant and M. L. Gomez, *Making Schools Multicultural: Campus and Classroom.* Upper Saddle River, N.J.: Prentice Hall, 1996.

Geertz, C. *The Interpretation of Cultures.* New York: Basic Books, 1973.

Gere, A. R. (ed.). *Roots in the Sawdust: Writing to Learn Across the Disciplines.* Urbana, Ill.: National Council of Teachers of English, 1985.

Ginsberg, M. B., Johnson, J. F., and Moffett, C. A. *Educators Supporting*

Educators: A Guide to Organizing School Support Teams. Alexandria, Va.: Association for Supervision and Curriculum Development, 1997.

Glanz, J. "Action Research." *Journal of Staff Development,* 1999, *20*(3), 22–23.

Glickman, C. D. *Action Research: Inquiry, Reflection, and Decision Making.* Video 4–95037. Alexandria, Va.: Association for Supervision and Curriculum Development, 1995.

Glickman, C. D., Hayes, R., and Hensley, F. "Site-Based Facilitation of Empowered Schools: Complexities and Issues for Staff Developers." *Journal of Staff Development,* 1992, *13*(2), 22–26.

Goodrich, H. "Understanding Rubrics." *Educational Leadership,* 1997, *54*(4), 14–17.

Grant, C. A., and Gomez, M. L. *Making Schools Multicultural: Campus and Classroom.* Upper Saddle River, N.J.: Prentice Hall, 1996.

Grant, C. A., and Sleeter, C. E. *Turning on Learning.* Upper Saddle River, N.J.: Merrill, 1998.

Hall, C. "Cultural Malpractice: The Growing Obsolescence of Psychology with the Changing U.S. Population." *American Psychologist,* 1997, *52,* 642–651.

Heath, S. B. *Ways with Words: Language, Life, and Work in Communities and Classrooms.* Cambridge: Cambridge University Press, 1983.

Hesselbein, F., and Cohen, P. M. (eds.). *Leader to Leader: Enduring Insights from the Drucker Foundation's Award-Winning Journal.* San Francisco: Jossey-Bass, 1999.

Highwater, J. "Imagination as a Political Force." General session address given at the annual conference of the Association for Supervision and Curriculum Development, Chicago, Mar. 1994.

Hilliard, A. G. "Teachers and Cultural Styles in a Pluralistic Society." *NEA Today,* 1989, *7*(6), 65–69.

Hirsch, S. (ed.). *School Team Innovator.* National Staff Development Council, [no date].

Hofstede, G. *Culture's Consequences.* (Abridged ed.) Thousand Oaks, Calif.: Sage, 1982.

Hofstede, G. "Cultural Differences in Teaching and Learning." *International Journal of Intercultural Relations,* 1986, *10*(3), 301–320.

Hopfenberg, W. S., Levin, H. M., and Associates. *The Accelerated Schools Resource Guide.* San Francisco: Jossey-Bass, 1993.

Hutchings, P. *Using Cases to Improve College Teaching: A Guide to More Reflective Practice.* Washington, D.C.: American Association for Higher Education, 1993.

Irvine, J. J. (ed.). *Critical Knowledge for Diverse Teachers and Learners.* Washington, D.C.: American Association of Colleges for Teacher Education, 1997.

Irvine, J. J., and York, D. E. "Learning Styles and Culturally Diverse Students: A Literature Review." In J. A. Banks and C.A.M. Banks (eds.), *Handbook of Research on Multicultural Education.* New York: Macmillan, 1995.

Jacobs, H. H. "The Growing Need for Interdisciplinary Curriculum Content." In H. H. Jacobs (ed.), *Interdisciplinary Curriculum: Design and Implementation*. Alexandria, Va.: Association for Supervision and Curriculum Development, 1989.

Jarvis, P. *Adult Learning in the Social Context*. London: Croom Helm, 1987.

Johnson, J., and Ginsberg, M. B. "Building Capacity for Change Through School Support Teams." *Educational Leadership,* 1996, *54*(3), 22–25.

Johnson, D. W., Johnson, R. T., and Smith, K. A. *Active Learning: Cooperation in the College Classroom*. Edina, Minn.: Interaction, 1991.

Journal of Staff Development, Summer 1998, *19*(entire issue 3: *Strategies to Move Hearts and Minds*).

Journal of Staff Development, Summer 1999, *20*(entire issue 3: *Powerful Designs: New Approaches Ignite Professional Learning*).

Kanter, R. M. *The Challenge of Organizational Change: How Companies Experience It and Leaders Guide It*. New York: Free Press, 1992.

Kasworm, C. E., and Marienau, C. A. "Principals of Assessment for Adult Learners." In A. D. Rose and M. A. Leahy (eds.), *Assessing Adult Learning in Diverse Settings: Current Issues and Approaches*. New Directions for Adult and Continuing Education, no. 75. San Francisco: Jossey-Bass, 1997.

King, A. "Inquiry as a Tool in Critical Thinking." In D. F. Halpern and Associates (eds.), *Changing College Classrooms: New Teaching and Learning Strategies for an Increasingly Complex World*. San Francisco: Jossey-Bass, 1994.

King, J. "'Thank You for Opening Our Minds': On Praxis, Transmutation, and Black Studies in Teacher Development." In J. King, E. Hollins, and W. Hayman (eds.), *Preparing Teachers for Cultural Diversity*. New York: Teachers College Press, 1997.

Kitayama, S., and Markus, H. R. (eds.). *Emotion and Culture: Empirical Studies of Mutual Influence*. Washington, D.C.: American Psychological Association, 1994.

Knapp, M. S., and Turnbull, B. J. *Better Schooling for Children of Poverty: Alternatives to Conventional Wisdom*. Vol. 1: *Summary*. Washington, D.C.: U.S. Department of Education, 1990.

Knowles, M. S. *The Modern Practice of Adult Education: From Pedagogy to Audiogogy*. (Rev. ed.) Chicago: Follett, 1980.

Ladson-Billings, G. "Beyond Multicultural Illiteracy." *Journal of Negro Education,* 1991, *60*, 147–157.

Ladson-Billings, G. *The Dream Keepers: Successful Teachers of African American Children*. San Francisco: Jossey-Bass, 1994.

Lambert, N. M., and McCombs, B. L. "Introduction: Learner Centered Schools and Classrooms as a Direction for School Reform." In N. M. Lambert and B. L. McCombs (eds.), *How Students Learn: Reforming Schools Through Learner-Centered Education*. Washington, D.C.: American Psychological Association, 1998.

Langer, S. *Philosophy in a New Key*. Cambridge, Mass.: Harvard University Press, 1942.

Lawrence-Lightfoot, S. *Portraiture*. San Francisco: Jossey-Bass, 1998.

Loeb, P. R. *Soul of the Citizen: Living with Convictions in a Cynical Time*. New York: St. Martin's Press, 1999.

Locke, D. C. *Increasing Multicultural Understanding: A Comprehensive Model*. Thousand Oaks, Calif.: Sage, 1992.

Loucks, S. "At Last, Some Good News from a Study of School Improvement." *Educational Leadership*, 1983, *41*(3), 4–5.

Manzo, A. V., and Manzo, U. C. "Note Cue: A Comprehension and Participation Training Strategy." *Journal of Reading*, 1990, *33*(8), 608–611.

Marzano, R. J. *A Different Kind of Classroom: Teaching with Dimensions of Learning*. Alexandria, Va.: Association for Supervision and Curriculum Development, 1992.

Massimini, F., Csikszentmihalyi, M., and Delle Fave, A. "Flow and Biocultural Evolution." In M. Csikszentmihalyi and I. S. Csikszentmihalyi (eds.), *Optimal Experience: Psychological Studies of Flow in Consciousness*. New York: Cambridge University Press, 1988.

McIntosh, P. "Curricular Revision: The Knowledge for a New Age." In C. S. Pearson, D. L. Shavlik, and J. G. Touchton (eds.), *Educating the Majority: Women Challenge Tradition in Higher Education*. New York: American Council on Education and Macmillan, 1989.

McLaughlin, M. W. "The Rand Change Agency Study Revisited: Macro Perspectives and Micro Realities." *Educational Researcher*, Dec. 1990, *19*, 11–16.

Meier, D. *The Power of Their Ideas: Lessons for America from a Small School in Harlem*. Boston: Beacon Press, 1995.

Mesa-Bains, A., and Shulman, J. H. *Facilitator's Guide to Diversity in the Classroom*. Hillsdale, N.J.: Erlbaum, 1994.

Molnar, A., and Lindquist, B. *Changing Problem Behavior in School*. San Francisco: Jossey-Bass, 1989.

Murphy, C. "Finding Time for Faculties to Study Together." *Journal of Staff Development*, Summer 1997, *18*(3), 29–32.

Newman, F. M., and Associates. *Authentic School Achievement: Restructuring Schools for Intellectual Quality*. San Francisco: Jossey-Bass, 1996.

Nieto, S. *Affirming Diversity*. White Plains, N.Y.: Longman, 1992.

Ogle, D. "The K-W-L: A Teaching Model That Develops Active Reading of Expository Text." *The Reading Teacher*, 1986, *39*, 564–576.

Oldfather, P. "Epistemological Empowerment: A Constructivist Concept of Motivation for Literacy Learning." Paper presented at the National Reading Conference, San Antonio, Tex., Dec. 1992.

Ovando, C. J., and Collier, V. P. *Bilingual and ESL Classrooms*. New York: McGraw-Hill, 1985.

Paley, V. G. *The Boy Who Would Be a Helicopter: The Uses of Storytelling in the Classroom*. Cambridge, Mass.: Harvard University Press, 1990.

Paul, R. "Socratic Questioning." In R. Paul (ed.), *Critical Thinking: What Every Person Needs to Survive in a Rapidly Changing World*. Rohnert Park, Calif.: Sonoma State University, Center for Critical Thinking and Moral Critique, 1990.

Raywid, M. A. "Finding Time for Collaboration." *Educational Leadership*, 1993, *51*(1), 30–34.

Rothwell, W. J., and Kazanas, H. C. *Mastering the Instructional Design Process: A Systematic Approach*. San Francisco: Jossey-Bass, 1992.

Sarason, S. *The Culture of School and the Problem of Change*. Needham Heights, Mass.: Allyn & Bacon, 1982.

Saxl, E. R., Miles, M. B., and Lieberman, A. *Assisting Change in Education*. Alexandria, Va.: Association for Supervision and Curriculum Development, 1989.

Saxl, E. R., Miles, M. B., and Lieberman, A. *Assisting Change in Education: Trainer's Manual*. Alexandria, Va.: Association for Supervision and Curriculum Development, 1990.

Schein, E. H. *Organizational Culture and Leadership*. San Francisco: Jossey-Bass, 1992.

Scott, J. P. "A Time to Learn." *Psychology Today*, 1969, *2*(10), 46–48, 66–67.

Senge, P. M. "The Leader's New Work: Building Learning Organizations." *Sloan Management Review*, 1990, *22*(1), 7–23.

Shade, B. J., Kelly, C., and Oberg, M. *Creating Culturally Responsive Classrooms*. Washington, D.C.: American Psychological Association, 1997.

Shor, I. *Empowering Education: Critical Teaching for Social Change*. Chicago: University of Chicago Press, 1992.

Shulman, J. H., and others. "Case Writing as a Site for Collaboration." *Teacher Education Quarterly*, Winter 1990, pp. 63–78.

Singham, M. "The Canary in the Mine: The Achievement Gap Between Black and White Students." *Phi Delta Kappan*, 1998, *80*(1), 9–15.

Smith, D. G. *The Challenge of Diversity: Involvement or Alienation in the Academy?* ASHE-ERIC Higher Education Report, no. 5. Washington, D.C.: Association for the Study of Higher Education, 1989.

Springfield, S. "Science, Cynicism, and the Diogenes Double-Edged Lamp." *Education Week*, 1998, *17*(43), 45–48.

Steele, C. M., and Aronson, J. "Stereotype Threat and the Intellectual Performance of African Americans." *Journal of Personality and Social Psychology*, 1995, *69*, 797–811.

Steinberg, A. "Adolescents and Schools: Improving the Fit." *Harvard Education Letter* (Reprint Series no. 1). Cambridge, Mass.: Harvard Graduate School of Education, 1993.

Sue, S. "Ethnicity and Culture in Psychological Research and Practice." In J. D. Goodchilds (ed.), *Psychological Perspectives on Human Diversity in America*. Washington, D.C.: American Psychological Association, 1991.

Takaki, R. Interview by J. M. Halford. *Educational Leadership*, 1999, *56*(7), 8–13.

Tatum, B. D. *"Why Are All the Black Kids Sitting Together in the Cafeteria?" and Other Conversations About Race.* New York: Basic Books, 1997.

Taylor, E. W. "Intercultural Competency: A Transformative Learning Experience." *Adult Education Quarterly,* 1994, *44*(3), 154–174.

Tiedt, P. L., and Tiedt, I. M. *Multicultural Teaching: A Handbook of Activities, Information, and Resources.* (4th ed.) Needham Heights, Mass.: Allyn & Bacon, 1995.

Tomlinson, C. A. *The Differentiated Classroom: Responding to the Needs of All Learners.* Alexandria, Va.: Association for Supervision and Curriculum Development, 1999.

Villa, R. A., and Thousand, J. S. (eds.). *Creating an Inclusive School.* Alexandria, Va.: Association for Supervision and Curriculum Development, 1995.

Voss, J. F. "Problem Solving and the Educational Process." In A. Lesgold and R. Glaser (eds.), *Foundations of Psychology of Education.* Hillsdale, N.J.: Erlbaum, 1989.

Vygotsky, L. *Mind and Society.* Cambridge, Mass.: Harvard University Press, 1978.

Walvoord, B. E., and Anderson, V. J. *Effective Grading: A Tool for Learning and Assessment.* San Francisco: Jossey-Bass, 1998.

Weiner, B. *Human Motivation: Metaphors, Theories, and Research.* Newbury Park, Calif.: Sage, 1992.

Whitehead, A. N. *Process and Reality.* New York: Free Press, 1979.

Wiggins, G. P. "A True Test: Toward More Authentic and Equitable Assessment." *Phi Delta Kappan,* May 1989, pp. 703–713.

Wiggins, G. P. *Educative Assessment: Designing Assessments to Inform and Improve Student Performance.* San Francisco: Jossey-Bass, 1998.

Wiggins, G. P. *Understanding by Design.* Alexandria, Va.: Association for Supervision and Curriculum Development, 1999.

Wilkerson, L., and Gijselaers, W. H. (eds.). *Bringing Problem-Based Learning to Higher Education: Theory and Practice.* New Directions for Teaching and Learning, no. 67. San Francisco: Jossey-Bass, 1996.

Williams, R. M., Jr. *American Society: A Sociological Interpretation.* (3rd ed.) New York: Knopf, 1970.

Wilson, E. A. *Reading at the Middle and High School Levels: Building Active Readers Across the Curriculum.* Arlington, Va.: Educational Research Service, 1995.

Wlodkowski, R. *Enhancing Adult Motivation to Learn.* (2nd ed.) San Francisco: Jossey-Bass, 1999.

Wlodkowski, R. J., and Ginsberg, M. B. *Diversity and Motivation: Culturally Responsive Teaching.* San Francisco: Jossey-Bass, 1995.

Wolfe, R. "A Model for Curriculum Evaluation." *Psychology in Schools,* 1989, *6,* 107–108.

Index

No-fault agreement, 100–101
Noli, P., 223
Northwest Regional Educational Laboratory, 241
Note cues activity, 68

O

Office liaison work sessions, 242–243
Ogbu, J., 4
Ogle, D., 82
Olson, L., 126

P

Paley, V. G., 2
Parents: teachers, student role-playing with, 156–158; teaching initiative involvement by, 241–242
Participation guidelines activity, 65–66
Partnership observation and dialogue, 23
Paul, R., 138
Peak performers study, 2–3
Pedagogical alignment, 50
Peer coaching: described, 248; rubric activity using, 183–184, 188
Planning guide for lesson design, 290–291
Positive attitude. *See* Developing positive attitude
Post-writes activity, 179–180
Poster conferences activity, 220–221, 224
Practicality beliefs, 11–12
Problem posing using personal challenges activity, 144–145
Problem-based learning, 143–145
Professional agreement activity, 66–68
Professional development topics: preliminary goals and activities for, 254–256; related to concept of culture, 256–258; related to school renewal processes, 258–259; related to building commitment, 259–261. *See also* Training institutes

Professional learning teams: activity for, 114–116; as teaching initiative element, 246–248. *See also* Teams
Profile of an effective organizational team, 118–122
Progress beliefs, 12
Providing prompts/cues, 87–88

R

"Race, Class, and Culture" (*Educational Leadership*), 141
Rags-to-riches stories, 11
Rating form for evaluation of school ethnic/cultural pluralism, 291–294
Rationality beliefs, 12
Reciprocal teaching, 88
Reflection logs activity, 194
Reflection trees for group projects activity, 195
Reframing activity, 101–104
Regulating difficulties, 88
Resistance: dealing with, 74–75; human dimension of change and, 124–125
Response cards activity, 61–62
Rethinking Our Classrooms: Teaching for Equity and Justice (Christensen), 137
Revolutionary War: example of cultural teaching of, 46–48; metaphor for, 133
Role-playing, 154–158
Roundtable dialogue on change activity, 123, 125–126
Rubric for expressing an idea clearly, 218
Rubric roundtables, 219–220
Rubrics: engendering competence using, 216–220; peer coaching, 183–184, 188
Ryan, R., 200

S

Sample school communication agreement, 67
Saxl, E., 126